# BEFORE MANIFEST DESTINY

# THE REVOLUTIONARY AGE
*Francis D. Cogliano, Christa Breault Dierksheide,
Eliga H. Gould, and Patrick Griffin, Editors*

# BEFORE MANIFEST DESTINY

THE CONTESTED EXPANSION OF
THE EARLY UNITED STATES

NICHOLAS G. DIPUCCHIO

UNIVERSITY OF VIRGINIA PRESS
*Charlottesville and London*

The University of Virginia Press is situated on the traditional lands of the Monacan Nation, and the Commonwealth of Virginia was and is home to many other Indigenous people. We pay our respect to all of them, past and present. We also honor the enslaved African and African American people who built the University of Virginia, and we recognize their descendants. We commit to fostering voices from these communities through our publications and to deepening our collective understanding of their histories and contributions.

University of Virginia Press
© 2025 by the Rector and Visitors of the University of Virginia
All rights reserved
Printed in the United States of America on acid-free paper

First published 2025

1 3 5 7 9 8 6 4 2

LIBRARY OF CONGRESS CATALOGING-IN-PUBLICATION DATA

Names: DiPucchio, Nicholas G., author
Title: Before Manifest Destiny : the contested expansion
of the early United States / Nicholas G. DiPucchio.
Description: Charlottesville : University of Virginia Press, 2025. | Series: The revolutionary age |
Includes bibliographical references and index.
Identifiers: LCCN 2024048642 (print) | LCCN 2024048643 (ebook) | ISBN 9780813952925
(hardcover) | ISBN 9780813952932 (paperback) | ISBN 9780813952949 (ebook)
Subjects: LCSH: United States—Territorial expansion—History. | United
States—Boundaries—History. | Republicanism—United States—History. |
United States—Historical geography. | United States—History—1783–1865.
Classification: LCC E179.5 .D58 2025 (print) | LCC E179.5 (ebook) | DDC 973.5—dc23/eng/20250207
LC record available at https://lccn.loc.gov/2024048642
LC ebook record available at https://lccn.loc.gov/2024048643

All maps by George E. Milne

*Cover art: The United States of America laid down from the best authorities, agreeable to the Peace of 1783*, John Wallis, London, 1783. (Library of Congress, Geography and Map Division)
*Cover design:* Joel W. Coggins

*To Katrina*

# CONTENTS

*List of Illustrations | ix*

*Acknowledgments | xi*

| | |
|---|---:|
| Introduction | 1 |
| 1. Bermuda | 11 |
| 2. The State of Franklin | 42 |
| 3. The Michigan and Upper Canada Borderlands | 79 |
| 4. Cuba | 114 |
| 5. The Pacific Northwest | 145 |
| Conclusion | 177 |

*Notes | 185*

*Bibliography | 217*

*Index | 239*

# ILLUSTRATIONS

| | |
|---|---|
| The Unrealized United States of America | 6 |
| The United States and Bermuda | 12 |
| Historic Map of St. George's, Bermuda | 30 |
| The Independent State of Franklin | 43 |
| The Michigan Territory and Upper Canada | 81 |
| Cuba and the US South | 116 |
| The United States Following the Transcontinental Treaty | 147 |

# ACKNOWLEDGMENTS

So many wonderful people helped me realize this book about unrealized ambitions. Their constructive feedback, guidance, and encouragement ensured this work would not be a thwarted endeavor. This book would not have been possible without them, and I thank them for their tireless support.

This book began as a dissertation under the supervision of Lorri Glover. Lorri is an exemplary scholar, mentor, and friend. A few weeks into my graduate school career, I confessed to Lorri that I was a fraud who lacked the skills necessary to write a dissertation. Lorri convinced me otherwise. Lorri has read countless drafts, provided insightful feedback, listened to me ramble about early US expansion, and challenged me to refine my arguments. She has offered encouragement throughout the dissertation's evolution into this current book. I am grateful to call her my doctoral advisor and friend.

I am also indebted to Todd Estes and Hal Parker. Todd has enthusiastically supported my academic career for over a decade. As an undergraduate at Oakland University, I took Todd's Jacksonian America course and seminar on the early American republic. Todd's teaching and encouragement convinced me to pursue graduate studies in the early United States. Todd served on my doctoral committee as an external reader, read several drafts, and talked through ideas with me. Hal's enthusiasm for world history inspired me to think beyond modern-day national boundaries and explore connections between empires. I am grateful that these two excellent scholars served on my doctoral committee and their advice ensured this project became a book.

I owe a great deal of gratitude to Nadine Zimmerli and the team at the University of Virginia Press. Nadine believed in this project before I did. She helped me navigate constructive feedback and sharpen my book's argument and historiographical intervention. She remained enthusiastic and supportive throughout the revision process. Nadine also arranged a Revolutionary Age Series workshop cohosted by the International Center for Jefferson Studies at Monticello and the University of Virginia Press. At the workshop, I received thought-provoking and crucial feedback from Frank Cogliano, Christa Dierksheide, Eliga Gould, Patrick Griffin, Peter Onuf, John Ragosta, and Lindsay Schakenbach Regele. Leslie Tingle carefully copyedited the manuscript and made excellent suggestions. If any mistakes are remaining, they are my own. I am thankful for the support of Nadine and the excellent scholars and staff at the University of Virginia Press.

I am privileged to have attended Saint Louis University, where I benefitted from the support of talented scholars and kindhearted colleagues. I greatly valued the advice of Michal Jan Rozbicki, who sadly passed away in 2019. His influence can be found throughout the book, especially in chapter 5, which I wrote in his graduate class on the Atlantic revolutions. I also benefitted from the encouragement of several professors, including Jennifer Popiel, Torrie Hester, and Flannery Burke. I am grateful to have learned alongside friends and talented historians including Nick Lewis, Joel Cerimele, Sam Klee, Bobby Olsen, Idolina Hernandez, Keegan Reynolds, Nate Caldwell, and Ángel Flores-Fontánez. Ángel graciously reviewed my translations for the Spanish-language sources in chapter 5.

My time as an undergraduate and employee at Oakland University has shaped me as a historian. James Naus deserves special recognition. James has been a mentor, friend, and advocate for my career. James offered me an opportunity to return to teach on campus and has been a constant supporter of my career plans. George Milne's expertise in historical cartography and Native America helped me think about North American spaces in new ways. His support is also reflected in the maps he created for this book. I also received constant encouragement from Derek Hastings, Don Matthews, Liz Shesko, Andrea Wenz, and Sara Chapman Williams. The faculty, staff, and students at Oakland University make it a wonderful institution to work at.

This book would not have been possible without the support of scholars across the field. The anonymous readers offered excellent feedback that helped me polish my argument, streamline sections, and add necessary context. My research on Bermuda benefitted immensely from feedback from François Furstenberg, Paul Gilje, Michael Jarvis, Grant Kleiser, Roderick McDonald, and Pernille Røge. Constructive critiques from Stephen Aron, Samuel Truett, Marc Rodriguez, and anonymous reviewers strengthened my chapter on the Pacific Northwest. Honor Sachs and Joseph Ross offered helpful feedback on my chapter about Cuba. My project has also benefitted from the thought-provoking conversations with early Americanists such as Heesoo Cho, Lawrence Celani, Ethan Gonzalez, and Katrina Ponti.

Several institutions helped support the making of this book. An Andrew W. Mellon Foundation Fellowship from the Library Company of Philadelphia and the Pennsylvania Historical Society enabled me to conduct critical research in Philadelphia in the summer of 2021. At the Library Company, Connie King and Ainsley Wynn Eakins pointed me to invaluable books and newspapers. Sarah Heim helped me navigate the vast manuscript collections held by the Historical Society of Pennsylvania. An Andrew W. Mellon grant from the Massachusetts Historical Society allowed me to find useful archival sources for my fourth and fifth chapters. Kanisorn Wongrichanalai and Katy Morris ensured that I could attend the archives after a delay caused by the COVID-19 pandemic.

Throughout the process of writing this book, I received endless support from my family. My parents, John and Kelly DiPucchio, have been a constant source of love. My father instilled the importance of heart and commitment. A successful children's book author, my mother taught me that failure is crucial to growth and success. My sisters, brothers-in-law, in-laws, grandparents, nieces, and my entire family have been constant joys in my life—and have given me much-needed breaks from writing. This book is dedicated to my wife, Katrina. A few months before departing for graduate school in St. Louis, I asked Katrina to be my girlfriend. To my surprise (and everyone else's), she said yes. She endured a long-distance relationship, found her vacations revolve around archival trips, and listened to me blather on about the book on our walks. This dedication cannot match the selflessness and unconditional love she has shown me. Thank you, Katrina. For everything.

An earlier version of chapter 1 first appeared as "Conquest for Commerce: American Policymakers, Bermuda, and the War for Independence, 1775–83," *Early American Studies* 18, no. 1 (Winter 2020): 61–89 (©2020 The McNeil Center for Early American Studies. Reprinted with permission of the University of Pennsylvania Press).

# BEFORE MANIFEST DESTINY

# INTRODUCTION

In July 1775, Benjamin Franklin articulated a grand vision of American expansion that never came to be. A few months after rebels and redcoats exchanged blows at Lexington and Concord, Franklin crafted an early version of the Articles of Confederation to organize the rebellion. In his draft, Franklin imagined *"The United Colonies of North America"* extending in all directions by planting "new Colonies when proper" and absorbing the British Empire. This colonial confederacy would invite "Ireland, the West India Islands, Quebec, St. Johns, Nova Scotia, Bermudas, and the East and West Floridas" to enjoy "all the Advantages of our Union." If Great Britain failed to address colonial grievances, Franklin warned that this confederation would be "perpetual."[1]

This confederation would become perpetual and independent. The course of the War for Independence, however, tempered Franklin's ambitions. In early December 1782, Franklin approached the negotiation table at the Hôtel d'York in Paris with a more modest proposal for the American union's boundaries. Afraid of British encirclement, the US diplomat demanded that Bermuda, Nova Scotia, and Canada be "declared free & Independent States, and at Liberty to join the Confederacy or remain separate." This proposal fell flat at the negotiation table. The American union would not span from the Irish Sea to the Mississippi River nor invite congressmen from Bermuda, Nova Scotia, and Canada. Nonetheless, these dynamic demands reveal the many unrealized territorial configurations imagined by US policymakers before their republic stretched from sea to shining sea.[2]

Franklin's unfulfilled plans, however, have been overshadowed by the triumphalist narrative of manifest destiny. In the 1840s, expansionists maintained that Providence destined the "Anglo-Saxon" race to spread their democratic culture across North America at the expense of "inferior peoples." Antebellum Americans espoused such bravado to mask deep fears about slavery's future, Indigenous resistance, manhood, industrialization, European colonialism, and disunion. Political writers such as John O'Sullivan and Jane McManus Storm Cazneau portrayed expansion as an unabated process that began with the first colonists of Jamestown and continued into their day with the adventurers bound for San Francisco. As a consequence, westward expansion became synonymous with inevitable, manifest destiny.[3]

Though they have deromanticized this narrative, scholars have generally followed this retelling. These historians have presented westward expansion as an unstoppable march across the continent with settlers in lockstep with state actors. They searched for signs of an embryonic vision of manifest destiny hidden in colonial charters or the founders' optimistic writings. These narratives traced US leaders' successful acquisitions of Louisiana, Texas, and California to convey a consistent plan for westward expansion. Consequently, manifest destiny has been flattened out to portray a continuity in thought from George Washington to James K. Polk. Indeed, several scholars have agreed that Franklin's 1751 *Observations on the Increase of Mankind* represented "the first conscious and comprehensive formulation of 'Manifest Destiny.'" Another historian argued that the nation began "successfully pursuing its grand, apparently inexorable, Manifest Destiny" at Hôtel d'York in 1782. This teleological narrative has left little room for thwarted expansionist episodes that distract from an uncompromising, unchanging drive to dominate North America.[4]

*Before Manifest Destiny* offers a new retelling of early republic expansion by exploring the unrealized visions of US policymakers. From the 1770s to the 1820s, policymakers pursued expansionist plans that were anything but manifest. Projecting manifest destiny back into these earlier decades erases these contested visions for the republic's future boundaries. This book traces these ambitions as they unfolded to recover the perspectives that informed how national leaders pursued territorial aggrandizement. Fearing for their republic's survival, US decision-makers from Thomas Jefferson to John Quincy Adams plotted expansionist schemes in all cardinal directions. At various moments, these dynamic imaginings included elusive territories such as Bermuda, Canada, and Cuba. US state actors also articulated foiled plans for regions that the United States claimed but struggled to control such as the Tennessee Valley in the late eighteenth century and the Michigan Territory and the Pacific Northwest in the early nineteenth century. In these peripheries, US officials struggled to achieve their aspirations in the face of on-the-ground circumstances and the ambitions of local inhabitants and geopolitical actors. Rather than being a static story of an unceasing march across the continent, the narrative of early US expansion is a tale of unfulfilled possibilities.[5]

This book recovers the unsuccessful plans for Bermuda, the Tennessee Valley, Upper Canada, Cuba, and the Pacific Northwest. To do so, it builds on a growing body of literature in Indigenous, continental, Atlantic, and global histories that underscore how US expansion was contested and was, as two historians recently put it, "a product of history." In hindsight, US designs for Bermuda, Upper Canada, and Cuba appear improbable, especially compared to the United States' demographic advantages to annex the West. But to early Americans, regions that seemed destined to join the republic did not always reflect the modern boundaries of the United States. At various moments, US citizens had closer ties with Bermudians, Canadians, and Cubans than with the Indigenous and colonial inhabitants of what would later become the states of Louisiana, Florida, and Texas. Conversely, as US efforts to annex the Tennessee Valley and the Pacific Northwest demonstrate, even regions that confederated with the United States were not guaranteed to join. Despite some optimists' predictions of continental domination, these contested spaces and adaptable mental maps undermine the notion that policymakers pursued clearsighted plans. Before manifest destiny, early US policymakers imagined many ever-evolving, unrealized destinies for the republic's expansion.[6]

Fear drove US policymakers to desire these elusive spaces. Far from shouting the bravado associated with manifest destiny, national leaders felt threatened in every direction. History taught the founders that republics were fragile. Beset with domestic, foreign, and ideological challenges, their republic proved no exception. By expanding their union, US policymakers could achieve security from neighboring nations, encourage state formation and economic development, gain new ports and resources for trade, and advance the cause of republicanism. A failure to expand, they feared, could imperil their republican experiment and possibly independence. At the same time, overextension and competing interests could collapse the already large union. Racial anxieties also animated expansion. Decision-makers worried that proximity to powerful Indigenous nations and free Black populations endangered the slaveholding nation. These wide-ranging fears compelled leaders like George Washington and James Madison to embrace a trial-and-error approach to expansion. Indeed, they reconfigured and abandoned their ambitions to keep their republican experiment alive.[7]

Geopolitical realities exacerbated these fears. In many ways, these contested territories illustrate the weakness of the early United States. Military, naval, and financial constraints dampened US policymakers' ambitions—even after the US Constitution strengthened the federal government. On the continent, Indigenous nations formed loose military confederacies and schemed with European powers to undermine US settler invasions. On the seas, the British Royal Navy stymied Americans' attempts to annex Bermuda and Cuba. Even in territories that joined the republic, US policymakers dreaded internal threats such as settler disloyalty and slave revolts that could subvert the territorial government.[8]

These realities forced early US leaders to engage with the visions expressed by local inhabitants and rival policymakers. The geopolitical chaos spawned by the late eighteenth- and early nineteenth-century Atlantic revolutions destabilized empires and rendered territorial boundaries fluid. In this context, the diverse inhabitants of the Americas articulated geopolitical schemes that clashed with and sometimes reinforced US policymakers' expansionist imaginings. As battlegrounds where these visions came face-to-face, these regions represented periphery centers—spaces whose inhabitants had to assess several options of confederation or independence. On the shores of British Bermuda, Bermudians dreamed that their archipelago would join the United States or become an independent free-trading hub. In the heart of North America, white separatists denied US authority in the Tennessee Valley, while Indigenous warriors sought to limit the United States to lands south and east of the Ohio River. In the Caribbean, people of African descent attempted to emulate Haiti's example near US shores. On the Pacific coast, Anglo-American settlers struggled to sustain a distant outpost and adapt to the commercial networks of the Chinookan-speaking peoples. In the wider hemisphere, Spanish American revolutionaries dreamed of the possibilities of their independent, transcontinental republics. These visionaries pressured US state actors to reevaluate how they practiced and envisioned expansion.[9]

These repeated contests over whose vision of the continent and its maritime dependencies and whose power within them would prevail shaped the ideas and objectives of US expansion. It is understandable why historians have found traces of an embryonic vision of manifest destiny taking shape before the antebellum era. After all, by the late 1820s, the United States had reached the edges of northern Mexico and staked claims to the Pacific coast. Consequently, *some* of the foundational ideological elements of manifest destiny had calcified between the American Revolution and the presidency of Andrew Jackson. During these formative decades, expansionists had begun shrouding racial, political, and economic fears by increasingly espousing the belief that Anglo-Americans were destined to spread republicanism across North America. By the 1830s, the stage appeared set for the contests over Texas, California, and Oregon.[10]

The story of westward expansion, however, cannot be fully understood without considering the unrealized alternatives for the nation's boundaries. The creation of a westward-bound, transcontinental republic was one of many potential destinies during the nation's first fifty years. Indeed, some US leaders imagined territorial configurations grander than the republic's modern continental boundaries. At the same time, many other visions gave little impression that the nation would stretch from the Atlantic to the Pacific. Amid the War for Independence, John Adams and Benjamin Franklin envisioned eastward expansion, hoping that annexing Bermuda would help retain their commercial relevance in the British Atlantic. As breakaway states and Indigenous confederacies threatened to halt the nation east of the Ohio River, the founders contemplated a republic nestled between the Atlantic Ocean and the Appalachian Mountains. In the early nineteenth century, the prospects for an independent Indigenous state in Michigan and free Black nations in the Caribbean inspired the desire to annex Canada and Cuba. Before the United States invaded northern Mexico, Missouri politician Thomas Hart Benton imagined expanding to the Pacific Northwest with the help of Mexican and South American allies.

The closing of these possibilities helped establish the playing field for antebellum expansionists. By the 1830s and 1840s, US decision-makers could not count on Mexican allies to secure the Pacific Northwest, nor were they launching invasions into the Cree homelands along Hudson's Bay. President James Polk could not use Bermuda and Cuba as launchpads to conquer the Caribbean, nor did he contend with a pan-Indigenous state in the Great Lakes. Ambitious policymakers remained interested in Canada and Cuba, but failure to annex these colonies helped direct the flow of US interest and settlers toward the Far West. The ideology of manifest destiny came

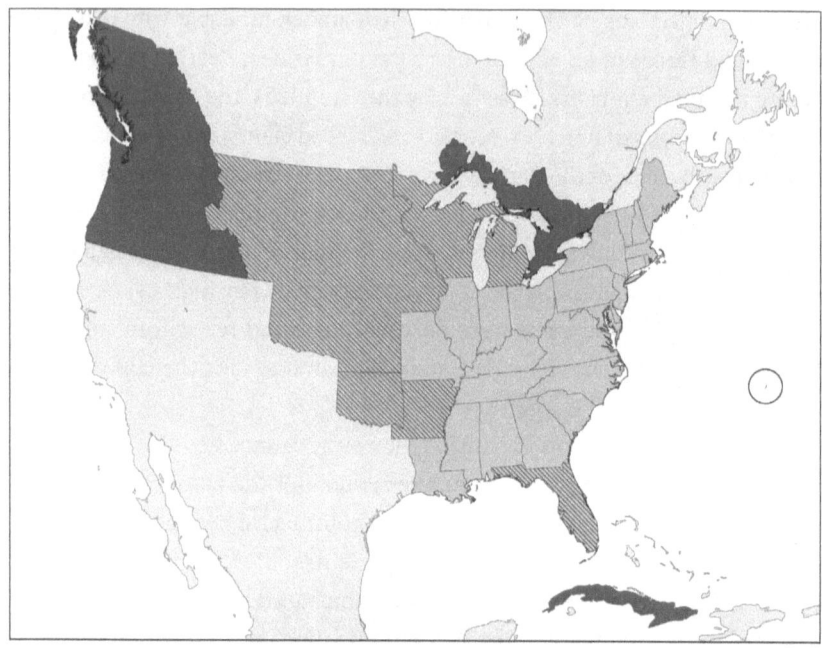

The Unrealized United States of America, circa 1820s.

in clearer focus because so many imagined fates that came before it did not. These thwarted possibilities set the stage for US expansionists to declare their manifest destiny to seize Texas, Oregon, and California.

The following five chapters interrogate pamphlets, newspapers, and diplomatic and private correspondence to trace this interplay of unrealized aspirations, competing visions, and geopolitics. These chapters recover the in-the-moment perspectives of early US policymakers to capture the contingency of their territorial plans. Chapters 1 and 2 explore how eighteenth-century policymakers struggled to define their new nation's future after declaring independence from Great Britain. Revolutionary Americans confronted several questions regarding their nation's expansion. How could aggrandizement secure their independent republic? How might they garner international respect? How would they navigate geopolitics in the Atlantic world and Native resistance on the continent?[11]

Chapter 1 focuses on Patriot-Bermudian efforts to liberate Bermuda from British rule and transform the archipelago into a free-trading hub. Fearing independence would shatter their longstanding commercial ties with the British Empire, revolutionary Americans imagined creating a free-trading, Atlantic-based republic that included Bermuda. The Royal Navy and Loyalist privateers denied this eastward expansion, but the foiled annexation of Bermuda convinced US revolutionaries that proximity to the British Empire threatened their survival.[12]

The second chapter recounts the short life of the postrevolutionary state of Franklin. The Treaty of Paris (1783) granted the new nation a claim to the vast lands between the Appalachian Mountains and the Mississippi River. However, the presence of powerful Indigenous nations and disloyal settlers on the ground undermined any notion of inevitable westward expansion. In the late eighteenth-century Tennessee Valley, the Franklinites invaded the Overhill Cherokees' territory, declared independence from North Carolina, attempted to gain statehood in the American union, and entertained war and confederation with the Spanish Empire. In the eyes of US policymakers, this de facto independent state portended a future of a breakaway, hostile trans-Appalachian West. If eastern policymakers ignored westerners' interests, the Franklinites threatened to spread republicanism across North America without the United States.[13]

Chapters 3 through 5 focus on the frustrated efforts to annex Upper Canada, Cuba, and the Pacific Northwest. These chapters focus primarily on the 1810s and 1820s—decades defined by rising sectional politics and the hardening of racial lines. These domestic developments intensified aggressive aggrandizement. In the contests for these elusive spaces, US policymakers engaged with revolutionary visions expressed by Indigenous Americans, Spanish Americans, people of African descent, and Europeans. The United States lacked a significant demographic and military presence in these regions, forcing policymakers to adapt their territorial schemes in response to these alternative fantasies.[14]

Chapter 3 details how a pan-Indigenous movement's dominance over the Great Lakes region drove and denied US northward expansion into Upper Canada during the War of 1812. In the Michigan Territory, Anishinaabe warriors undermined Thomas Jefferson's dream of an "empire of liberty" by cooperating with Shawnee chief Tecumseh's confederacy and British officials in Canada. In the 1800s and the early 1810s, Tecumseh and his confederates attempted to halt the United States at the Ohio River and create a pan-Indigenous state in the Great Lakes region—a vision that contributed to the United States' failed invasion of Upper Canada in 1812. The possibility of a pan-Indigenous state, the near loss of Michigan, and the foiled conquest of Canada urged US policymakers to perform a dress rehearsal for Indigenous removal along the Michigan and Canadian border.[15]

The fourth chapter explores how fears of a repeat of the Haitian Revolution elsewhere informed US policy toward Cuba. As Cuba began to mirror Haiti on the eve of the revolution, US leaders from John Quincy Adams to James Monroe increasingly feared a slave revolt on the island would disrupt white supremacy and slavery in the Gulf region. Unable to direct the course of Caribbean geopolitics at a distance, US expansionists struggled to acquire Cuba. To this end, American policymakers endeavored to shield the island from abolitionist nations by advocating for the preservation of Spanish colonialism. The contest for Cuba helped racialize the republic's neighborhood policy. This racialized policy intended to influence the fate of their geopolitical neighbors to prevent slave revolts and the creation of free Black nations near US shores.[16]

The final chapter examines the frustrated efforts to establish a distant settlement on the Pacific coast in the 1810s and 1820s. The Transcontinental Treaty of 1819 recognized US claims to the Pacific Northwest. On maps, the United States stretched from sea to sea. Yet many policymakers feared that the vast distance between the Atlantic and Pacific coasts rendered a transcontinental nation impossible. Even optimistic expansionists believed that Fort Astoria—a fur-trading outpost in the Columbian River basin—would break away and assumed that the region would remain under the control of the Chinookan-speaking peoples. To overcome distance and settler disloyalty, US policymakers contemplated developing a Pacific coast settlement with the assistance of the emerging Spanish American republics. Amid an era of Pan-American unity, US leaders embraced Spanish Americans' beliefs that their commerce and ocean-connecting canals would accelerate US expansion to the Pacific coast. These hopes did not materialize, but such high expectations for the newly independent republics provided economic rationales to seize northern Mexico.[17]

When antebellum expansionists celebrated manifest destiny in the 1840s, they attempted to shroud a history of fits and frustrations with a static story of an unstoppable westward movement. The proponents of manifest destiny rejected the uncertainty of early US expansion by touting inevitability. They hid unfulfilled alternatives by describing a Providential design for

America's past and future. This narrative became possible, however, because many other destinies failed to materialize. The abandonment and adaptation of these alternatives helped set the stage for antebellum aggrandizement. Halted to the North, South, and East, antebellum Americans touted their manifest destiny to seize the West. *Before Manifest Destiny* recounts the murky, unmanifest tale that came before.[18]

## ONE

# BERMUDA

In the summer of 1775, George Washington searched desperately beyond the thirteen colonies to acquire muskets and munitions for the Continental Army. Receiving word about a supply of unguarded gunpowder on British-held Bermuda, he wrote to the island's inhabitants, reminding them that "the Cause of Virtue & Liberty is confined to no Continent or Climate." Instead, he continued, "it comprehends within its capacious Limits the wise & good however dispersed & separated in Space or Distance." Bermudians sharing Washington's convictions were already at work. On the night of August 14, 1775, a band of Bermudians helped US sailors secure their colony's gunpowder. Hoping to maintain trade with the mainland colonies, these Bermudian rebels sparked US interest in annexing their archipelago. Like the revolutionary cause, the territorial ambitions of US policymakers reached beyond North America.[1]

Hidden beneath the grand narrative of westward expansion lay the United States' unsuccessful effort to expand eastward. In hindsight, revolutionary Americans' interest in Bermuda seems fanciful. After all, US diplomats failed to acquire the archipelago in peace negotiations, quixotic plans for invasion never materialized, and the feeble Continental Navy could not compete with the powerful Royal Navy. Fantastical as the efforts to incorporate Bermuda may have been, they reveal much about revolutionary Americans' territorial intentions. US interest in Bermuda unveils not an incipient manifest destiny but instead a deep anxiety about leaving behind the British Empire. Fearing independence would shatter commercial ties, revolutionary policymakers envisioned a free-trading, commercial republic that would supplant the British Empire in North America. Located 650 miles off the coast of North Carolina, Bermuda could realize this expansionist imagining. Conversely, US policymakers worried that a British-held Bermuda would threaten their nation's independence and commerce. Though they expanded their republic westward, revolutionary policymakers faced east for empire to remain relevant in the Atlantic world's commercial networks.[2]

Bermudians reinforced revolutionary Americans' vision with their dream of a free-trading, independent Bermuda. Before the American Revolution, Bermuda united the British Atlantic through intercolonial carrying trade and by its strategic location between North America and the Caribbean. Dependent on the Royal Navy for protection and North America for food, Bermudians witnessed the American Revolution collapse their commercial

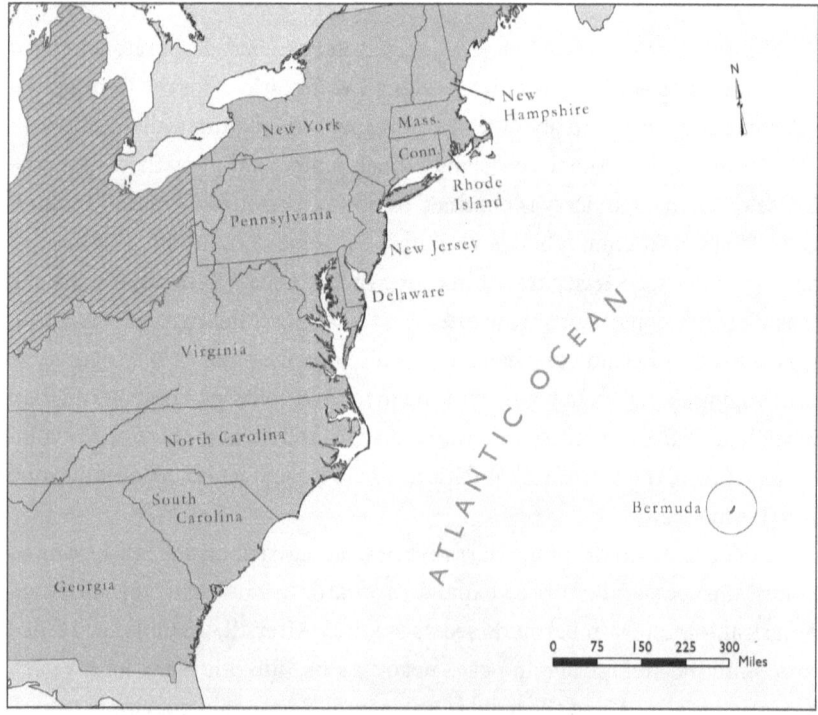

The United States and Bermuda, 1776.

businesses and imperil their role as the bridge of the British Atlantic. Seeking to retain their significance, many Bermudians sought to transform their archipelago into an independent, commercial emporium of the Atlantic world. US policymakers embraced this vision to justify an invasion of Bermuda.[3]

British policymakers thwarted the realization of these imagined destinies. British officials remade the archipelago into a privateers' nest to prevent an invasion, and they cultivated Bermudian elites' loyalty. Such policies ensured Bermuda's attachment to the British Empire. Denied eastward expansion, revolutionary Americans proved unable to realize their imagined destiny to recover the commercial networks of the British Atlantic. Instead, revolutionary leaders found their newly independent republic surrounded by the British Empire on land and at sea.[4]

## BREAKDOWN OF THE BRITISH ATLANTIC

Revolutionary Americans imagined several visions of confederation leading up to independence. These imaginings were not based on an embryonic manifest destiny but rather on their personal experiences as colonial subjects of the British Empire. As the rebellion over taxation and mercantilist policies spiraled into a war, Patriot leaders such as Benjamin Franklin and John Adams recognized a confederation would encourage collective security, centralize diplomatic efforts, and promote economic development. Born British subjects, Adams and Franklin had always looked east toward the metropoles of Great Britain and Western Europe. Their world was the British Atlantic, where they forged commercial and cultural ties with London and the British Caribbean. To this end, Franklin envisioned a confederacy that included Ireland and all the British colonies of the Americas, warning that this union would become "perpetual" if the Patriots' grievances remained unaddressed by Parliament. In the summer of 1776, Adams outlined an American union based on British North America's boundaries before the revolution. In his plan for treaties, Adams hoped that European powers would recognize the thirteen colonies' claims to Canada, Newfoundland, Nova Scotia, the Floridas, and Bermuda. If they did not reconcile with the mother country, Americans hoped to recreate the British Empire in North America.[5]

Commerce proved central to revolutionary Americans' understanding of the British Empire and their expansionist plans. In the eighteenth century, Britons celebrated the commercial focus of the empire. British philosophers such as Adam Smith and David Hume distanced their empire from the colonialism of Spain and France. In contrast to the Catholic empires built on conquest, Great Britain "planted" colonies for commerce. As subscribers of Montesquieu's theories, Britons adhered to the French philosopher's belief that if a nation "sends colonies abroad it must rather be to extend its commerce than its dominion." Britons on both sides of the Atlantic constructed a myth of a benevolent British Empire based on the trade of agricultural commodities. These Britons, however, obscured the ruthless, exploitative labor system that produced these commodities. Anglo-Americans prided themselves on being champions of commerce, believing their North American colonies supported Great Britain's ascendancy and economic supremacy. The supposed politeness that accompanied international trade mattered to them, as white colonists tried to counter accusations of inferiority and worried about their proximity to the "wilderness," Indigenous Americans, and enslaved Black workers.[6]

On the eve of independence, Patriot leaders imagined that their colonies would thrive by escaping the constraints of British mercantilism. The enthusiasm behind America's commercial potential led even the pessimistic John Adams to ask: "Will not the American Trade, once free, spread beyond even my most sanguine Expectations?" US policymakers believed free trade would compel the Great Powers to recognize their republic as a treaty-worthy nation. Such optimism masked widespread trepidation. Many of America's first policymakers, including merchant John Hancock and planter Henry Laurens, feared losing their deep commercial ties with Britons in London, Liverpool, Kingston (Jamaica), Bridgetown (Barbados), and the broader British Atlantic. Patriot leaders endeavored to reconcile these lost imperial connections and legitimize their longstanding clandestine trade with rival European colonies by encouraging free trade. In *Common Sense* (1776), Thomas Paine argued that "our plan is commerce, and that, well attended to, will secure us the peace and friendship of all Europe."[7]

Revolutionary leaders argued that confederating with the remaining British colonies would help them realize their vision of a commercial republic. This conquest for commerce outlook drove the hopes and fears of policymakers. In a 1778 letter to Patrick Henry, John Adams boasted that British subjects trembled at the prospect of the United States as "a dangerous Rival in Commerce and naval Power," especially if the republic annexed "the West India Islands . . . Canada Nova Scotia and the Floridas." Failure to annex these colonies, however, would limit their exports and threaten their navigation of the Atlantic Ocean. Pennsylvania congressional delegate Robert Morris worried that the "Eastern States had little fit for exportation to Europe" unless they acquired Nova Scotia and Newfoundland, whose fisheries provided "Oil, Fish, whale Bones &c." In short, he surmised, "there is nothing for an European market." As the war dragged on, Americans would be reminded that these British colonies mattered to their republic's commercial prosperity and stability.[8]

Bermudians shared North Americans' dismay about a shattered British Atlantic world. On the eve of the American Revolution, Bermuda and the mainland colonies shared roughly a century and a half of entangled history. In the seventeenth century, Bermuda became England's second "new world" colony—established five years after Virginia. Destined for Jamestown in 1609, the English ship *Sea Venture* shipwrecked on Bermuda, paving the way for eventual English colonization of the archipelago. Englishmen viewed Virginia and Bermuda, both briefly under the control of the Virginia Company, as keys to challenging Spanish hegemony in the Americas. Whereas Virginia established a foothold on the continent, Bermuda could control the navigation of European ships in the Atlantic world. Near North America's shores, Bermuda proved a convenient waypoint for Atlantic voyages to and from the Caribbean. Since wind patterns determined shipping routes, one Bermuda governor estimated that roughly nine out of ten European and North American ships passed the archipelago on their voyages to the highly profitable Caribbean sugar colonies. Such a strategic location worked to the advantage of British privateers. During the Seven Years' War, Bermuda was used as a base for privateering that Massachusetts delegate James Lovell recalled was "troublesome" for French vessels.[9]

Geography also tied the archipelago closer to North America. Bermudians associated their identity and economy with their colony's position in the Atlantic world. Indeed, Bermudian poet Nathaniel Tucker celebrated the "enchanted isle" as "Nature's darling spot" due to its favorable climate and distance from "instant harms." Bermudians devoted their economy to seafaring—especially after the restrictive Somers Islands Company dissolved in 1684—and built their colony's significance around the intercolonial carrying trade. Most Bermuda sloops sailed for the British Caribbean to carry shipments of sugar and coffee to Atlantic markets. However, the pursuit of commerce and seafaring left few colonies to pursue large-scale agriculture. Royal governor George James Bruere remarked in 1763 that Bermudians produced "nothing near enough" to feed the colony and thus had to make one- to two-week voyages to North America for "Corn, Pork, Lumber &c." To receive provisions, white colonists and enslaved people of African descent undertook shipbuilding and extracted salt from the Turks Islands, providing North Americans with swift sloops and an essential supply of preservatives. Bermuda's economic connections with North America grew as Bermudian colonists helped settle port cities including Norfolk, Virginia, and Charleston, South Carolina. These Bermudian expatriates formed trading ties with their relatives and friends back home. Official Bermuda traffic records showed that 59 ships arrived from North America and 41 departed from Bermuda's ports en route to the mainland in 1772. These modest numbers, however, do not reflect the many Bermudian sloops that unofficially entered and departed the archipelago.[10]

The American Revolution thus jeopardized the Bermudian way of life. In the 1760s and early 1770s, many Bermudians shared the North American Patriots' revolutionary sentiments. But for Bermudians, the American Revolutionary War posed less ideological questions about liberty and political representation and instead more practical challenges such as food shortages. Their trepidations were magnified when the First Continental Congress passed the Continental Association Agreement of 1774, which threatened to ban exports to Great Britain and the loyal colonies after September 10, 1775. Nonexportation intended to remind Britons of North America's invaluable role in feeding the other colonies and fueling Atlantic commerce.[11]

Prominent Bermudian families tapped into their economic and familial ties with North America to exclude Bermuda from the commercial boycott. The Tucker family led the charge. Amassing wealth through intercolonial trade, the Tuckers had established themselves as pillars of the colony and held a profound influence over other Bermudian families. Some family members had resettled to Norfolk, Virginia, and kept the Bermuda branch of the Tuckers apprised of the revolutionary turmoil. Their wealth, influence, and connections made them the archipelago's primary interpreters of the events in North America. Notable families such as the Bascomes, Gilberts, Harveys, and Jennings fell in line with the Tuckers, which in turn rendered Bermuda's colonial assembly supportive of the American Revolution.[12]

The Tuckers sympathized with prominent Patriots. St. George Tucker, a former student of Virginia delegate George Wythe at the College of William and Mary, stressed this support in a 1775 letter to Thomas Jefferson. "The Inhabitants are a people, who from their immediate Connection and frequent Intercourse with the Continent," he explained, "have contracted an affection for this Country." As the most "Zealous Friends to the Cause of America," Bermudians considered "the Cause as their own, and with pleasure behold every step that has been taken in support of it." The scion of the Tucker family stressed that the Bermudians monitored developments in North America and even joined the Patriots in their refusal "to admit the Stamps in 1765." However, Tucker lamented that his fellow colonists were "incapable" of joining the Patriots because "a single Ship of War might cut off all Communication whatsoever with the Continent, and reduce the Island to the most horrid state of Distress." Hoping to exploit this revolutionary camaraderie, St. George Tucker pleaded that the archipelago's limited fertile fields left Bermudians dependent on North America for "the *absolute* Necessaries of Life."[3]

Henry Tucker of the Grove joined his son's efforts. As his expatriate son was immersed in the revolutionary politics of Virginia, the elder Tucker felt "very uneasey at the Situation of America" and feared "thousands must be Sufferers if not totally ruined" as a consequence of the Continental Association Agreement. Henry assured his son St. George that Bermudians wished "well to their cause" but admitted that they dared not to "offend Engd for fear of their resentment." These anxieties convinced Tucker and a Bermudian delegation to travel in July 1775 to Philadelphia, where they begged the Continental Congress to reconsider nonexportation. Unlike the sugar colonies of the British Caribbean, Bermuda lacked an influential lobby in London, forcing Bermudians to turn to Congress for support. The head of the Tucker family warned that nonexportation would starve hundreds of Bermudians. Congress instructed Benjamin Franklin, Robert Morris, and the Pennsylvania Committee of Safety to respond to the distressed delegation. Though low on nourishment, the archipelago possessed what the revolutionaries desperately needed: gunpowder. Following the Battle of Bunker Hill in June 1775, politicians and military officers of the rebellious colonies searched every corner of the Atlantic world for weapons and munitions. Aware of the empty gunpowder storages, the Tuckers apprised Jefferson and Virginia delegate Peyton Randolph of "a considerable Quantity of powder" at the archipelago's capital of St. George's. Franklin promised the Tuckers that the gunpowder would rescue Bermudians from starvation.[14]

Word of the archipelago's gunpowder stash spread through congressional circles and private correspondences. George Washington requested that Rhode Island governor Nicholas Cooke provide several vessels to take Bermuda's gunpowder to the mainland. "The Voyage is short, our Necessity is great," Washington stressed. The commander in chief of the Continental Army believed that "the Expectation of being supplied by the Inhabitants of the Island under such Hazards as they must run, is slender." "The only Chance of Success," he surmised, "is by a Sudden Stroke." Believing the gunpowder shortage necessitated the voyage, Cooke selected Abraham Whipple, a captain of the Continental Navy, to undertake it. In the late summer of 1775, Whipple sailed for Bermuda aboard his sloop, *Katy*, with instructions to seize supplies and recruit Bermudians.[15]

By the time Whipple reached Bermuda in late September, the gunpowder had already been secured for the American cause. On the night of August 14, a coalition of Bermudians and American sailors secretly loaded the gunpowder onto two ships bound for Philadelphia and Charleston. This successful heist enraged Bermuda's royally appointed governor, George James Bruere, who offered monetary rewards and even freedom to enslaved people who came forward with information. St. George Tucker escaped Bruere's wrath but later recalled that a Loyalist noticed his dusty coat and insinuated his involvement. "I will confess," Tucker reminisced, "I never put on that coat again, while I remained in Bermuda."[16]

The Continental Congress responded more favorably, restoring trade with Bermuda on October 2 and promising to provide the islanders with bushels of food in return for salt, ammunition, field pieces, or arms. Bermudians escaped the Continental Association Agreement but incurred the fury of Bruere and the British policymakers. However, their actions also garnered the attention of revolutionary policymakers. To the congressional delegates, Bermudians appeared "friendly to the cause of America" and therefore "ought to be supplied with such and so great a quantity of the produce of these colonies." This friendship, coupled with Bermuda's dependence on North America, allowed Patriot leaders to imagine revolutionizing Bermuda. And, as they inched closer to independence in the spring of 1776, Americans wondered if they could make the archipelago the fourteenth state.[17]

## AMERICANS, BERMUDIANS, AND THE REVIVAL OF THE BRITISH ATLANTIC

The gunpowder plot revealed the great lengths that Bermudians went to restore the British Atlantic. Throughout the war, Bermudians vacillated their support for Philadelphia or London, portraying themselves as revolutionary sympathizers to Patriots and loyal subjects to Britons. This precarious double-dealing felt necessary to Henry Tucker, who worried that Bermudians "cannot Support [themselves] Without Cloaths from [England] & Victuals from America." Whether in a memorial to the Crown or a letter to a congressional delegate, Bermudians lamented the destruction of the interconnected commercial networks of the British Empire. In a 1776 memorial to George III, the Bermudian Council and Assembly expressed "the utmost anxiety" over the ongoing war's disruption of commerce. Whereas the Continental Association Act threatened to sever trade with the North Americans, Bermudian assemblymen now loathed Great Britain's Prohibitory Act (1775), which prevented loyal colonies from trading with the rebellious thirteen colonies. The islanders felt that their archipelago's strategic location left them threatened on "every side." Though dependent on the British Navy for protection, Bermudians believed that food and intercolonial trade tied them closer to the North Americans. As such, Bermudians defied Parliament and smuggled supplies, sloops, and salt to the Patriots at North American ports and on the Dutch island of St. Eustatius. Through smuggling, Bermudians retained some semblance of the prewar British Atlantic.[18]

Prorevolutionary Bermudians ironically entertained independence and free trade to revive the interconnectedness of the British Atlantic. Led by the Tuckers, this pro-American faction recognized that the independence of the thirteen colonies seemed like a real possibility and therefore sought to secure their significance as the midway point of Atlantic voyages. In a 1775 letter to Benjamin Franklin, Henry Tucker envisioned Bermuda as a free port for the rebellious colonies, the Caribbean, and Europe. Before Parliament passed the Prohibitory Act of December 1775, Tucker argued that making the "Island a Medium for Trade of Non-enumerated goods between the American Colonies and Foreign Ports" would be an "Advantage of America." North Americans could exchange their "large Quantities of produce" for "Powder" from the French and Dutch. Even after Great Britain outlawed trade with the rebels, the Tuckers clung to this dream of transforming Bermuda into a free-trading hub. Indeed, in October 1777, Henry Tucker and the Bermudian assembly appealed to Governor Bruere, hoping he would permit them to "go in search of Provisions to any Port or place" in the Atlantic world.[19]

The Tuckers and their fellow prorevolutionary islanders had another opportunity to pitch this vision when US diplomat and Connecticut merchant Silas Deane visited Bermuda en route to France in April 1776. Immersed in the Atlantic economy, the Connecticut merchant championed the virtues of free trade. In a memoir submitted to the French court in August 1776, Deane envisioned a free-trading Atlantic world where Americans received "the Manufactures of others for the produce of their country." Free trade would erode British hegemony and prevent a "Rivalship" between America and the Great Powers of Europe. These beliefs made Deane receptive to the Bermudians' hopes for the archipelago. Congressional delegate Robert Morris instructed Deane to "directly apply to Henry Tucker," who would apprise him of "everything you wou'd wish to know respecting that Island."[20]

Deane received a warm reception from prorevolutionary Bermudian families, who sold him on the archipelago's potential to expand free trade. Deane left the conversations convinced that the Patriots should revolutionize Bermuda. Based on the advice from "the informers . . . who have discoursed" with him, Deane stressed to Morris that placing Bermudians under American protection "will Cost, neither Time, nor Money" and "might be very beneficial." At St. George's, then the capital of Bermuda, Deane met with inhabitants "zealous in the American Cause," who appeared "willing to do every thing in Their power to promote it." Confident that Bermudians would receive Americans as "their best Freinds," Deane believed that if the thirteen colonies could not capture the archipelago, the revolutionaries could at least recruit sailors and employ "one hundred & Twenty vessels." The future president of the Continental Congress, Henry Laurens of South Carolina, shared this sentiment. "We have been informed," he told sailor Elisha Sawyer, "that Seaman Arms Ammunition & Vessels may be procured at Bermuda." Laurens instructed Sawyer that upon his arrival he should "lose no time but immediately endeavor to enlist for the Service & defence of this Colony, two hundred . . . able Seaman." Laurens advised Sawyer "to purchase a proper Vessel on Account of this Colony" if he managed "to enlist more Men than [he could] conveniently & Safely accommodate."[21]

By capturing Bermuda, Deane suggested that the Americans could establish a naval base on the archipelago. Deane's interest in the archipelago undermines the neat transition from agrarian, continental expansion to commercial imperialism that defines most histories of the US Empire. Bermuda lacked the land and soil for commercial-scale agriculture. "The Land is absolutely fit for Nothing," Deane complained, "but the growth of Cedar." But that cedar—used for shipbuilding—certainly complemented the island's strategic position to secure and promote Atlantic commerce. Governor Bruere noted how Bermudian sloops "sail so well" and reasoned that Bermudians would eventually build "very good Frigates of War." Deane believed that American sailors could rest safely on the archipelago, which would "make a safe Harbor for Our Cruisers." Its harbors, he continued, "are the most difficult to access in the World, & some of the safest when entered." Bermuda's potential to be a shipbuilding and a free-trading waypoint for America aligned with what would later be called the "Hamiltonian" vision: a republic committed to economic development and deeply tied to the Atlantic commercial networks.[22]

Deane argued Bermuda could also ward off the Royal Navy's blockade of the continent. Following the skirmishes at Lexington and Concord, British policymakers responded to the escalating American rebellion by blockading the Eastern Seaboard. This "seize and detain" blockade—authorized by the Prohibitory Act of 1775—cut off port cities, ruined American commerce, captured Patriot vessels, impeded smuggling with the West Indies, and prevented food and munitions from reaching the desperately undersupplied Continental Army. When news of the blockade reached the rebel colonies in February 1776, members of Congress reacted with clamors for independence and free trade with foreign nations. Confessing that the colonies lacked a sizeable navy, Virginia delegate Benjamin Harrison doubted whether American exports could ever reach Europe considering that Patriot frigates were "much restrained by the heavy ships of the enemy" that had been "placed at the entrances of our Bays." Deane argued that occupying Bermuda could mollify Harrison's concerns. In a letter to Robert Morris, Deane suggested that the maritime colony could aid in "drawing off" the Royal Navy from "blocking up the ports, on the Continent." At the very minimum, Deane reasoned, capturing Bermuda would temporarily distract the Royal Navy.[23]

Bermuda's location afforded opportunities for raiding British trade. In response to the Prohibitory Act, Congress authorized privateering in the spring of 1776. To this end, Deane informed Morris that "every Vessel passing Great Brittain & the West Indies, unless drove out, of their Course, sails within about One Hundred Leagues" of Bermuda. A conquest of Bermuda would allow Americans to disrupt Great Britain's trade with its sugar colonies in the Caribbean. As the crown jewels of the British Empire, sugar colonies such as Barbados and Jamaica filled imperial coffers and energized British subjects. "It must be the policy of America," Deane continued, "to intercept, as far as possible, their intercourse between each other as well to supply Ourselves." With "Vessels proper for privateers," Bermuda presented American sailors with the attractive prospect of severing the sugar trade. Though Patriots were unsuccessful in realizing this goal, displaced Loyalists would later capitalize on the island's privateering potential.[24]

After declaring independence in July 1776, US policymakers embraced Deane's and the Bermudians' thinking. Revolutionary leaders hoped to create a free-trading, independent republic as articulated in John Adams's Model Treaty (1776), which insisted that Americans "Shall enjoy the Rights, Liberties, Priviledges, Immunities and Exemptions in Trade, Navigation and Commerce." Under Deane's influence, Benjamin Franklin included the archipelago in his earliest (and most audacious) peace propositions. In addition to demanding American independence and granting reciprocal free trade, Franklin insisted that Britain cede "the provinces or Colonies of Quebec, St. John's, Nova Scotia, Bermuda, East and West Florida, and the Bahama Islands, with all their adjoining and intermediate territories." These British colonies mattered to the new republic's commerce, geopolitical security, and independence. If they remained in British hands, Franklin worried that "occasions of misunderstanding" would arise between the new republic and the monarchy. Patriot leaders imagined an American-occupied or independent Bermuda would advance their vision of a commercial republic that succeeded the British Empire in North America and garnered international respect among the powers of the world.[25]

This expansionist vision of the United States was greatly influenced and encouraged by the aspirations of Bermudians. Patriot policymakers and pro-revolutionary Bermudians hoped to recover connections disrupted by the US War for Independence. Bermuda would empower the Patriots to spread their commerce and thwart British efforts to trade with their Caribbean colonies. Aware of these complementary ideas, US diplomats Franklin, Deane, and Arthur Lee suggested that the United States "take Possession, with the Consent of the Inhabitants of that Island, and fortify the same as soon as possible." America's first policymakers assumed that Bermuda's destiny lay with their new republic. American and Bermudian leaders, however, would soon find themselves adapting their ambitions within the context of a large-scale, global war. If the United States ignored Bermuda, Deane warned Congress in October 1776, "Great Britain will seize it this winter, or France on the first rupture."[26]

## GREAT BRITAIN, FRANCE, AND THE GEOPOLITICS OF US EXPANSION

British policymakers shared Deane's appraisal of Bermuda. The gunpowder plot enraged British officials, who feared an American invasion of the archipelago. While Britons were horrified by the "seditious, libellous, and unchristian Spirit" of the Bermudians and Americans, the missing gunpowder also reminded British policymakers of the colony's strategic position within their Atlantic empire. The Royal Navy still dominated the waters of the Atlantic. But with a torn empire, Britons recognized Bermuda's value as a naval base. In a letter to Lord George Germain, Rev. Thomas Lyttelton stressed the need to fortify Bermuda, which he considered "of great importance in Time of War." Having previously lived on the archipelago, Lyttelton touted Bermuda's potential to showcase the naval and military might of the British Empire. Whereas injured soldiers could recover in the archipelago's warm climate, the Royal Navy's vessels could "benefit from a Number of good ship Carpenters." British vessels and Bermudian sloops stationed there, Lyttelton believed, could plunder the trade of Spain and France, too. Since the archipelago was "in the Tract of all West India Trade," Lyttelton, like Deane and the Tuckers, pictured it as a privateering haven.[27]

Lyttelton and other Britons expressed grave concerns about Bermuda's vulnerability to American attacks. Lyttleton worried that "defenceless" Bermuda was "at the Mercy of every Armed Vessel from the Continent of America." Despite these fears, Governor Bruere ordered Captain Tollemache of the *Scorpion* to remove the archipelago's cannons, fortifications, weaponry, and anything "the Rebels will endeavor to carry off." By taking everything that could be "applyed against His Majestys army," Tollemache exposed the colony to an invasion, and Bruere's shortsighted decision left him begging the pro-American Bermudian assembly to fund the fortification of the archipelago and appealing to British officials for a garrison. Lacking

"Public money" to "Remedy the Inconveniences," Bruere and loyal Bermudians trembled at rumors circulating around the British Atlantic of potential American incursions. After all, in March 1776, Americans invaded the Bahamas "in defence of trade of the Eastern colonies." Thereafter, Britons "conjectured that they intend their next visit to Bermuda."[28]

Royal Governor Bruere repeatedly begged London to send redcoats and warships. British policymakers occasionally met his requests. To enforce the Prohibitory Act, Admiral Lord Howe sent two warships—HMS *Nautilus* and HMS *Galatea*—to suppress smuggling between Bermudians and Americans in the summer of 1776. Lord George Germain, the secretary of state for the Colonies, believed that the presence of the Royal Navy "prevented the Rebels, in any designs they might have had, to possess themselves of the Bermuda Islands." Germain advised the irate governor to avoid policies that would enrage Bermudians and warned him that "any Orders or Instructions from the King would only be exposed to Insult & Indignity." Rather than accommodating the colonists' demands, Bruere urged Germain in the spring of 1777 to send "Soldiers here for the better Support of Internal Government."[29]

Bruere's requests received greater attention after France entered the war in 1778 and recognized American claims to Bermuda. Instructed by Congress, the commissioners in Paris—Benjamin Franklin, Silas Deane, and Arthur Lee—sought France's military assistance to achieve independence. Aiming to shake up Atlantic geopolitics, the commissioners collaborated with the French foreign minister, Charles Gravier, Count of Vergennes, to divide the territories of the British Empire. To provide economic and geopolitical "Security" for France and the United States, American policymakers proposed "that the Conquest of Canada Nova-scotia, Newfoundland, St. Johns, the Florida's Bermuda, Bahama & all the West India Islands now in Possession of Brittain be attempted by the joint Force of France & the United States." If successful, "half the Fishery of Newfoundland together with all the Sugar Islands shall thereafter Appertain to France, the rest to the United States." The Treaty of Alliance, signed on February 8, 1778, promised these territories if France and the United States defeated Great Britain. The alliance also affirmed the "absolute and unlimited" independence of the United States "in Matters of Gouvernement as of commerce." Commerce also pertained to the fifth and sixth articles of the treaty, which recognized American claims to British America and Bermuda.[30]

The French willingly renounced any future claims to Canada and Bermuda. Viewing the fledgling republic as just a client state, Vergennes preferred that Bermuda and Canada be held by friendly Americans rather than France's old rivals across the English Channel. French policymakers proved less concerned about repossessing Canada and more interested in gaining new colonies in the Caribbean to protect Saint-Domingue (modern-day Haiti). They also believed that the expansion of American trade would fill France's coffers. At the very least, Vergennes hoped to restore the balance of powers that existed before the Seven Years' War. Though pawns in a European game, the American commissioners reassured congressional delegates that "France is determined to protect her Commerce with you." France's navy would shield American vessels in the Atlantic Ocean from the British navy. Some Frenchmen pressed their country to invade Bermuda for the United States. In the summer of 1779, the Marquis de Lafayette proposed to Vergennes that "in the winter we might give Bermuda to the Americans." One year later, he again suggested that the French "put in at Bermuda and establish the cause of liberty there."[31]

The Treaty of Alliance intensified Americans' territorial aims. In several letters to the *Pennsylvania Gazette,* for example, a writer who called himself the "Honest Politician" lauded the treaty with France, especially the articles that guaranteed free trade and "the possession of Bermuda, as well as of any part of the continent of North America." This anonymous Patriot wanted any captured British West Indies colonies ceded to France, and while revealing how US ambitions extended beyond the continent, indicated that the republic's expansion for commerce did not necessarily equate to territorial sovereignty. Since "we cannot yet hold one West India island by our fleets," the Honest Politician averred, "it is our interest, that they be held by those who are our allies, and from whom we can receive from the free ports every article of commerce without duty, import, or custom, more than we are at liberty to establish in like case upon articles exported from the continent to those islands."[32]

Before his notorious betrayal of the Patriot cause, Maj. Gen. Benedict Arnold shared this sentiment in his proposed invasion of Barbados and Bermuda in September 1778. In the autumn of 1778, Arnold had been stationed at Philadelphia to protect Congress and the city, which had just been abandoned by British forces in June. Upon reading the treaty's stipulations, he sensed an opportunity for military glory and pitched the plan for conquest to Congress. Hoping to form a coalition of French battleships and American frigates, Arnold numbered among several Continental Army officers who wanted French aid in an invasion of Bermuda. Arnold plotted to "undertake an expedition against Barbados, and, in returning from that Island to take possession of Bermudas in the name of the United States." The major general suggested that if successful, the Americans would sacrifice "the right of conquest to the Island if [the French] shall think proper to send a sufficient and timely force to keep possession of it." Like the Honest Politician, Arnold assumed that American commerce would benefit from an increased presence of France in the Caribbean. After Barbados, "the fleet should immediately proceed for the Islands of Bermudas." If they took "possession" of Bermuda, Arnold continued, "a swarm of privateers may be fitted out to cruise upon the [British] West India commerce." Congress approved Arnold's proposals, but the French diplomat Conrad Alexandre Gérard rejected the plan in favor of achieving American independence in the North American theater.[33]

Arnold's unrealized plans underscored how geopolitical considerations factored into how US politicians and military officers imagined their republic's expansion. By 1778, US leaders' territorial and commercial ambitions had become bound to European competition and warfare. Rather than imagining a Western Hemisphere free of European powers, Patriot policymakers adapted their territorial schemes to the diplomatic and military decisions of European powers. British policymakers surrounded Bermuda with warships, hampering Americans' prospects of smuggling or invading the colony. Diplomatic developments such as the Franco-American alliance intensified the desire to revolutionize Bermuda. But revolutionary Americans' designs on Bermuda depended on France's willingness to provide naval support, given the weakness of the United States' fleet. Unbeknownst to the Americans, France's entry into the war would transform Bermuda into a dangerous neighbor. As Arnold warned the congressional delegates, the Bermudians "must from necessity become formidable enemies to our commerce" if the United States failed to annex the archipelago.[34]

## "OUR TRADE HAS NEVER BEEN SO DISTRESSED"

Even as Arnold was contemplating betraying the American cause, geopolitical circumstances drove many Bermudians to turn on the Patriots. France's entry into the war in 1778 and Spain's in 1779 transformed a contest over

American independence into a global conflict, which expanded into the East and West Indies and along the coast of West Africa and even threatened an invasion of England itself. Consequently, the British dispersed their military and naval resources around the globe. With the war shifting to the southern colonies and the Caribbean, the strategic importance of Bermuda escalated. In October 1778, British general Sir Henry Clinton finally responded to Governor Bruere's cries for a garrison by sending two detachments that would remain in the colony until the conclusion of the war.[35]

The redcoats were not the only newcomers to Bermuda. From 1778 onward, Loyalist refugees from the rebellious colonies migrated throughout Great Britain and its empire, relocating to London, the Caribbean, Canada, and Bermuda. Bermuda's food shortages, high prices, and Patriot-friendly inhabitants made the island an unattractive home. With limited opportunities, Loyalists including Virginian John Goodrich and his family took to privateering. Fulfilling the potential touted by Deane and Arnold, the Loyalist privateers turned Bermuda into a paradise for plundering. Thereafter, to avoid Patriot and Loyalist privateers, merchants covertly transported goods between the continent and Bermuda. Bermuda merchants James and William Perot instructed ship captain Thomas Prizgar to "make the first port you can on the Continent say Virginia or Maryland" if unable to reach Philadelphia in late April 1779. After exchanging "tobacco" for the "West India Market," Prizgar was expected to arrive to Bermuda "in the night."[36]

Loyalist privateers based in Bermuda destroyed the Chesapeake tobacco trade. After losing the British as their primary consumers, plantation owners of the Chesapeake sought to distribute their cash crop in French markets. Their aspirations evaporated, however, as the British strengthened their blockade and urged Loyalist privateering. Led by Goodrich and his sons, privateers haunted their former neighbors, ensuring that "few [American vessels] escape that are sailing out or into Chesapeake Bay." Loyalist raiders memorized the North American coast and the sea routes taken by their former neighbors, preventing significant quantities of tobacco from reaching Bordeaux and the French Caribbean. "We consider it an Object of importance to destroy the infamous Goodrich," the Marine Committee wrote to the Eastern Navy Board. The Goodrich family's success in seizing tobacco and other commodities inspired other Loyalists and even Bermudians to join in the raid. The Bermuda-based privateers, the Marine Committee complained, "infested our Coast." The privateering particularly troubled the port of Baltimore, since the size of its bay made the city's merchant ships easy targets. Privateering in 1779–80 caused Baltimore's clearances to plummet: by the last four months of 1780, clearances had fallen by nearly two-thirds. As one Virginian grumbled, "'Tis true the number of privateers that avarice and enmity have equipped from N. York & Bermuda to cruise on our trade is very great indeed."[37]

The privateering convinced the governors of Maryland and Virginia to seek the aid of the Continental Congress. Thomas Jefferson, then Virginia's governor, wrote several times to John Jay, president of the Continental Congress, requesting letters of marque authorizing armed vessels to capture enemy ships. He complained that "our trade has never been so distressed since the time of Lord Dunmore as it is at present." With Bermuda raiders swarming the seas, frustrated Chesapeake residents urged their leaders to do more than write letters. Virginia militiaman Alexander Dick wrote Jefferson with an offer to lead a conquest of Bermuda. Captain Dick thought that a small detachment of militiamen, "State Ships," and a frigate could effortlessly capture the archipelago.[38]

Congress responded to the rampant privateering by revoking trade with Bermuda in March 1779. Congressional leaders hoped they might alienate the Loyalist privateers from other Bermudians by cutting off the archipelago's primary source of food. Although an ardent ally of Bermuda, George Washington agreed with Congress's decision. Why, he wondered, should Americans continue to ship flour and other commodities to Bermudians, when those supplies "contribute to the support of that swarm of Privateers [who] infest our Coast" and "annihilate our trade"?[39]

Sympathy and salt, however, saved Bermudians from starvation. Philadelphia merchant John Green informed Franklin that "a Sloop arrived in Philada from the inhabitants of Bermudas beging assistance from Congress." These Bermudians claimed that "several hundreds of the Inhabitants had already perished for want of food, that many had not tasted bread for several weeks." The *Pennsylvania Gazette* reported that "the inhabitants were in a starving condition." This crisis prompted even Governor Bruere to allow "salt to be exported to this continent, upon condition that the vessels return with nothing but provisions." Bermudians understood the Patriots' desperate need for salt. Virginians especially relied heavily on the salt mined by Bermudians on the Turks Islands, which they needed to preserve the Continental Army's food supply as well as the provisions—salted beef, pork, and fish—exported throughout the Atlantic world. If Bermudians could deliver "bushels of salt," Jefferson informed St. George Tucker, "I imagine the same measure might be meted to [the island]." Salt and friendship convinced delegates, mostly from the southern and middle states, to restore trade with Bermuda.[40]

Bermudians experienced not only the possibility of food shortages but also the wrath of a new governor. George James Bruere passed away in 1780, likely due to the stress caused by the defiance of Bermudians and the prospects of an invasion. His son, George Junior, succeeded him in October 1780. Seeking revenge against the Bermudians, George Junior installed military officers and Loyalists in the Bermuda council and constructed outposts on the island's west end to prevent smuggling. Like his father before him, Bruere the younger irked prominent Bermudian families. The prorevolutionary sect of Bermuda remained steadfast in their sympathy for the Americans. In a 1780 letter to Continental Board of War member Timothy Pickering, Bermudian captain B. Joell attached a map of St. George's, Bermuda, marking twenty-three of the small port town's buildings with Xs to label their occupants as "friends of America." Despite ongoing privateering, American policymakers also recognized Bermudians, in the words of delegate James Lovell, as "our friends."[41]

This friendship and privateering served as justifications to invade Bermuda. Brig. Gen. Samuel Parsons proposed a naval expedition in the autumn of 1780 to capture "Nova Scotia Penobscott & Bermuda." "Many very important Advantages," he wrote, "will result from our Success." The advantages that Parsons alluded to revolved around geopolitical and economic security. In 1780, the British increased their naval presence along the North American coast. As Loyalist privateers from Bermuda raided the Chesapeake, their northern counterparts in Nova Scotia disrupted the New England trade. Halifax, the capital of Nova Scotia, served as the headquarters for the Royal Navy in North America. British naval forces docked at Halifax and privateers in Bermuda, East Florida, and the West Indies encircled American ports. Seeking to prevent blockades and privateering in future wars, Parsons relayed this message to Gen. Nathanael Greene, believing that these territories, along with Canada, would provide "protection to the Country." If the United States failed to gain "any important Advantages," Parsons warned Washington that the republic's "Character as a Nation will be exceedingly lessen'd in the Eyes of the People of Europe." Bermuda and the North American colonies mattered to the United States' security and reputation.[42]

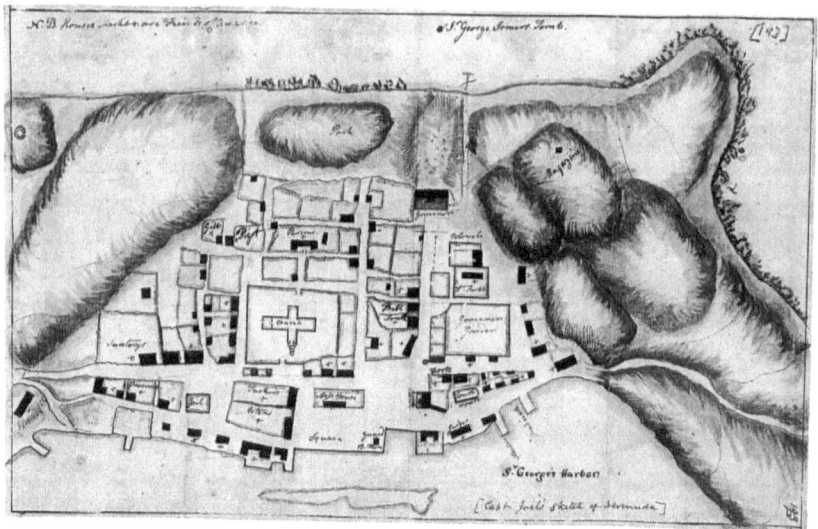

Captain B. Joel's map of St. George's, Bermuda, July 1780. The houses marked with an X signify the Bermudian families friendly to the Patriot cause. (Collection of the Massachusetts Historical Society)

Parson's push for Bermuda and other maritime colonies conveys the dangers posed by the proximity of Great Britain to the future peace of the United States. After the globalization of the US War for Independence in 1778, Britons redeveloped their war plans. The entry of France and Spain threatened the British Caribbean, which compelled British policymakers to station soldiers and Loyalists on Bermuda. Loyalist refugees transformed the pro-revolutionary island into a hub for privateering, devasting American trade. But such privateering fueled Americans' designs on the archipelago. After the Battle of Yorktown, Americans, Bermudians, and Europeans would scramble to reconfigure territorial boundaries and realize their visions for the future of the Atlantic world.

## AFTER YORKTOWN

The surrender of Lord Cornwallis at the Battle of Yorktown in the autumn of 1781 led British prime minister Lord North to decry "Oh God! It is all over!" But for revolutionary leaders, the last two years of the conflict were vital to securing their republic's prosperity. During and after the siege of Yorktown, military officers and politicians inundated Washington's secretaries with proposals to retake New York City and other British holdouts. But many revolutionary leaders thought beyond the thirteen states. Generals, merchants, and diplomats plotted invasions of nearby British colonies in hopes of eroding British hegemony in and around North America. As the war neared its end in the early 1780s, Patriot policymakers sought to annex colonies before signing a peace treaty with Great Britain.[43]

Many of these proposals included Bermuda. As Washington commanded the siege at Yorktown in October 1781, James Mitchell Varnum, a retired brigadier general and Rhode Island delegate to Congress, pointed out Bermuda's potential to extend the republic's burgeoning commerce and naval presence in the greater Atlantic. Aware that Washington was "well acquainted with the natural and political Situation of the Island of Bermuda," Varnum "tho't a Conquest of that Island Necessary." He justified the invasion because Bermuda's "Inhabitants are generally friendly to the united States, and are loudly dependent on them for Subsistence." and he argued that the island "was intended to be annexed to them when the Treaty of Alliance was formed with France." Like many policymakers, Varnum warned that the archipelago was "every way calculated to annoy us. . . . Our Commerce is greatly annoyed by the Privateers which rendesvous there." He added: "A Conquest might relieve us from that Inconvenience & convert it into a Place of Arms for our own Vessels." He also thought Bermuda would "form an excellent Barrier against naval Operations in a future War." At the very least, Varnum suggested that Bermuda could be exchanged for New York City "should the British strenuously insist upon retaining some Possessions." Overall, Varnum envisioned Bermuda serving to protect American commerce and repel Britons seeking to meddle with their nation-building efforts.[44]

St. George Tucker shared Varnum's belief that Bermuda mattered to America's peace, but he also considered the interests of his fellow Bermudians. An officer of the Virginia militia, Tucker had devoted himself to the cause of America, even serving at the Battle of Yorktown. However, the Bermudian expatriate remained attuned to the interests of the Bermudians through his correspondence with family and friends. An American conquest, he reasoned, would help realize Bermudians' dream of a free-trading archipelago. In a series of letters to Washington shortly after Yorktown, Tucker outlined a plan of invasion. He reminded the commander in chief of the

Continental Army that the hearts of Bermudians "glow with the warmest Sentiments of Friendship." Tucker informed Washington "that a fifty Gun ship and three or four Frigates with a few Land Forces would accomplish this End in less than three Days."[45]

Tucker provided Washington with a plan to achieve Bermuda's independence. After capturing the archipelago, American forces would enforce Bermuda's neutrality. He suggested that "the Island of Bermuda shall remain in a neutral State untill the End of the War." Thereafter, a treaty would determine "whether it shall be restored to the Crown of Great Britain or annexed to the united states of America." Regardless of their affiliation, Bermudians would be "permitted to trade without molestation, with Great Britain or any of her Depenncies as well as with France & her Depenncies and the united states of America." Tucker also included a draft of articles to send to "some respectable Gentlemen" who would be "the best Judges of the Interests of the people." The Americans would allow Bermudians "a free Trade with France, America, Spain, Holland & all neutral powers" and even propose a "Secret Article" to them. The secret article stated that "the Island of Bermuda" would be "considered as an Independant State, perfectly free to establish such form of Government, and to enter into such political Connections as the Inhabitants may think proper." Tucker hoped to open the door for Bermudians to join the United States or gain independence. Though idealistic, Tucker's vision attempted to salvage the commercial connections lost by the War for Independence and gain new trading partners for the Bermudians.[46]

Washington embraced these proposals and included the conquest of Bermuda in his military plans in 1782. Uncertain of the outcome of the diplomatic negotiations in Paris, he prioritized recapturing New York City and Charleston, but he also advocated for the annexation of Bermuda and Nova Scotia because he understood the value of these territories to postwar transatlantic trade. Washington's commercial agriculture interests as well as his military experience shaped that vision. As a planter, Washington monitored and adapted to the Atlantic economy, even shifting from tobacco to wheat production in the 1760s. In the decade before the Revolutionary War, he expanded his shipments to the Caribbean and witnessed his profits grow as years of bad harvests in Europe fueled growing demand. He was more innovative than most Chesapeake planters, and he directed his plantation managers and enslaved workers to produce silk, hemp, corn, flax, alfalfa, and buckwheat. Immersed in Atlantic commerce, Washington believed that a conquest of Halifax "would add much, not only to the security of the trade of Canada, but the United States in General." Whereas annexing Nova Scotia added "greatly to the security of our Shipping," Washington thought that a successful invasion of Bermuda would prevent privateers from continuing to "annoy our Trade." Adhering to Tucker's advice, Washington boasted that a conquest "might be carried without much if any opposition."[47]

Philadelphia merchants joined the Virginia planter in proposing an invasion of Bermuda. In the late summer of 1782, as peace negotiations dragged on, a cadre of unnamed Philadelphian businessmen asked the Pennsylvania congressional delegates to "press an attempt upon Bermuda to secure their commerce." Reminiscent of the expedition proposed by Arnold, the Pennsylvania delegates sought French assistance for the enterprise. After all, the French fleet "was now off the Capes of Delaware" and "had sent up a message that if the ships in the harbor were ready to put to sea [they] would afford them a convoy from the Coast." Congressmen including James Madison shared the merchants' aspirations, hoping that American trade would "at least receive some transient advantages from [the fleet's] visit to the American Coast." Absorbing these proposals, Secretary of Foreign Affairs Robert Livingston informed the Minister of France, Anne-César de La Luzerne, that "the security and possession" of Bermuda would protect "our commerce and that of France." Congress rejected the proposal out of fear that the French would occupy the archipelago for themselves. Congressional delegates had also learned from Washington of "a superior British fleet" headed for Philadelphia, which made the French naval presence off the capes of Delaware a necessity. Washington hoped this information would save them "the trouble of making arrangements."[48]

Interest in Bermuda reached American newspapers, too. In a 1782 letter to the *Freeman's Journal or The North-American Intelligencer*, "Harpax," who was perhaps a disgruntled merchant or congressional delegate, relayed the benefits of acquiring Bermuda to his Philadelphia audience. This anonymous author hoped to conquer the archipelago before the conclusion of the ongoing peace negotiations in Paris. Harpax evoked a rhetoric similar to Silas Deane's in stressing Bermuda's geographic location and commercial potential. "Bermuda is extremely well situated for an enemy to annoy the European and West India commerce of North America in time of war," Harpax noted, "as we have already pretty well experienced in the present between the United States and Great Britain." Like Tucker and Varnum, Harpax foretold the archipelago's postwar commercial potential. "Being once in possession of the Bermuda islands and St. Augustine," Harpax explained, "Great Britain, in any future war, would have little or no check upon our trade to and from the Carribees."[49]

Harpax encapsulated the sentiments of military officers, diplomats, and merchants regarding Bermuda. In wake of widespread privateering, revolutionaries witnessed how dangerous a hostile Bermuda could be to American trade. But such danger compelled Americans to imagine how annexing Bermuda would bolster their commercial prospects in the postwar era. Revolutionary Americans' vision complemented the free-trading aspirations of Bermudians. If the Americans could secure trade with Britain's Caribbean islands, Harpax anticipated fashioning Bermuda as an "emporium or grand repository of West India and European commodities" where American merchants could send "their vessels with the produce of this country to exchange for that of others." Harpax feared that these commercial opportunities would be squandered if the United States failed to capture Bermuda before Americans and Britons reached a peace agreement. The unknown expansionist eyed public readership and the congressional delegates in Philadelphia when concluding that "it is plain these islands ought to be considered as a consequence to the United States, and the measures taken to sever them from the dominion of Great Britain before a peace may render it impracticable."[50]

## "AT LIBERTY TO JOIN THE CONFEDERACY": A FAILED PITCH FOR AN AMERICAN BERMUDA

Peace, in fact, rendered the annexation of Bermuda impracticable. As late as December 1782, the American commissioners at Paris—Benjamin Franklin, John Adams, Henry Laurens, and John Jay—included Bermuda in their demands for a definitive peace. Attempting to salvage the British Atlantic, Franklin's draft insisted on the protection of merchant vessels, fishing rights, and free trading rights for American citizens and British subjects. But for the future geopolitical security of the United States, Franklin demanded that "Canada, Nova Scotia, and Bermuda should be declared free & Independent States, and at Liberty to join the Confederacy or remain separate."

US policymakers did not require that Bermuda confederate with the United States, as long as the archipelago did not block American navigation and trade.[51]

The American commissioners, however, lacked any justification for annexing an archipelago they had failed to capture. In hindsight, US efforts to confederate with Bermuda seem fantastical. Budget constraints prevented the revolutionaries from building a naval fleet that could launch an invasion and maintain control of the archipelago in the event of a British counterattack. Moreover, wartime Americans constructed frigates carrying twenty-eight to thirty-six-guns, which paled in comparison to the sixty-four- and seventy-two-gun warships employed by the British. By contrast, Lord Sandwich, First Lord of the Admiralty, expanded the Royal Navy significantly in the latter half of the war. In 1781, 105,000 men served in the Royal Navy, which enabled the British to contend with the Continental Navy and their European rivals. As such, many schemes to invade Bermuda depended on French naval support. In his plan to capture the maritime colony, Varnum asked Washington whether "French Frigates can be employed in the Co-operation?" Though French policymakers recognized the value of a friendly Bermuda, they prioritized winning the war on the continent and transforming the new republic into a vassal. Overall, the British Navy proved an insurmountable obstacle to any maritime conquest.[52]

Political change in Bermuda at the war's climax gravitated the archipelago away from the revolutionaries and toward the British Crown. Some Britons and Bermudians held out hope that Bermuda would be fashioned into a free-trading waypoint that would welcome merchants throughout the Atlantic world. "If America becomes independent," a Briton on Bermuda thought wishfully in early 1783, "this heap of sand will become of greater utility to [Great Britain] than half a dozen West India islands." However, the political environment had changed profoundly under the new leadership. Following the stress-induced death of Governor Bruere and the short governorship of Bruere's son George Bruere Jr. (1780–81), the British Crown appointed an amiable Salem Loyalist and merchant, William Browne, as the royal governor of Bermuda in January 1782. Coupled with the efforts of Bruere, who undercut smuggling and promoted privateering, Governor Browne gained the favor of Bermudians, leading the once pro-American Bermudians to reconcile with London. The former Salem merchant selected several Bermudians to his council and reinstated prominent Bermudians back to leadership positions in the militias and parish magistrates. Browne encouraged Bermudians to establish deeper commercial connections with Canada and the British Caribbean, weakening the archipelago's ties with the rebellious colonies. By the war's end, Browne believed that his policies convinced Bermudians to abandon their dream of an independent archipelago that would be "the storehouse of the Western World" and richer "than half a dozen West India islands."[53]

Bermuda's fate was also sealed by the deterioration of US-Bermudian relations by 1782. Bermuda's trade with the United States had ceased that year, leading even prorevolutionary Bermudians to embrace privateering. From January 5 to September 19, Bermudian privateers seized ninety-three prizes from American ships. Sympathy waned on both sides. Congress refused to consider Bermudian pleas and sought to conquer the archipelago until peace had been resolved by treaty. The deterioration of US-Bermuda relations makes sense when considering the original motives of the prominent Bermudian families. They had been open to the revolutionary cause. But for them, survival remained the primary objective. Bermudian George Bascome explained to St. George Tucker that adapting to the aspirations of both Patriot and British leaders saved "the lives of 14,000 souls." Bermudians had entertained confederation with the American republic or independence to escape the mercantilist constraints of the British Empire. By the war's end, friendly relations with Governor Browne and profitable privateering seemed more beneficial to their well-being than independence—despite the ambitions of revolutionized expatriates such as St. George Tucker. Ironically, the visions of the Americans and Bermudians to promote free trade in the Atlantic world gave way to the refashioning of Bermuda into the "Gibraltar of the West." Rather than an open free port, Bermuda would serve as a naval base where Britons could frustrate American efforts to expand their boundaries and trade in the Atlantic East.[54]

## ATLANTIC AIMS: REEXAMINING AMERICAN EXPANSION FROM BERMUDA'S SHORES

American diplomats, military officers, and politicians failed to acquire or revolutionize Bermuda. The fortunes of this small island, however, provide an opportunity to reconsider the territorial ambitions of early American leaders whose greatest commonalities were their shared commercial imperatives and their British identity. Their expansionist imagining at the outset of the War for Independence unveils not an embryonic vision of manifest destiny but instead a fear to leave behind the commercial networks of the British Atlantic. Revolutionaries such as Adams and Franklin envisioned a free-trading republic that would erode British hegemony in North America and command Atlantic commerce. In the colonial era, North Americans believed that nearby colonies such as Canada, the Floridas, Nova Scotia, Bermuda, and the Bahamas mattered to the British Empire's economic prosperity and geopolitical security. The War for Independence reminded Patriot policymakers of the threat that these colonies posed to their union. As a consequence, US policymakers emerged from the conflict with Anglophobia—a fear that would haunt US expansionists in the decades that followed independence.[55]

As their interest in Bermuda shows, revolutionary policymakers believed that the loyal British colonies would foster free trade. Beyond the continent, John Adams argued that nature justified the promotion of free trade with the British Caribbean. "The commerce of the West India Islands is a part of the American system of commerce," Adams insisted. "They can neither do without us, nor we without them." Furthermore, he asserted that "obstinate attempts" to block trade might "lay a foundation for intimate combinations between the islands and the continent which otherwise would not be wished for or thought of by either." Hidden beneath this boastful language lay a fear of losing commercial ties with the British Caribbean. "If We should agree to revive the Trade upon the old Footing," Adams conceded, "it is the Utmost that can with a colour of Justice or Modesty be requested of Us." Admitting that this restoration of previous commercial arrangements was "not equal," Adams did not want to "deny ourselves the Freight from the West Indies to Europe, at least to G. Britain." Rather than restoring ties with their former subjects, British policymakers trembled at the prospect of losing the sugar colonies to the United States. Sir Henry Clinton, for example, was sure that the United States desired to annex Canada and the Caribbean. He predicted that US territorial interests would result in another war with the ambitious new republic.[56]

US policymakers believed that the loyal British colonies undermined the security and independence of their new republic. New England revolutionaries worried that a British-controlled Canada and Nova Scotia could threaten American commerce, relations with Indigenous nations, and independence. Searching "for a permanent Peace," Samuel Adams feared that New England "will never be able to afford Protection to her Trade" unless the republic seized Canada and Nova Scotia. As such, Adams asked: "Will it not be wise then for us to wrest those Possessions from her, if it be in our Power?" By controlling Nova Scotia, Adams endeavored to establish a naval base to "become formidable or respectable" in the eyes of European powers. As a result, congressional delegates considered the acquisition of Nova Scotia and Canada as being of the "utmost importance to the peace and commerce of the United States."[57]

Dread of encirclement by the British transcended regionalism. With the British disrupting the Carolina indigo and rice trade, Charleston merchant Henry Laurens spent the early years of the war advocating for the annexation of St. Augustine, the capital of East Florida. "Carolina sees the destruction of her Commerce," Laurens complained, "from Bahama & Florida in the hands of an Enemy." During the war, St. Augustine was a nest for the Royal Navy and Loyalist privateers, whose constant presence along the coasts of the Carolinas caused American policymakers to launch several campaigns in the spring of 1776 and the summer of 1777. "While St. Augustine remains in the possession of the Enemy," Laurens stressed, "Georgia will be unhappy.... South Carolina too will be continually galled by Rovers and Cruizers from that Pestiferous nest." He concluded that an "expedition must therefore be undertaken."[58]

Thomas Jefferson shared Laurens' sentiment about eliminating British influence in North America. Whereas they loathed Bermudian privateers raiding American commerce, revolutionary leaders such as Jefferson panicked about British intrigue with Indigenous nations in the trans-Appalachian West. Americans had long feared a European presence in Canada, where French fur traders and British officials supported Indigenous resistance to Anglo-American settlement. In a letter to military officer George Rogers Clark on Christmas Day 1780, the prominent Virginian imagined a republican empire that would check British influence in North America. "We shall form to the American union a barrier against the dangerous extension of the British Province of Canada," Jefferson continued, "and add to the Empire of liberty an extensive and fertile Country thereby converting dangerous Enemies into valuable friends." Like their fears about Bermuda, revolutionary leaders maintained that the prosperity of their republic depended on the removal of the British Empire in North America.[59]

Jefferson's "Empire of liberty" conveys a desire to dominate North America. However, Patriot leaders proved willing to share the continent and seas with independent Britons and friendly European powers. Immersed in Atlantic geopolitics, wartime politicians and diplomats tempered their territorial demands to adjust to European interests. In fact, Patriot leaders offered to invade the Floridas on behalf of Spain in exchange for access to waterways for trans-Appalachian settlers. Reiterating Congress's official statement, Benjamin Franklin wrote to a Spanish ambassador that "if his Catholic Majesty will join with the United States in a war against Great Britain, they will assist in reducing to the possession of Spain the town and harbor of Pensacola." In return, however, "the inhabitants of the United States shall have the free navigation of the Mississippi, and the use of the harbor of Pensacola." As long as the French and Spanish opened their ports to American merchants, Franklin had little concern about a Spanish Florida.[60]

Virginia governor Patrick Henry joined Franklin's efforts to secure access to the Mississippi River. In 1778, Henry begged the Spanish governor of Louisiana, Bernardo de Gálvez, to allow western Americans to ship their produce down the Mississippi River. Revolutionary Americans dreamed that the trans-Appalachian West—which Americans claimed through the Treaty of Paris (1763) but which remained under the control of Indigenous nations—would serve as a breadbasket for a free-trading Atlantic world. If the young republic could gain access to the Mississippi River, congressional delegates argued, this western land could "not only supply an abundance of all necessaries for the West India islands, but serve for a valuable basis of general trade, of which the rising spirit of commerce in France and Spain will no doubt particularly avail itself." But this expansionist imagining did not exclude friendly European powers from the continent. Henry reassured Gálvez that Virginians had "more Land than can be settled for many Ages to come" and lacked designs on Spanish Louisiana. Instead, western Americans and East Coast policymakers sought the "inland Navigation of Mississippi & Ohio" because "British Cruizers cannot infest it." Patrick did not anticipate Spain's closure of the Mississippi River to American settlers nor the aggressive push by westerners into Spanish Louisiana in the 1790s. Nonetheless, Henry's comments reveal a desire to secure commerce and escape the terror of British privateers.[61]

US policymakers' ideas about Bermuda mirrored their expectations for the rest of the British Empire. Eighteenth-century British Americans had always feared proximity to dangerous European powers, particularly

Catholic France and Spain. However, US policymakers emerged from the War for Independence with an Anglophobia that proved far more potent than fear of neighboring Catholics. Once proud of their heritage, the former British subjects understood Great Britain to be the strongest and wealthiest nation in the Atlantic world. At the outset of independence, the Royal Navy patrolled American seas and British garrisons surrounded (and even occupied) American settlements in the West. Though unable to create a commercial republic that would replace British North America, Americans left the War for Independence dreading British encirclement—a fear that would persist well into the nineteenth century.[62]

The far-reaching interest in Bermuda illuminates the dynamic, contingent plans for the republic's first territorial boundaries. Reading manifest destiny back into the revolutionary era misses the ways in which Patriot leaders imagined expansion in the context of the eighteenth-century Atlantic world. Uncertain about leaving behind the British Empire, Patriot leaders believed that annexing or revolutionizing Bermuda would enable them to realize their vision of a free-trading republic. From 1775 to 1783, revolutionary Americans conspired to conquer Bermuda. Diplomats such as Silas Deane and military officers such as James Mitchell Varnum entertained the idea of Bermuda safeguarding American vessels and transforming into a commercial emporium. Bermuda, along with colonies such as Nova Scotia and the Bahamas, would enable the republic to safely navigate in the Atlantic world.

Revolutionary policymakers' plans for Bermuda did not develop solely in congressional circles or military councils. Sharing British North Americans' fear of a broken British Atlantic, Bermudians sought to reassemble lost commercial ties. Prorevolutionary Bermudians envisaged an independent Bermuda becoming a neutral marketplace for all the powers of the Atlantic world. By promoting free trade, Bermudians would be safe from an invasion and would receive all the necessities for survival on an isolated archipelago. Bermudians expressed this dream in their pleas to Patriot leaders, who believed that this vision for the archipelago reinforced their expansionist goals in the Atlantic East. Widespread Bermudian support for the War for Independence led Patriot diplomats to demand the annexation or independence of Bermuda in their peace negotiations with Great Britain.

The nascent republic, however, was unable to realize the hopes of Americans and Bermudians. The Articles of Confederation constrained the republic's financial and military resources, preventing it from mounting an invasion of Bermuda without French assistance. As the War for Independence globalized in 1778, British policymakers restored the loyalty of Bermudians by accommodating local interests and sending garrisons to instill order. Ultimately, the American commissioners recurred to their demands for Bermuda during the negotiations in Paris in 1782–83 but could not pry the valuable colony away from the British Empire. British hegemony in the Atlantic Ocean denied the United States' eastward expansion into Bermuda.

Although Bermuda remained a British colony (and remains an overseas territory today), the archipelago illuminated the British threat to American commerce and independence. After 1778, Loyalists transformed Bermuda into a privateering haven, devasting Chesapeake and mid-Atlantic commerce. As diplomats and military officers had predicted, a hostile Bermuda could impede maritime navigation, obstruct trade, and endanger US nationhood. Their anxieties about nearby British colonies came to fruition in the decades that followed the War for Independence. In 1803, Thomas Paine stressed to President Thomas Jefferson that "Burmuda ought to belong to the United States" because "in its president condition it is a Nest for piratical privateers." During the War of 1812, the British launched the Chesapeake campaign from the shores of Bermuda. And, amid the US Civil War, Confederate merchants evaded the US blockade of the Confederacy's coast by trading with Bermudians. Unable to remove the British Empire in North America, US policymakers dreaded their British neighbors well into the nineteenth century.[63]

After the War for Independence, American policymakers continued to imagine expansion within the realm of Atlantic competition and commerce. They believed that the trans-Appalachian West would keep them relevant in the Atlantic world and enable them to repay their debts with land sales. But their revolution kickstarted an era of political, social, and territorial change that shook the geopolitical order of the Atlantic world. As this revolutionary age unfolded in the late eighteenth and early nineteenth centuries, competing visions for the future of the Americas would transform how Americans imagined and practiced expansion. US policymakers would soon find themselves clashing with the ambitions of settlers in the Ohio and Tennessee Valleys.

## TWO

# THE STATE OF FRANKLIN

The upheaval rocking the Tennessee Valley prompted Adam Stephen to write frantically to James Madison in late 1787. Observing the violent clashes between Anglo-American settlers and the Cherokees south of the Holston River, the western Virginian warned Madison about the self-proclaimed state of Franklin (1784–ca. 1788), which had declared independence from North Carolina a few years prior. "The Wild men of Franklin State," Stephen complained, "have an intention to drive the Cherokees out of their Country." Stephen worried that the Franklinites' conflict with the Cherokees would ignite a general war with Native nations that would endanger the American republic's presence in the trans-Appalachian West. Stephen had good reason to fear the calamitous state of Franklin. In the 1780s, Franklin separatists ignored national and state laws, conducted brutal raids against southeast Native nations, demanded war with Spain while contemplating confederation with its empire, and lost a decisive short battle against North Carolina loyalists. No wonder, then, that Franklin attracted few supporters east of the Appalachians.[1]

The state of Franklin was not what the nation's founders had in mind for the West. In the aftermath of the War for Independence, the founders envisioned transforming the Native lands between the Appalachians and the

Mississippi River into a breadbasket for their commercial republic. Farmers would purchase acres to repay wartime debts, and veterans would receive land as a reward for their wartime service. Postrevolutionary Americans attempted to realize this destiny north of the Ohio River. In that fertile land, the Northwest Ordinances promised to add equal western states to the union, while military officers of the early republic professionalized the US Army in response to repeated military defeats at the hands of Native confederates. The Northwest Territory would seemingly become the launchpad for the American empire.[2]

The state of Franklin thwarted this vision for expansion. Most settlers flocked south of the Ohio River, where a dream of orderly settlement collapsed in the face of rapid migrations. In hindsight, these settlers could be considered early agents of the republic's manifest destiny. For state actors and settlers in the 1780s, however, the Franklinites raised doubts about whether the United States would expand west of the Appalachian Mountains.

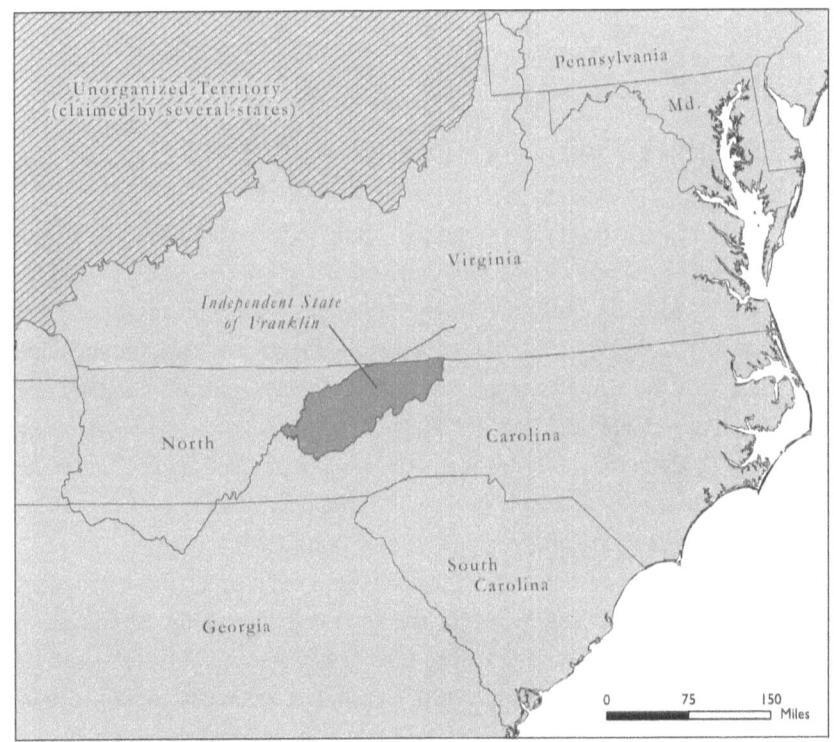

The Independent State of Franklin, circa 1784.

Rejected by North Carolina and Congress, the state of Franklin was a de facto independent republic of the founders' making. Franklin acted as an independent, "breakaway" republic that contested US authority in the trans-Appalachian West. To the founders, Franklin portended a future of unruly rival republics spread across the West and undermined any notion that US expansion would be inevitable.[3]

Fear of western separatism forced the founders to reconfigure their expansionist imaginings. By the end of the 1780s, the founders' and the Franklinites' imagined destinies for trans-Appalachia had been foiled. But the Franklinites' vision of westward expansion would live on. Portraying their movement as a continuation of the American Revolution, westerners argued that pursuing their political and economic interests would enhance rather than corrupt republicanism. Afraid of breakaway republics, national leaders such as James Madison believed that appeasing western interests would advance US empire and strengthen the union. Franklin, however, served as a cautionary tale that settlers could spread republicanism across North America without the United States.[4]

## FACING EAST AND EXPANDING WEST

The Treaty of Paris (1783) extended the newly independent republic to the Mississippi River but halted its boundaries south of the Great Lakes. Despite the Patriots' military struggles in the West, British prime minister Lord Shelburne conceded the vast, Native-controlled lands to maintain amicable relations with the United States. Britain's diplomats rejected US demands for Bermuda, Nova Scotia, and Canada, but the nation's founders still clung to their ambitions for a free-trading Atlantic. Postrevolutionary Americans believed that trade would elevate their republic to the status of treaty-worthiness within the European sphere of geopolitics.[5]

While they craved commerce, postrevolutionary Americans struggled to realize their grand ambitions for the territory beyond the Appalachian Mountains. The founders intended to sell these western lands—claimed by several states, including Virginia, North Carolina, and Pennsylvania—to alleviate the national debt. However, white Americans ignored the complexities of a region dominated by Indigenous nations, coveted by European powers, and invaded by unruly settlers. Despite these obstacles, George Washington viewed the trans-Appalachian West within the Atlantic-based, commercial outlook of the revolutionary era. Washington maintained that securing access to the Mississippi River for western settlers would increase exports to the Caribbean and Europe. "Smooth the road once, & make easy the way for them," Washington remarked, "& then see what an influx of articles will be poured in upon us—how amazingly our exports will be encreased by them." Yet Spain stunted these ambitions by closing the Mississippi River in 1784 to Anglo-American settlers.[6]

British policymakers balked at the founders' aspirations. Lord Shelburne's efforts to reconcile with the United States triggered a flurry of postwar diatribes. Living in London in the mid-1780s, Abigail Adams complained how "the Americans are so much secreetly feard, but openly hated." Seeking to avoid commercial agreements favorable to the United States, John Baker Holroyd, 1st Earl of Sheffield, tore into the founders' optimism in his *Observations on the Commerce of the American States* (1783). Sheffield insisted that the trans-Appalachian West constituted the young nation's Achilles heel. Conventional wisdom stressed that republics must remain small to survive. History supported this theory. After all, the overextended Roman republic descended into the dictatorship of Julius Caesar. Sheffield reassured readers that Americans would not have to worry about an overextended republic. Instead, the West would break away and form separate republics. "The authority of Congress," Sheffield mocked, "can never be maintained over those distant and boundless regions, and her nominal subjects will speedily imitate and multiply the examples of independence."[7]

Sheffield reasoned that settler expansion would benefit British economic and imperial interests. Recent history showed how the American population flocked west of the Appalachian Mountains, where they "cannot become commercial." British manufacturers stood to become the greatest beneficiaries of this population movement. Farmers in "the inland parts of the continent will require an inexhaustible supply" from British manufacturers over the next few decades. Maintaining the Navigation Acts, rather than easing trade restrictions, would strengthen the restructuring of the British Empire and potentially return the former colonies under London's control.[8]

Sheffield's predictions about the ignominious fate of the United States enraged Americans. US elites craved the approbation of their British and European counterparts. They attempted to present themselves as progenitors of a republican experiment that would inspire the Old World to embrace liberal politics and commerce. Crucial to this vision was the extension of free trade and access to new markets. Sheffield's *Observations*, however, dampened these ambitions. Many Americans shared Richard Henry Lee's disdain for "all the silly, malign commercial restraints upon our trade with her W. India islands, that are to be found in Lord Sheffield's book on the Commerce of the two countries." Sheffield's writings reflected the postwar reality. Parliament excluded American ships from British Caribbean ports, limiting the markets for American merchants and farmers. Writing under the pseudonym "Common Sense," Thomas Paine argued in 1784 that "the ground of security which Lord Sheffield has chosen to erect his policy upon, is of a nature which ought, and I think must awaken, in every American, a just and strong sense of national dignity." Only by "acting in Union," Paine argued, could Americans overcome "the usurpations of foreign nations on the freedom of trade."[9]

Unfortunately for Paine, Americans diverged in response to Sheffield's *Observations*. Northerners feared Sheffield was right when he contended that the trans-Appalachian West would drain the north's population at the expense of their commerce and political significance. Masked under the pseudonym "Nestor," Pennsylvanian Benjamin complained that "there is but one path that can lead the United States to destruction; and that is their extent of territory. It was probably to effect this, that Great Britain ceded to us so much waste land."[10]

By contrast, Virginians eschewed Sheffield's theories. Virginian elites were already planning canals and roads that would link the Tidewater to their western land claims. Virginians surmised that the population movement from the Northeast to the Southwest would brighten their economic future. Because the trans-Appalachian West seemed "more convenient to receive it's government from Virginia than from any other state," Thomas Jefferson contemplated improved connections between the Potomac River and the western waters. While he feared the potentially corrupting nature of commerce, Jefferson recognized in 1784 that "all the world is becoming commercial." Jefferson understood that "we cannot separate ourselves from [the world], our citizens have had too full a taste of the comforts furnished by the arts & manufactures to be debarred the use of them." This reality led Jefferson to conceive an expansive republic of virtuous farmers spread across North America who would trade with the world but avoid the concentrated commerce that plagued the urban centers of Europe. In creating internal improvements, Virginians would link the West with the Atlantic coast and reject Sheffield's claim that Americans could not become commercial.[11]

Whether they agreed with Sheffield or not, the founders all feared that a failure to successfully transform the West into a site for intensive commercial agriculture would undo westward expansion. The inability to develop new states and manage the vast migration of settlers could spawn lawlessness, separatism, destructive wars with Native nations, and ultimately the downfall of the republic. As political thinkers far removed from the geopolitical and economic realities in the trans-Appalachian West imagined its destiny, events on the ground in the Tennessee Valley began to unfold. Anglo-American settlers penetrated Cherokee lands to exploit their economic resources. They ushered in an era of instability, intrigue, conflict, and removal that seemingly confirmed Sheffield's worst predictions.

## FOUNDING FRANKLIN, 1784-1785

The Tennessee Valley endured tremendous demographic and political changes in the late eighteenth century. The fertile soil and abundant game suited the Overhill Cherokees (bands distinct from the Cherokees living in South Carolina), who controlled the valley as their hunting grounds. But beginning in the late 1760s, white settlers spread across present-day eastern Tennessee, searching for trade goods, natural resources, and land. Fertile, rain-drenched lands offered endless opportunities to grow grains and raise cattle while the mountains hid valuable metal resources. A semi-subsistence agricultural, slaveholding settler society emerged in the eighteenth-century valley. These economic possibilities outweighed the dangers of wars with Native nations and the geographic isolation felt by incoming settlers, who formed the Watauga Association in 1772 for mutual defense. These settlers, John Adams remarked in 1775, brought with them "Republican Notions—and Utopian Schemes."[12]

These possibilities convinced the North Carolina General Assembly to annex the Tennessee Valley on July 5, 1776, despite exerting little authority over the region. Nonetheless, the assembly organized the valley into the Washington District, adding administrative structure and courts to provide stability. During the War for Independence, North Carolina's administrative struggles led to the division of the Washington District into Washington, Sullivan, and Greene Counties. These counties later formed the basis of Franklin statehood. The general assembly envisioned their state's western claims as a path toward paying down wartime debts that had wrecked North Carolina's economy by 1782. National leaders agreed. In addition to its agricultural and commercial potential, these lands could be sold to speculators and granted to soldiers to fulfill promised pensions. Whereas the Northwest Territories would "extinguish about 10 Millions of the pub[lic] debt," Virginian Richard Henry Lee estimated, "the remaining lands, going southward to the Mississippi, [would] nearly discharge all the domestic debt."[13]

But who "owned" the right to claim western lands: settlers, states, or the union? In April 1784, the North Carolina General Assembly joined the state legislatures of New York and Virginia in ceding their claimed western lands to the Confederation Congress. Consequently, the North Carolina Cession Act of 1784 left Tennessee Valley settlers without a state.[14]

The western settlers of the Tennessee Valley reacted to the land cession with apprehension and opportunism. In response to these uncertainties, valley settlers assembled at the log courthouse in Jonesboro (in what is now Washington County, Tennessee) in late August 1784 to form a system for defense and law and order. The convention delegates devised plans that went beyond providing a short-term solution. For emerging valley elites—including Stockley Donelson, Joshua Gist, Charles Robertson, and David Looney—North Carolina's cession offered opportunities to control the valley's land speculation and the natural resources. In fact, many of the leading Franklinites supported North Carolina's cession, hoping to remove political barriers to Native lands in the Tennessee Valley. A few days after declaring independence, Franklinite David Campbell purchased "thirteen hundred acres of land on the French Broad," which he regarded "a great addition" to his "fortune." Franklinites such as Campbell invoked an old property-law doctrine called preemption rights that was recognized by southern states, whereby settlers who "improved" the land had the right to purchase it. Using the land cession and the American Revolution's language of self-government, valley leaders justified separatism and violence against Overhill Cherokees to control the political and economic fate of the Tennessee Valley.[15]

These political and economic desires, fueled by wars with Native peoples and land speculation, drove the settlers to reconvene at Jonesboro on December 14, 1784. Perturbed by the August meeting, North Carolina's

General Assembly had revoked the land cession. In response, delegates at the Jonesboro convention pushed for independence, hoping statehood would improve their economic and political fortunes. After a contentious debate, the delegates voted to reform Washington, Sullivan, and Greene Counties into the state of Franklin, honoring Benjamin Franklin.[16]

Franklin elites rationalized their movement as a continuation of the American Revolution. Amid the statehood debate, an unnamed delegate pulled out a copy of the Declaration of Independence and compared North Carolina's inept policies to George III's inactions and corrupt ministers during the imperial crisis of the 1760s and 1770s. By declaring independence in late 1784, the Franklinites articulated a new vision of American expansion—one where settlers could invoke the language of popular sovereignty, establish coequal states, and spread republicanism.[17]

In March 1785, the Franklinites selected Revolutionary War hero John Sevier as their governor. Serving as the brigadier general of North Carolina's Washington District, Sevier had initially opposed separatism. However, the allure of governorship and land speculation combined with North Carolina's indecisiveness swayed him to Franklin's cause. Already claiming hundreds of acres, Sevier sought more land. Beyond personal motives, he conceded that North Carolina failed to protect the westerners and represent their interests. In a letter to North Carolina governor Alexander Martin, Sevier stressed that the Franklinites felt "illy treated" by the general assembly's cession and retrocession of the Tennessee Valley. "Indian War will ensue this summer," Sevier warned Martin, "and it is the Western people alone that must suffer and undergo all the hardships and cruelties that usually attend a savage and bloody war." In reality, Overhill Cherokees' retaliation against the Franklinites' incursions occurred immediately upon independence. Franklinite David Campbell complained in late 1784 that "there are some for immediately attempting the utter Extirpation of the Indians."[18]

The Franklinites undermined the orderly expansion imagined by the nation's founders. Rather than transforming the West into a breadbasket to the benefit of the eastern states, the Franklinites crushed the aspirations of North Carolinian speculators and politicians when they invaded Cherokees' lands and declared independence. Over the next few years, the Franklinites would articulate an imagined destiny for the West that would favor settler interests and bolster republicanism. Sevier considered Governor Martin "a friend of the Western Country" and thus hoped he would embrace this vision.[19]

## FRANKLIN SEPARATISM AND THE DESTINY OF THE WEST

Alexander Martin was not a friend of the western country. The North Carolina governor viewed the Franklin movement as a "black and traiterous revolt" and sought to "convince the people of the Western Country, that the State still retained her affection for them." Franklin separatism had few supporters in North Carolina. Franklin's statehood challenged North Carolina's sovereignty, disrupted its debt repayment, and thwarted the ambitions of coastal speculators. In April 1785, Martin issued a fiery manifesto aimed at breaking up the "western revolt." Martin argued that Franklinites tarnished the "laurels they so gloriously won at King's Mountain"—where western militiamen defeated Loyalist soldiers and forced Lord Cornwallis to retreat to South Carolina in October 1780. Franklin statehood, however, had "designs of a more dangerous nature." Aware of Franklinites' land-speculating motives, Martin pointed to "a restless ambition and a lawless thirst of power" that "may at last bring down ruin upon themselves and our country at large." Indeed, Martin stressed that Franklin separatism would establish "a precedent for every district, and for every County of the State to claim the right of separation and independency." Martin feared that Franklin foreshadowed a future of breakaway states that would untether the union.[20]

Martin's manifesto enflamed tensions between Franklinites and North Carolinians. Though masking their identity under a pseudonym, "A Freelander" blasted Martin's manifesto as "Big words! and mighty doings upon paper!" If a civil war erupted in the Appalachian Mountains, Freelander reasoned that North Carolina aristocrats would be unable to "deal with men, that were on the memorable expeditions to King's mountain, and through the Cherokee country." In contrast to the "Good eating and good drinking" found in North Carolina, Franklinites strove for "frugality and temperance" and managed public affairs that achieved "the dignity of republican government." Writing to his North Carolinian friend Richard Caswell, Sevier stressed that westerners preferred a new state receptive to local concerns over North Carolina's hapless authority. Therefore, Franklin statehood would "prevent anarchy, promote our own happiness, and to provide against the Common Enemy . . . that always infest this part of the World." Hatred and cruelty toward Native peoples underpinned their separatism.

Sevier believed that violence toward "those bloody savages ... who have frequently murdered the wives and children of the people of this country" embodied "that manly and soldierly spirit that becomes an American." Whereas easterners were divided on policy toward Indigenous peoples, westerners considered warfare with Native nations essential to self-government and regional interests.[21]

The separatist sentiments brewing in the Tennessee Valley in 1785 garnered the attention of leading Virginians. After all, Virginians had to deal with a separatist movement in their westernmost county. Kentucky County emerged amid the Cherokee-American wars and the US War for Independence. The invasion of the Ohio River Valley by white settlers and the forced migration of enslaved African Americans provoked Cherokee, Shawnee, and Creek warriors. The retaliatory raids by Native warriors required a local government to handle the county's defenses and development. Unlike their North Carolina counterparts, Virginian planters such as George Washington, Thomas Jefferson, and James Madison recognized that separation between Kentucky and the Old Dominion was necessary. To this end, Virginians believed that Kentucky provided the ideal model of state-making through cooperation between easterners and westerners. As Richard Henry Lee put it, when Kentuckians "found themselves compitent to the business of Self Government" and "properly applied to our Assembly, no good objection could be made to a separation." James Madison agreed, viewing Kentucky as a "useful example for other Western Settlemts."[22]

Virginians attempted to draw stark distinctions between Kentucky and Franklin. In a September 1785 letter to Thomas Jefferson, Virginia governor Patrick Henry compared Kentucky separatism with its Franklin counterpart. Whereas "the Separation of Kentuckie into a distinct Government" seemed likely "to be accomplished in a good Humour," Henry stressed that "very different is the Condition of No. Carolina" because "Her people settled on the western Waters, have assumed sovereign Power" in defiance of the general assembly. Indeed, whereas Kentuckians and Virginians approached separation through bilateral agreement (which dragged on until 1792), Franklin statehood rebuffed North Carolina's jurisdictional authority. Henry predicted that the "severe Bickerings between them and their Brethren eastward of the great Mountains"—combined with "the present poverty of the Inhabitants"—would ultimately deter "people from settling there." Franklin separatism imperiled state sovereignty, destabilized the frontier, and represented the democratic elements that frightened postwar policymakers.[23]

These efforts to distinguish the independent state of Franklin from Kentucky county did not alleviate anxieties. Virginian elites feared that western Virginia could *become* the next state of Franklin. Word about Franklin extended far beyond the rugged Appalachian Mountains to the refined circles of Paris. Though a champion of westward expansion, US minister to France Thomas Jefferson wrote to George Washington that "the late example of the state of Franklin separated from N. Carolina increases my anxieties for Virginia." Often regarded as an optimistic expansionist, Jefferson dreaded that Virginia-Kentucky relations would descend into the bitter, hostile interactions that defined North Carolina's troubles with Franklin. Jefferson worried that Franklin and Vermont would start a trend where the slightest difference would break up a state—and possibly the union. "If Congress are not firm on that head," Jefferson wrote to Richard Henry Lee, "our several states will crumble to atoms by the spirit of establishing every little canton into a separate state." Jefferson painted a bleak future for the trans-Appalachian West. With Franklin on his mind, he trembled at the prospect of breakaway states in the West that acted as "our worst enemies instead of our best friends."[24]

Virginian policymakers would have to confront their fears about Franklin when southwestern Virginians in Washington County contemplated joining the new state in 1785. Lee deduced that the movement within Washington County was "stimulated by a troublesome person who for self aggrandisement appears willg: to dismember that part also, & join with the Revolters from N. Carolina." This troublesome individual, Col. Arthur Campbell of Virginia, had direct ties to Franklin and ambitious plans for the West. When his brother and Franklin judge David Campbell informed him about the separatist movement, Arthur Campbell endeavored to attach Washington County to Franklin. "A new scene is now opening that calls for the aid of every patriot," Campbell said of the West in 1783. Campbell believed if US policymakers took "proper establishment," the West would "serve as a balance of power" and would secure "the liberties of the eastern States." Franklin could help realize this vision.[25]

Campbell's pro-Franklin crusade exposed prominent Virginian policymakers to emerging ideas about western interests and expansion that developed on the southwestern frontier. Contrary to Henry and Lee, Campbell maintained that the events in Franklin, rather than Kentucky statehood, provided a model for Virginia regarding their "distant and disputed territory." As historian Peter Onuf has noted, Campbell's letters to prominent Virginians such as James Madison helped shape their ideas about separatism and territorial expansion. Madison even considered the settlers "from the Western side of the Alleghany praying for a separate Government" to be "the children of A.C.'s ambition." The content of these letters fixated on Campbell's efforts to annex Virginia's Washington County to Franklin. Thus, Madison's ideas about westward expansion had been formulated not only by Kentuckians but also by the Franklin statehood controversy.[26]

In a series of proclamations and letters to Virginian notables, Campbell championed the attachment of Washington County to Franklin. Settled along the Holston River, Campbell attended several sessions at the Jonesboro courthouse when the Franklinites declared statehood in late 1784. He and his Washington County allies shared similar regional interests and land-speculating ambitions with the Franklinites across the Holston River. Franklinites and western Virginians complained that they paid excessive taxes and received inadequate protection or benefits in return. Campbell, western Virginians, and some Franklinites crafted a memorial to Congress in late 1784 (received in January 1785) detailing the necessity of creating a sizable state in the southwest. "We are too much elated at the prospect before us not to wish that we very speedily enjoy the advantages of such government as will be exercised over a convenient territory," the memorialists wrote.[27]

The memorialists criticized Congress's current system of state-making in the trans-Appalachian West. While they appreciated that new states north of the Ohio River would be admitted as equal republican states under the Northwest Ordinance of 1784, the southwestern memorialists argued that sketching new states on maps ignored geographical and topographical realities. The memorialists implored Congress to enforce the land cessions of Virginia and North Carolina to create an equal state that extended from the Ohio River to the Tennessee Valley. The memorialists further called on Congress to "likewise confirm and guarantee to the inhabitants all their equitable rights and privileges acquired under the laws of the States lately claiming this territory." In return, the western state would use funds acquired from the land sales "towards the payment of the national debt."[28]

Within the context of Franklin separatism, Campbell and his allies also maintained that new western states—receptive to regional interests and appeasing the private ambitions of local leaders—would ultimately strengthen the union. "It is as possible that one state shall aim at an undue influence over others," western memorialists petitioned to the Virginia House of Burgesses, "as that any individual should aspire after the aggrandisement of himself." New states in the trans-Appalachian West added "obstacles" impeding a region from dominating its neighbors. "Your memorialists conceive that an increase of states in the federal union will conduce to the strength and dignity of that union," they wrote, "just as our increase of individual citizens will increase the strength and dignity of a state." New western states would address regional inequalities while preventing the majority from dominating the minority. By extending the sphere, these aspiring separatists believed that new states would improve republican institutions at the local and national levels and secure the union. The Franklin advocates thus argued that, contrary to contemporary political thought, territorial expansion would bolster rather than endanger republicanism.[29]

Campbell reiterated these arguments in letters to Henry and Madison. "If we wish for a separation it is on account of griviancies that daily become more and more intolerable," Campbell informed Henry. "It is from a hope that another mode of governing will make us more useful than we now are to the general Confederacy," Campbell continued, "or ever can be, whilst so connected." These westerners would safeguard the union by binding "themselves by every *holy tie* to support republican principles" and avoid "ignorance and barbarism" by implementing "local independent Institutions."[30]

Campbell articulated his vision for expansive western states in a letter to Madison. In it, he claimed that Franklin was just the beginning. "Virginia will follow the example of North Carolina," he boasted, "and fix her limits on the highths of the Allegany." Campbell proposed allocating Virginia's western lands to Kentucky, Franklin, and a new state called Washington (comprising present-day West Virginia and western Pennsylvania).[31]

The formation of these new states ran counter to the arguments made by European intellectuals and eastern politicians that the trans-Appalachian West would destroy the American union. James Madison spent his entire political career recognizing the importance of a stable frontier that would protect the union from Indigenous nations and European empires. Campbell helped sharpen Madison's ideas. In the wake of Spain's closure of the Mississippi River, Madison dispelled the notion that western Americans would break away from the United States. Rather, he contended that "the ties of friendship" would unite eastern and western Americans. Building on this discourse, Campbell maintained that western states "would vastly increase the strength, riches, and population of the United States" and check European intrigue. "Washington . . . would soon become a firm barrier against any attempts from the Western parts of Canada," he boasted. At the same time, he imagined how "Kentuckey, and Frankland, would circulate eastwardly some of the riches of Mexico, and keep the Spaniards, the Southern and Western Indians in awe." Campbell reasoned that these western states would refute the arguments made by pessimists who wanted to dissolve the American confederacy. He asked: "Is not there much less difficulty, and far less danger, to limit the large States to a convenient, and suitable bounds; and then parcel out the Western territory, into proper divisions for free Communities?" Efforts in Franklin would secure the frontier and prevent European powers from "aiming at our destruction."[32]

Arthur Campbell's pro-Franklin separatism, however, terrified Virginians. When word of Campbell's scheme to wrestle Washington County from Virginia reached him in early 1785, Gov. Patrick Henry resolved to crush the conspiracy. Henry received reassurance from Sevier—who sought Virginia's approval—that the Franklin government would not "Encourage any part of The people of your state to join us." The Virginian governor employed a recently passed militia reorganization bill that authorized him to replace militia leaders. He replaced Campbell from his post as county lieutenant of Washington County with his rival, William Russell. Henry also formed a special commission to conduct an administrative investigation of Campbell, who was soon charged with urging citizens to separate from Virginia and avoid paying taxes and voting in elections. By the end of 1785, Henry had quashed separatism in Washington County.[33]

Nonetheless, the pro-Franklin separatism in Washington County underscored the contested, un-manifest fate for the trans-Appalachian West. Although Campbell's plot never materialized, it exposed influential Virginians—James Madison, Thomas Jefferson, Patrick Henry, George Washington, and Richard Henry Lee—to the ideas that justified Franklin's statehood. In the wake of Franklin separatism, westerners confronted the founders' plans and grave predictions for the West. Indeed, the West would not simply be a font of wealth for eastern speculators and politicians. Instead, Campbell and his Franklinite allies saw the creation of coequal states as a source of geopolitical security and a means to spread republicanism. But this vision for the West was precarious. As the state of Franklin demonstrated, repeated attempts to deny westerners' political and economic interests could create more unrecognized, breakaway states that would increasingly turn hostile. Between the summer of 1785 and early 1786, the Franklinites' state-building and treaty-making efforts made the state more autonomous and independent. In doing so, these efforts would create more chaos and confirm the founders' worst fears about the West.

## MAKING A BREAKAWAY REPUBLIC

Amid the interstate scheming in 1785, the Franklinites attempted to establish their state's internal functions and external relations. The Franklinites craved approval from Congress and sought to become the fourteenth state of the United States. Yet throughout 1785, these efforts to be recognized by Congress and stabilize their state only further solidified their status as a de facto independent republic. This budding autonomy allowed the Franklinites to impose an unfair land treaty on the Overhill Cherokees and encroach on their lands. External recognition, though, meant nothing if the Franklinites failed to maintain order within their state. Internal conflicts beset Franklin from the outset of independence. The statehood campaign never represented a unified movement in the Tennessee Valley. Upon the North Carolina General Assembly's repeal of the land cession, Revolutionary War hero John Tipton and his allies worked to return Franklin to North Carolina. To quell divisions, Sevier and the Franklinites desired to legitimize Franklin by crafting a state constitution and winning the approval of Congress. However, internal and external pressures would ultimately overpower any effort to sustain the state of Franklin's incorporation into the union. Consequently, this breakaway republic destabilized the Tennessee Valley and undercut US authority in the West.[34]

In the spring of 1785, William Cocke traveled to the bustling streets of New York City (then the capital of the United States) to present the case for Franklin statehood before Congress. Like separatists in Vermont, Maine, and Kentucky, the Franklinites longed for a strong national government to secure their statehood by overriding the jurisdictional claims of large states. In mid-May, Cocke presented a memorial that detailed the reasons for separation from North Carolina—much to the chagrin of North Carolina representative Richard Dobbs Spaight. The Franklinites' memorial encapsulated the postrevolutionary sentiments in the West: easterners disregarded western interests and, in an effort to exonerate themselves of settler violence, left them directionless in Indian affairs. The settlers claimed that "the Indians were daily murdering our friends and relatives without distinction of age or sex." The memorial's authors, Landon Carter and William Cage, also emphasized that the repeal of the cession act indicated North Carolina's disregard for Tennessee Valley settlers. Like Sevier and Campbell, Carter and Cage prayed that Congress would "adopt such suitable measures as may promote the peace and prosperity of those who wish ever to be found a zealous and useful part of the people that form so dignified a union."[35]

Unfortunately, the Franklinites' prayers went unanswered by Congress. After several representatives formed a committee to consider Franklin's statehood, Congress voted on the fate of Franklin on May 20, 1785—a decision that excluded North Carolina from casting a vote. Under Article XI of the Articles of Confederation, a new state required the approval of a two-thirds majority (nine states) in Congress to be admitted to the union. Congress upheld North Carolina's land cession but denied Franklin statehood. Whereas New Jersey, Rhode Island, Connecticut, New York, New Hampshire, Pennsylvania, and Georgia voted to recognize Franklin, several southern states rejected a new state in the Tennessee Valley. William Cocke stayed in New York City for a short time after the vote, continuing to seek support for Franklin. However, his overall mission proved, as Patrick Henry put it, "fruitless."[36]

While denied statehood by two votes, the Franklinites nevertheless received dubious recognition from another regional power: the Overhill Cherokees. The explosive settler population growth in the eighteenth-century Tennessee Valley had inflamed tensions between the Overhill Cherokees and Euro-Americans. In the revolutionary era, US settlers considered Native lands beyond the Appalachian Mountains as key to (white) liberty and independence. US policymakers such as Thomas Jefferson also championed this message, viewing the spread of yeomanry farmers as quintessential to a healthy, virtuous republic. An empire of liberty, Jefferson reasoned, would avoid corruption by providing ample land for independent farmers. After all, as he put it, "Those who labour in the earth are the chosen people of God, if ever he had a chosen people, whose breasts he has made his peculiar deposit for substantial and genuine virtue." These chosen agriculturalists employed such lofty rhetoric to justify speculating, squatting, and violence at the expense of Indigenous nations. By June 1785, the Franklinites had negotiated a peace and land deal with Overhill Cherokees.[37]

The Treaty of Dumplin Creek, as this agreement became known, proved problematic. Unrestricted and autonomous, the Franklinites pressured younger Cherokee leaders to accept an unfair land deal. As the first treaty between white Americans and the Cherokees after the War for Independence, the Treaty of Dumplin Creek granted the state of Franklin "all the lands lying and being on the South side of Holston and French Broad Rivers, as far south as the ridge that divide the waters of Little River from the waters of Tennessee." These fertile lands would help secure settlers' vision of independence and liberty and appease speculators' economic schemes. In the wake of the treaty, Franklinites pursued violent removal. US agent Joseph Martin complained that he "had more trouble with the Indians in the course of the Summer, than I ever had, owing to the rapid encroachment of the people from the New State (Franklin)."[38]

Leaders with real authority in American and Cherokee circles refused to recognize the treaty's legitimacy. Under the Articles of Confederation, the national government and state governments could make treaties with sovereign Indigenous nations. Yet Congress did not recognize Franklin as an American state and thus denounced the Treaty of Dumplin Creek. Despite Congress's rejection of Franklin's statehood, Sevier averred that he acted on "behalf of the white people, and for and in behalf to the State or Government, or the United States." But for Congress, Sevier did not act on behalf of the United States. In the eyes of US policymakers, Sevier negotiated with Cherokees to legitimize the Franklinites' illegal squatting on land claimed by the United States.[39]

Chief Kaiyah-tahee (Old Tassel) worried that encroaching Franklinites and faulty treaties would undermine any real effort at peace. From the Cherokee town of Chota, Kaiyah-tahee had worked tirelessly to avoid pulling the Overhill Cherokees into Chickamauga Cherokee leader Dragging Canoe's war with Anglo-American settlers. The Franklinites' land-grabbing schemes, however, threatened to undo his efforts. In a speech to US officials in September 1785, Kaiyah-tahee remarked that his villagers were "very uneasy on acc't of a Report that is among the white people, that call themselves a New People, that lives on French Broad." Typical of Anglo-American negotiations with Indigenous nations, the Franklinites secured land cessions through deals with chiefs who lacked authority in their nations. Since the Treaty of Dumplin Creek, Kaiyah-tahee stressed that the Cherokees "are told they claim all the Lands on the waters of Little River, and has appointed men among themselves to settle their disputes on our Lands and call it their Ground." Kaiyah-tahee hoped that "the Great Council of America" would use its power "to move them off."[40]

Cherokee and US leaders negotiated a separate treaty, which captured the contrasting visions of westward expansion held by westerners and easterners. In November 1785, Kaiyah-tahee and thirty-six other Cherokee chiefs met with US diplomats Benjamin Hawkins, Joseph Martin, Andrew Pickens, and Lachlan McIntosh along the Keowee River in South Carolina. Seeking peace and stability in the West, the US commissioners affirmed Cherokee boundaries in the Treaty of Hopewell. To the chagrin of the Franklinites, the treaty permitted the Cherokees to punish any settler who trespassed on their lands. A victory for both Cherokee and American leaders, the Treaty of Hopewell nullified the Treaty of Dumplin Creek. As Cherokees already knew and eastern Americans would learn, western settlers ignored treaties and resorted to violence to obtain land.[41]

Although US policymakers denied the Treaty of Dumplin Creek, westerners hailed their negotiations with the Overhill Cherokees as an extension of the American Revolution. One Franklinite described the discussions between their state and the Overhill Cherokees as a "project" that would "startle" the "rigid secretaries" of the east because the Franklinites intended to "incorporate [the Cherokees], and make them useful citizens." Amid the destruction and discussions of incorporation, Franklin judge David Campbell hoped "to save the well disposed of the Cherokee Nation." This belief aligned with the views of some policymakers such as Thomas Jefferson, who theorized that Indigenous Americans would eventually assimilate with white Americans upon embracing Euro-American culture. And, in the early stages of settler colonialism, this sort of uneasy coexistence seemed plausible given the overlap of Native villages and Euro-American towns in the West. With "the Indian and Whiteman, at their works of industry at one and the same time," Franklinites intended to expand "the fruits of the glorious American revolution!" Rumors about incorporation had been disseminated by westerners, potentially to appease easterners who feared uneasy borderlands. In addition to the US commissioners' peace negotiations with southern Native nations, the treaty would allow peace to "prevail on all our borders," as another westerner argued. In reality, the Treaty of Dumplin accelerated the violent removal of the Overhill Cherokees.[42]

As they tussled with the Confederation Congress and the Overhill Cherokees, the Franklinites attempted to reframe their government. In November 1785, Franklinite leaders convened at Franklin's new capital of Greeneville to revise the constitution, which had emulated North Carolina's constitution. At Greeneville's Presbyterian Church, constitutional delegate Rev. Samuel Houston proposed a radical frame of government, which promised a Declaration of Rights and a democratic constitution. Houston relied on the support of Virginian Arthur Campbell and his former teacher Rev. William Graham. The Houston-Graham constitution vowed to expand political suffrage to all free white men while checking politicians' authority by implementing term limits and allowing direct elections of representatives. Houston and Graham wanted the constitution to encourage education in the Tennessee Valley, including provisions to erect a university and use tax revenues to establish grammar schools in each county. Such progressive reforms alarmed Franklinite elites. For established elites such as John Sevier and William Cocke, the proposed constitution's democratic principles undermined their control over the political and economic future of the Tennessee Valley. Using their regional influence, conservative Franklinites secured the original frame of government by preventing the passage of the radical Houston-Graham constitution by a 24–19 vote. Nonetheless, westerners depicted Franklin as the epitome of the American Revolution. "I am not without hopes," a Franklinite remarked, "that the next generation in Frankland will vie with Athens itself."[43]

Before they could vie with Athens, the Franklinites still had to deal with North Carolina. After Alexander Martin's term ended in May 1785, Richard Caswell became governor of North Carolina. Fortunately for the Franklinites, Caswell had business ties with John Sevier. They had even applied together for two hundred acres in Greene County in 1784. Easing direct tensions between North Carolina and Franklin, Caswell instead aimed to exacerbate internal divisions within Franklin by encouraging settlers to rejoin North Carolina without penalty. This strategy also gave Franklinites, including "a gentleman in Frankland," a misguided sense that North Carolina begrudgingly accepted their independence. "We have now the most friendly assurances from North Carolina," he wrote, "since governor Martin's administration has expired." In reality, Caswell would spend the next two years working to pull the Franklinites back into North Carolina's orbit.[44]

The state of Franklin was left unrecognized in 1785. Despite efforts to present themselves as a continuation of the American Revolution and to develop a state constitution, the Franklinites failed to appeal to Congress. Congress not only denied Franklin its statehood but also dismissed its treaty with the Overhill Cherokees. These efforts to create the fourteenth state in the Tennessee Valley unintentionally bolstered Franklin's de facto independence from both North Carolina *and* the United States. Though operating within land claimed by the United States, the Franklinites received no support from Congress, crafted their own treaties with the Cherokees that ran counter to US interests, and decided on a frame of government.

Franklin's state-making and treaty-making efforts foreshadowed a West unattached to the American union and conveyed the weaknesses of the Articles of Confederation. Far from their lofty expansionist imagining of the West, US policymakers feared a breakaway West and a dismantled union. Massachusetts merchant Tristram Dalton warned John Adams in late 1785 that "the fondness of people in certain districts to declare themselves independent States," such as "the State of Franklin in N Carolina," imperiled the "political Security and Happiness" of Americans. While he argued that "Our confederacy must be viewed as the nest from which all America, North and South is to be peopled," Jefferson feared that "the people of Kentucké think of separating not only from Virginia . . . but also from the confederacy." Such fears extended to the state of Franklin. The dangers of a collapsing and unaligned Franklin became increasingly apparent when a proposed treaty between the United States and Spain threatened to close the Mississippi River to US settlers for twenty-five years.[45]

## CRISES ABOUND: THE JAY-GARDOQUI TREATY AND THE VOLATILE STATE OF FRANKLIN, 1786–1787

By mid-1786, the Tennessee Valley had become a site of clashing, multinational visions for the West. From their capital at Greensville, Sevier and the Franklinites envisioned the budding of a western state that would spread republicanism beyond the Appalachians. At Chota, chief Kaiyahtahee attempted to maintain the Overhill Cherokees' autonomy over the land promised to them by the Treaty of Hopewell. Far away in New York City, congressional delegates sought to navigate the disorderly westward expansion that threatened their fragile union. Yet new geopolitical actors in and around the Tennessee Valley entered the contest by 1786. In the valley, North Carolinian loyalists created an operational government to undercut Franklin's legitimacy. Situated in New York City or New Orleans, Spanish officers scoured their information networks to exploit East-West tensions and transform Franklin and Kentucky into vassals of the Spanish Bourbons. No incipient manifest destiny could have been truly anticipated by the founders amidst this geopolitical chaos.[46]

These geopolitical realities deflated the cautious optimism that defined the first year of the Franklin statehood movement. In June 1786, judge William Cocke wrote to Benjamin Franklin, seeking assistance from the state's influential namesake. "I make no doubt but you have heard that the good people of this country have declared themselves a separate State from North Carolina," Cocke noted, "and that, as a testimony of the high esteem they have for the many important and faithful services you have rendered to your country, they have called the name of their State after you." After obsequiously praising Franklin, Cocke hinted that his state sought to capitalize on his influence in Congress, wanting his "sentiments and advice on so important a subject."[47]

Unfortunately for Cocke, Benjamin Franklin ignored the flattery and instead gave the Franklinites a response typical of eastern politicians. He thought that the Franklinites were "perfectly right in resolving to submit them to the discretion of Congress, and to abide by their determination." While many Franklinites equated the Confederation Congress to the British Parliament for ignoring western interests, Franklin reminded the Franklinites: "It is happy for us all that we have now in our country such a council to apply to . . . without being obliged, as formerly, to carry them across the ocean to be decided." Benjamin Franklin's response further confirmed that few eastern politicians supported their cause.[48]

These rebuffs compromised Sevier's authority and the statehood movement. To make matters worse, North Carolina struck back. Partisanship— between the settlers loyal to North Carolina and those aligned with Sevier and independence—flared up in the Tennessee Valley between 1785 and 1787. Despite the belief that Governor Caswell supported Franklin, North Carolina's policy of exciting preexisting tensions worked against the Franklinites. In November 1785, the North Carolina General Assembly passed legislation that would pardon Franklin settlers for their supposed treason. North Carolina also established regional elections to send representatives from Washington, Sullivan, and Greene Counties to the legislature. The legislation allowed for the appointment of loyal regional, civil, judicial, and military officials in counties that constituted Franklin. This strategy essentially resulted in two de facto state governments in the Tennessee Valley. In response to this legislation, Franklinites held elections—separate from the western settlers who pledged loyalty to North Carolina—to send their delegates to the general assembly. Despite rebelling against North Carolina, Franklinites hoped that pro-Franklin representatives in the assembly could advance independence. Two state governments, each denying the legitimacy of the other, sparked intense conflicts in the valley. In the late summer of 1787, anti-Franklinite leader and North Carolina loyalist John Tipton and approximately 50 militiamen raided Sevier's courtroom in Jonesboro, prompting Sevier and 150 Franklinites to storm Tipton's courthouse in Buffalo. Witnesses at the courthouse claimed that the raid exemplified "the Superiority of Franklin."[49]

As they battled with Tipton and his fellow North Carolina loyalists, the Franklinites continued to encroach on Cherokee territory, ignoring the boundaries established by the treaties of Dumplin Creek and Hopewell. With "many families settled within nine miles of the Cherokee nation," David Campbell wondered, "what will be the consequence of those emigrations?" A thousand Chickamauga Cherokee warriors answered Campbell's question. Under the leadership of Chief John Watts (Kaiyah-tahee's nephew), Cherokee warriors raided several settlements near present-day Knoxville in early 1786. One Franklinite warned that the brewing conflict would lead to "one general calamity" for hostile and neutral Indigenous nations alike. In July, Sevier ordered the Franklin militia to destroy Cherokee settlements in retaliation for the murder of white settlers. When the militia approached Chota, Kaiyah-tahee and Chief Hanging Maw offered to turn in the murderers, who supposedly lived in the Cherokee village of Cawatie. Instead, the Franklinites burned down Cawatie and demanded that surviving chiefs sign the Treaty of Coyotee, dispossessing Cherokees of the land between the French Broad and the Little Tennessee Rivers. After opening a land office in the newly acquired territory, the Franklinites settled, as Kaiyah-tahee put it, "much Faster on our Lands after a Treaty than Before." Despite US agent Joseph Martin's efforts to impede Franklin's expansion, the Franklinites aggressively annexed Cherokee lands, exacerbating tensions with the Overhill and Chickamauga Cherokees.[50]

While aggressive diplomacy with the Cherokees worsened Franklin's volatile conditions, US relations with Spain raised doubts about the breakaway state's future in the American union. In the decade that followed the War for Independence, the young republic struggled to obtain treaties and recognition by European powers. This postwar reality particularly hampered northern merchants, who had previously relied on established trade connections in the British Empire. Secretary of Foreign Affairs John Jay brought these insecurities to the negotiating table. French diplomat Louis-Guillaume Otto conveyed Jay's (and other American elites') sentiment about the United States' international reputation. Jay informed Otto that "the commerce of America is so reduced that extraordinary efforts are necessary to extricate it from its present embarrassments." This belief compelled Jay to negotiate a treaty with Spanish diplomat Diego de Gardoqui that would open Spanish ports in Europe and the Caribbean to American commerce. This agreement, however, came at a cost: the United States would have to recognize Spain's sole right to navigate the Mississippi River for twenty-five years. By controlling the Mississippi River, Spanish officers could slow the tide of Anglo-American settlers spiraling toward Louisiana and New Spain.[51]

The proposed treaty nearly shattered the fragile American union. The Jay-Gardoqui negotiations underscored the competing commercial and political interests between North and South and East and West, casting doubt on the union's longevity. Northern merchants celebrated the treaty's commercial arrangements, hoping to nourish the Spanish Empire with provisions such as cod and wheat. Spain's exclusive right to the Mississippi River would retain the north's prominence in national politics by discouraging westward migrations out of New England. "The fertility of those countries would insensibly attract the most industrious inhabitants of the northern states," Otto surmised, "who would not hesitate an instant to exchange the arid rocks of Massachusetts and of New Hampshire for the smiling plains of the Ohio and the Mississippi." Otto noted that "this emigration doubly enfeebles New England" because "it adds to the population of the southern states." For northerners, the treaty could secure the Atlantic-based, commercial republic envisioned during the War for Independence.[52]

Enraged westerners and southerners derided the treaty as a northern ploy that sacrificed their economic interests. While southerners certainly believed the negotiations with Spain threatened their political and economic ambitions, westerners understood the Jay-Gardoqui Treaty as a culmination of antagonistic eastern policies aimed at the West. Franklinites such as William Graham had already felt that opponents of Franklin statehood were advocates of "absolute government and unlimited Empire." Now, US policymakers forfeited westerners' convenient access to the Mississippi River for commercial incentives with Spain. Under this treaty, westerners would have to transport their products across the Appalachian Mountains. In the late eighteenth century, this eastward journey proved an arduous, if not impossible, task. Indeed, the Appalachian Mountains could only be crossed through the Cumberland Gap, Forbes Road (linking the Susquehanna to the Ohio Valley), Braddock's Road (connecting the Potomac to the Monongahela Valley), and two routes along the Mohawk River. The Mississippi River therefore proved vital to their economy, and access to it underlay their fidelity to the American union.[53]

Some US policymakers feared westerners would separate from the union. Southerners informed Otto that "the navigation of the Mississippi . . . is perhaps the most important object for the United States" because "the inhabitants of the vast and fertile regions of Kentucky, and of the neighboring countries, have no other outlet than New Orleans." Otto reported a grave outcome for both the United States and France. "If congress is unable to procure for them an entrepôt in that city," Otto predicted, "they will regard its protection as wholly useless, and we are informed, in the most positive manner, that they are disposed to separate from the confederation and to throw themselves into the arms of England." Far away in Paris, Jefferson offered a similar assessment in a letter to Madison, believing that "the act which abandons the navigation of the Missisipi is an act of separation between the Eastern and Western country." Rather than stretching from sea to shining sea, the United States would cling to the Atlantic seaboard while upstart, breakaway republics in the West would extend beyond the Mississippi River. After all, westerners "are able already to rescue the navigation of the Missisipi out of the hands of Spain, and to add New Orleans to their own territory."[54]

Franklinites, Kentuckians, and other westerners schemed to realize Jefferson's fears in late 1786 and 1787. In early 1787, rumors swirled throughout the American republic about a plot to seize New Orleans. While in New York, Otto reported that "the situation of congress with respect to the treaty with

Spain becomes more embarrassing from day to day." He worried that stories of western settlers stopping Spanish vessels on the Wabash River marked only the beginning. "The inhabitants of Kentucky and of Frankland do not merely insist on the free navigation of the Mississippi," Otto continued, "but they threaten to commit hostile acts against the inhabitants of Louisiana unless Spain renounces its exclusive system." Armed Franklinites and Kentuckians might even "make a way for themselves across the colony of Santa Fé."[55]

Fantastical as an invasion of Santa Fe might have been, westerners nonetheless circulated several letters promoting secession and invasion during the Mississippi crisis of 1786–87. In late 1786, an anonymous man residing south of the Ohio River, likely frontiersman George Rogers Clark, wrote fiery letters condemning eastern policymakers. "The late commercial treaty with Spain," he proclaimed, "has given this western country an universal shock." Eastern policymakers behaved worse than British imperial officials by sacrificing settlers' "liberty of transporting [their] effects" and rendering them "vassals to the merciless Spaniards."[56]

As postrevolutionary policymakers envisioned their commercial republic, westerners argued that the Providential destiny of the republic lay not in the Atlantic world but in the vast trans-Appalachian West. This vision encapsulated the western settler sentiment—one that mistakenly depicted the West as a virgin wilderness ready to be cultivated by white Americans. "Shall the best and largest part of the United States be uncultivated, a nest for savages and beasts of prey?" he asked. "Certainly not," the westerner answered. "Providence has designed it for some nobler purposes." By abandoning the West for commerce with Spain, the United States proved "ignorant of this country as Great-Britain was of America."[57]

This anonymous westerner reasoned that the proposed Jay-Gardoqui Treaty justified separatism and war with Spain. "I cannot but remind you of the danger into which the United States are plunging themselves," he warned. "Spain has placed the rock upon which they are like to split." Unless US policymakers abandoned the treaty, westerners appealed "to justice and to arms, for the defence of their just rights" in their efforts to separate from the eastern states and invade Spanish America. While "the State of Franklin are ready to fly arms," Kentuckians called for "Liberty or Death." Unless Congress voted against the treaty, westerners predicted that "America is ruined . . . inevitably ruined!"[58]

By March 1787, this separatist conspiracy reached members of the Confederation Congress, who learned of letters circulating in Franklin. Madison feared that the unity of the West might, like the state of Vermont, result in settlers entering "insensibly into a communication and latent connection with their British Neighbours" or falling prey to ambitious individuals. As such, Madison and his allies persuaded enough delegates to vote against ratifying the Jay-Garodqui Treaty in the spring of 1787.[59]

The rejection of the Jay-Gardoqui Treaty did not calm western settlers, who still clamored for war with Spain. In addition to closing the Mississippi River, Spain supported southeastern Native nations in their resistance against Anglo-American expansion. Spanish officials in Louisiana and Florida supplied Indigenous warriors such as Creek leader Alexander McGillivray with arms and munitions to repel Franklinites and Kentuckians from encroaching on their lands. Westerners interpreted Spain's efforts to close the Mississippi River and its support of Native nations' warfare as a broad strategy to halt US expansionism. Unlike their western counterparts, the Franklinites lacked formal attachment to the United States, removing any restraints for a potential war with Spain. By late 1787, the *Maryland Gazette* reported that Franklinites had assembled to "take into consideration the hostile behavior of his Catholic Majesty's subjects in the Floridas and Louisiana, towards the good citizens of that state in particular, and the other western states in general." The Franklin assembly was determined to raise "a body of 1,500 men" to "to *thrash* (by the Divine Blessing) those perfidious Castilians into a better conduct towards the subjects of those States."[60]

Proposed separatist plots, imagined invasions of Spanish America, and real violence toward southwestern Native peoples simultaneously underscored Franklin's instability and the national government's inability to control the trans-Appalachian West. For the founders, Franklin exposed the worst elements of postrevolutionary America. In their calls for independence, Franklinites touted regionalism and democratic principles of self-representation. These unruly Tennessee Valley settlers ignored the authority of state legislatures and Congress, pursued treaties and war with Native nations that conflicted with national policy, threatened secession, and clamored for war with Spain. In the summer of 1787, many leaders of the founding generation determined that a stronger national government would remedy the ills ushered in by separatism in the West. At the Philadelphia convention, delegates specifically contemplated ways to prevent another Franklin. More generally, they created a federal government sufficiently powerful to manage territorial expansion and address the interests voiced by Franklinites and like-minded westerners.

## REDEFINING EXPANSIONISM AMID FRANKLIN'S COLLAPSE, 1787-1789

In the fall of 1787, Franklinites waited anxiously to hear the outcome of the Philadelphia convention. They hoped any potential revisions to the Articles of Confederation would address their statehood movement and force North Carolina to honor their land cession. David Campbell believed that "if the Federal Convention does nothing unfriendly," the Franklinites would "surely yet do well." In a letter printed in the *Maryland Journal*, one Franklinite dreamed that "the Federal Convention will invest Congress with power to have a deed executed to them for the territory ceded by the State of North Carolina." Many western settlers anticipated that the framers would also devise a constitution that would strengthen national authority, resolve interstate jurisdictional controversies, and provide government and military protection in the backcountry. In doing so, the new federal government might resolve the dilemma of Franklin statehood. "I am happy to hear of so much unanimity in the late Convention," Sevier wrote to Benjamin Franklin, "and have sanguine hopes you have adopted a plan of government that will add dignity to the Rising greatness and happiness of our American Empire." Sevier expected the convention delegates to address the "general uneasiness among a number the Western Americans" who felt that "their interest is neglected."[61]

Unfortunately for Sevier, the new Constitution rejected Franklin's statehood. Under Article IV, Section 3 of the US Constitution, "No new State shall be formed or erected within the Jurisdiction of any other State; nor any State be formed by the Junction of two or more States, or Parts of States, without the Consent of the Legislatures of the States concerned as well as of the Congress." Responding to separatism throughout the union, this language quashed any hope of federal support for Franklin's statehood. Article IV, Section 3 responded to the jurisdictional controversies surrounding Franklin separatism. After all, the Franklinites and western Virginians sought to carve out part of Virginia to attach to Franklin, and Congress had previously denied their statehood in 1785. Despite efforts by Sevier and his allies, Franklin statehood seemed impossible after September 1787.[62]

During the ratification debates of 1787–88, the Federalists argued that the proposed Constitution would prevent democratic insurrections. Whereas Franklin undermined North Carolina's authority, Shays's Rebellion—an insurrection led by farmers and war veterans against debt collectors—threatened the Massachusetts countryside. Alexander Hamilton believed the new Constitution would remedy these ills. In *The Federalist No. 6*, Hamilton maintained that the "revolt of a part of the State of North Carolina" along with "the actual insurrections and rebellions in Massachusetts" resulted from "a lax and ill administration of government." The Constitution not only delegitimized Franklin statehood, but it also granted the national government authority to crush rebellions and confront jurisdictional tensions between states.[63]

While they rejected the process of Franklin statehood, the framers of the Constitution debated the equality of new western states. Although the Northwest Ordinances proposed creating new states coequal to the original thirteen, many founders contemplated limiting the number of western representatives in Congress and making western states inferior to their Atlantic counterparts. Sheffield's logic that the West would drain the resources and population of the Atlantic coast continued to occupy easterners' minds. During the 1787 Philadelphia convention, North Carolina delegate Hugh Williamson argued that new states in the West should be treated as inferior to the original thirteen. Pennsylvania delegate Gouverneur Morris agreed with Williamson. He warned that if the Constitution did not set a number limit for representation, the Atlantic states would be at the mercy of new western states.[64]

These arguments failed largely because many Federalists echoed the vision of the Franklinites and other westerners: that the future of the American republic lay in the West. James Madison warned that the westerners would refuse to join a union that denied them their interests and equality. During the ratification debates, many Federalists embraced a forward-thinking vision of the United States, whereby the Constitution would empower policymakers to govern the trans-Appalachian West. "We are representatives," James Wilson declared, "not merely of this present age, but of future times; not merely of the territory along the seacoast, but of regions immensely extended westward." Wilson acknowledged that Americans will "fill, as fast as possible, this extensive country, with men who shall live happy, free, and secure." Achieving this future required ratifying the Constitution. Denying westerners of their equality and interests would guarantee a future of breakaway republics in the West.[65]

Anti-Federalists reminded the Federalists of the dangers of an overextended republic and a consolidated government to their liberties. Drawing from eighteenth-century political science, the Anti-Federalists believed that republics needed to remain small to survive. While a stronger national government would help govern the trans-Appalachian West, the Anti-Federalists feared that such reforms would come at the expense of republicanism and liberty. Many Anti-Federalists also feared that a union that benefitted larger states would lead to the tyranny of the majority over the minority. Maryland Anti-Federalist Luther Martin worried that smaller states would be at the mercy of larger states that claimed land beyond the trans-Appalachian West. Large states would deny "the *erection of new within their territory*" and demand that smaller states assist in "subduing the inhabitants of Franklin, Kentucky, Vermont, and the provinces of Main and Sagaohock."[66]

James Madison countered these conventional notions about territorial expansion and republicanism in *Federalist No. 10*. There, Madison argued that extensive territorial domains strengthened republics. In a vast republic, distinct political and economic interests would emerge that would prevent a majority from dominating a minority. "Extend the sphere," Madison maintained, "and you take in a greater variety of parties and interests; you make it less probable that a majority of the whole will have a common motive to invade the rights of other citizens." Whereas smaller republics posed fewer obstacles for majorities to arise, large republics would force representatives to compromise with different regional interests in the union.[67]

The "Father of the Constitution" wrote his famous pamphlet amid widespread discussions in the West about republicanism and expansionism. Throughout the 1780s, westerners, including the Franklinites, argued that new western states would do more to spread and secure republicanism than harm the republican union. *Federalist No. 10* did not directly address Franklin statehood. However, Madison's novel interpretation of republicanism and territorial expansion drew on the logic of both David Hume and Arthur Campbell (who articulated similar ideas as early as 1783). When he wrote to Madison in late 1785, Campbell attempted to sway Madison and other

Virginian elites in favor of attaching Virginia's Washington County to Franklin. Campbell argued that new western states would increase obstacles for large states attempting to dominate their smaller counterparts while also preventing the need for separate confederacies. The western Virginian rejected both the idea of having "a consolidated Empire under one head" and the proposition that "one, or a few States . . . erect a separate government, and dissolve the present Confederacy." In his efforts to win support for his pro-Franklin scheme, Campbell reasoned that there would be "less difficulty, and far less danger" in limiting the size of states and parceling "out the Western territory, into proper divisions for free Communities." In the eyes of Campbell, the creation of new states would enable Americans to "unite in the closes[t] bands of amity."[68]

The last years of Franklin statehood raised doubts about the United States' destiny to extend the sphere, however. Revenge precipitated the state's downfall. Serving as colonel and clerk of court for North Carolina in the Tennessee Valley, John Tipton retaliated against his rival Sevier in early 1788. Tipton ordered Sheriff Jonathan Pugh to seize Sevier's property for unpaid taxes to North Carolina and send the Franklin governor's enslaved laborers and livestock to his home on Sinking Creek. When Tipton's orders reached him in the southern Tennessee Valley, Governor Sevier marched the Franklin militia away from fighting Chickamauga Cherokee leader Dragging Canoe to surround Tipton's farm in late February. The *Poughkeepsie Journal* reported that after Sevier "had besieged Col. Tipton's house," Col. George Maxwell "surprised the Governor and his party by the first fire, and forced the Governor to retreat without his boots." Fought on the fields surrounding Tipton's house, the Battle of Franklin in late February 1788 resulted in the capitulation of Sevier and crushed support for the statehood movement in Washington and Sullivan Counties.[69]

Sevier escaped justice by retreating to southern Franklin, where separatist fervor remained strong. After the skirmish on Tipton's farm, Franklin existed as a rump state, constituting the former separatist state's territory south of the French Broad River. "The governor fled below the mouth of French Broad out of the lines of Carolina, where his warmest friends live," the *Columbian Herald* reported. The paper added: "Matters seem now pretty well settled, and laws of the old state established." Near Cherokee territory and Spanish America, Lesser Franklin (as historians called it) bonded over a mutual hatred of Native peoples and Spaniards.[70]

Sevier remained popular in the south for his brutal campaigns against the Cherokees. Sevier and the Franklinites had amplified tensions with the Cherokees before the surrender of northern Franklin. In early 1787, the Franklin Assembly had passed a law that allowed its citizens to settle south of the French Broad to the Little Tennessee River. These encroachments exceeded the boundary lines established by the treaties of Dumplin Creek and Coyotee. Western Virginian Adam Stephen warned Madison that that the Franklinites' disregard for treaties would provoke a general war—whereby a coalition of southwestern Indigenous nations would wage war against the United States. "Should these ill advisd people force them into a War, we shall have all the Southern Indians against us," Stephen continued, "and among other Evills they will infect the Navigation of the Mississippi, which would greatly distress our people settled on the Waters of the Ohio." Once an advocate of Franklin statehood, Arthur Campbell agreed with Stephen. In a late 1787 letter to Virginia governor Edmund Randolph, Campbell dreaded "the consequence of a very irregular Militia from Franklin going through the Cherokee Country" en route to supporting Georgia's war against the Creeks. He feared that the Franklinites would undo any progress made between the United States and the southeastern Native nations. Overhill and Chickamauga Cherokees retaliated against the Franklinites, conducting raids and committing murders. Ignoring his state's atrocities, Franklinite David Campbell concluded that the Cherokees were "devoted to destruction."[71]

The Franklinites' policy in 1788 toward the Cherokees was one "devoted to destruction." By the spring of 1788, the Franklinites had been backed into a corner. Operating with limited resources and having gained many enemies, the Franklinites maximized their cruelty and brutality. In May 1788, a band of Cherokee warriors enflamed this sentiment after murdering eleven members of John Kirk's family. Sevier responded with fury. In late summer 1788, Richard Winn reported to Secretary of War Henry Knox that "a party from North Carolina (called Franklin State) with Servier at their head, came over and destroyed several [Overhill Cherokee] towns, killed near thirty of the Indians, made one prisoner, and obliged the remainder to fly with their families to some of the Lower towns for protection." Overhill Cherokee chief Kaiyah-tahee, who had worked tirelessly to maintain Cherokee territory amid Franklinite incursions, pleaded with Sevier's men that Chickamauga and Creek warriors committed the murders. Kaiyah-tahee joined Chief Abram in attempting to arrange a truce with the Franklinites. At the Cherokee village of Chilhowee, Maj. James Hubbard lured the chiefs into a home to discuss peace, only for them to be tomahawked by John Kirk. The death of Kaiyahtahee urged many Overhill Cherokees to relocate to northern Georgia or join Dragging Canoe's war against Anglo-American settlers. Even after the downfall of Franklin and the Constitution's ratification, self-proclaimed Franklinites continued to wage war against the Cherokees. War with Indigenous nations kept Sevier popular in the South and the Franklin statehood movement alive.[72]

Spanish officials sensed that the violent rump state of Franklin could be used to their advantage. Throughout the 1780s and 1790s, Spanish officials including diplomat Diego de Gardoqui imagined transforming the transAppalachian West into a buffer zone where loyal Anglo-American settlers and Indigenous warriors would shield the silver mines of New Spain from the upstart United States. For example, in one proposal to western Americans, Louisiana governor Esteban Rodríguez Miró y Sabater urged that they "obtain their independence from the United States." These vassals would be expected to convert to Catholicism and pledge loyalty to the Spanish Crown. In return, the settlers would be rewarded with land opportunities in Louisiana and access to the Mississippi River. Gardoqui saw an opportunity following the Battle of Franklin. To this end, he sent James White to convince Franklinites to align with Spain. Gardoqui reported that "the discord is confirmed in [the State of] Franklin, whose Inhabitants are so involved in difficulties." Therefore, White will "arrive in good time."[73]

Despite the anti-Spanish sentiment brewing in the West, Sevier entertained an alliance with the Bourbon monarchy that would mean independence from the United States. Sevier's contact with Spain was not unusual in the late eighteenth century. Anglo-American adventurers had been tempted by the allure of economic opportunity in Louisiana, while prominent westerners such as Gen. James Wilkinson of Kentucky had covertly served as paid agents of the Spanish crown. But unlike Kentucky, Franklin was on the verge of total collapse. In September 1788, Sevier desperately contacted Gardoqui about a potential alliance. Despite the ardent anti-Spanish sentiment in the West, Sevier informed the Spanish diplomat that the Franklinites "have come to realize truly . . . upon which nation depend their future happiness and security" and determined "the interest and prosperity of it depend entirely upon the protection and liberality of your government." To this end, the Franklinites anticipated "the future probability of an alliance and concession of commerce" with Spain. Sevier stressed that it appeared a "favorable" moment to execute this plan. After all, North Carolina had "rejected the constitution, and at the least a considerable time will pass before it becomes a member of the Union." An alliance now, he reasoned, would only incur the wrath of North Carolina and not the entire United States. He begged for a passport to access Spanish ports and any supplies to prepare for an invasion from the East. For a moment, the war hero of a republican revolution contemplated transforming the Tennessee Valley into a puppet state of the Spanish monarchy.[74]

Negotiations to align Franklin with Spain quickly fell apart, however. Miró questioned the motives of Sevier and White, believing the latter to be too attached to republicanism to pledge genuine loyalty to the Spanish Crown. For this reason, Spanish authorities feared that an alliance would empower Franklin to become an expansive, independent republic. After all, Sevier had requested that Spanish officials use their influence to prevent the Creeks, Chickasaws, and Choctaws from halting Franklinites' establishment of "new settlements on the Tennessee or near Muscle Shoals." Sevier had long coveted Muscle Shoals—a resource-rich area on the Tennessee River that had served as a hunting ground for the Cherokees—and schemed with North Carolinian and Georgian speculators to shore up the lands. Spanish officers thus lost interest in White's schemes and hoped to avoid replacing the United States with an even more aggressive settler republic.[75]

Whether he dreamed of a vast independent country or a Spanish puppet state, Sevier had to abandon his intrigue by the end of 1788. In July 1788, North Carolina leaders issued a warrant for Sevier's arrest. After his arrest and trial, North Carolina's general assembly issued an act of pardon that granted general clemency to the Franklinites except for Sevier. On November 30, after a special committee considered the Franklin governor's fate, North Carolina pardoned Sevier. As Lesser Franklin fell at the end of the decade, Sevier quickly reestablished himself as a leading figure in the Tennessee Valley. The North Carolina Senate elected Sevier to serve as the District of Washington's brigadier general, granting the former rebel a prestigious position. The state of Franklin had collapsed, but not the career of its leading statesman.[76]

The North Carolina Senate also selected Sevier to represent the western districts for the state's second ratifying convention. Outsiders such as John Brown Cutting believed North Carolinians would eagerly embrace the new

Constitution, given their state's "internal and ferocious disturbances." For Cutting, "the conflicts for independent power between those who denominate themselves citizens of Frankland and the residue of their neighbours" would convince Carolinians to support a powerful government that would prevent "the worse sort of unsubdueable anarcy." However, North Carolina did not ratify the Constitution at the Hillsborough Convention in the summer of 1788, fearing the new federal government would undermine states' rights and therefore slavery. But shortly after the Hillsborough Convention and the collapse of Franklin, North Carolinians reconsidered their western policy and constitutional leanings. In a letter to Washington, Madison noted that North Carolinians increasingly worried about western interests, especially as they felt excluded from the union after the majority of the states had ratified the new Constitution. In response to the demands beyond the Appalachian Mountains, North Carolina appointed Sevier to represent western interests during the Fayetteville Convention of late 1789, where he and the majority voted in favor of the Constitution.[77]

The fates of the state of Franklin and of John Sevier illustrate how US policymakers reimagined their expansionist plans for the West. In the eyes of the founders, the chaotic finale of Franklin statehood portended a bleak future for the trans-Appalachian West. Their short-lived civil war against Tipton's men, ruthless invasions of Cherokee lands, and intrigue with Spain underscored how US expansion beyond the Appalachian Mountains was far from manifest or destined. Despite leading this chaos, Sevier's career lived on, culminating in his appointment as the first governor of Tennessee in 1796. The contested and un-manifest nature of westward expansion forced the founders to embrace men like Sevier and their interests. The Federalists embraced the Franklinites' and other westerners' arguments that advancing western interests would strengthen the fragile republican union. The Franklinites and their western allies reminded US decision-makers that their visions had to reconcile the aspirations of ambitious settlers and Indigenous nations. Failing to recognize these realities would undermine the American empire west of the Appalachian Mountains.

After repeated efforts to quash the Franklin separatist movement, North Carolina ceded their land claims in the trans-Appalachian West in December 1789. To avoid another Franklin, Congress organized the Tennessee Valley into the Southwest Territory in 1790, providing the region with an administrative organization for its rapidly growing population. These settlers continued to raid Native settlements, participate in transimperial schemes, and loathe eastern politicians' decision-making. Nonetheless, US policymakers made strides in appeasing western interests by permitting slavery (in contrast to the Northwest Territory) and offering appointments to former Franklinites. Though he was a wealthy eastern Carolinian, William Blount quickly won the favor of former Franklinites by selecting John Sevier as brigadier general of the Washington District (comprising the former Washington county of Franklin) in the Southwest Territory, David Campbell as a territorial judge, and William Cocke as attorney general. Accommodating western interests, Blount remained popular in the Tennessee Valley, even after his murky support of a British invasion of Spanish Florida and Louisiana leaked to the public. When Tennesseans secured statehood in 1796, the newly elected governor Sevier and his fellow ex-Franklinites finally secured a recognized state beyond the Appalachian Mountains—one achieved at the expense of Indigenous nations and enslaved African Americans.[78]

Westerners' interests could shape national policy east of the Appalachian Mountains, too. In September 1789, James Madison drew on his recent interactions with Kentuckians, Franklinites, and other westerners to argue that the nation's capital should be placed along the Potomac River. His proposal stemmed less from southern intrigue than a desire to accommodate western interests. Responding to fears that "within so great a space, no free government can exist," Madison argued that the best means to diminish inconveniences and regional inequality "is to place the government in that spot which will be least removed from every part of the empire." Whereas selecting a northern capital might lead to two warring nations, a capital on the Potomac River would secure the American empire. "From the fertility of soil, the fineness of climate, and every thing that can favor a growing population, we may suppose the settlement will go on with every degree of rapidity which our imagination can conceive." He continued, "If the calculation be just, that we double in twenty-five years, we shall speedily behold an astonishing mass of people on the western waters."[79]

As Madison's comments suggest, the founders had increasingly imagined that the future of the republic lay west. But far from imagining a clear-sighted manifest destiny, Madison and the founders recognized that this future was contested and uncertain. In the 1780s, eastern policymakers envisioned transforming the land between the Appalachian Mountains and the Mississippi River into a breadbasket for the Atlantic. This dream would be achieved through an orderly process of state-making and land distribution, as laid out in the Northwest Ordinances. The founders feared that a failure to realize these goals would permit lawlessness, destructive wars with Native nations, and European schemes.

The state of Franklin proved a manifestation of these anxieties. Emerging from the political and economic chaos of postrevolutionary America, the Franklin statehood movement thwarted the expansionist imaginings of eastern politicians. The Franklinites justified their land claims, war with the Cherokees, and separatist movement as a continuation of the American Revolution in the West. Rejected by Congress and North Carolina, the state of Franklin had become a de facto independent republic. While they sought admission into the American union, the Franklinites defied US policymakers' authority in the West by disrupting US relations with southeast Native nations, plotting a war against and alliance with Spain, and contemplating independence. The volatile state of Franklin presaged what Kentucky and the wider trans-Appalachian West *could* become. The eighteenth-century Tennessee Valley forced the founders to imagine the possibility of their republic being halted east of the Appalachian Mountains and the West dominated by independent states.[80]

The breakaway, trans-Appalachian West never came to be, nor did Franklin statehood last. Yet the turmoil of the trans-Appalachian West pressured the founders to reimagine their expansionist visions for the West. Although they rejected the state of Franklin, the founders would soon embrace many of the Franklinites' ideas about western interests and republicanism. Like their fellow westerners, Franklinites taught crucial lessons to members of the founding generation about the importance of appeasing their interests, especially in the wake of the unrealized Jay-Gardoqui Treaty. The Franklinites and their western allies championed the creation of new coequal states that would in turn balance the competing interests that imperiled the republican union. They hoped for a strong national government that could advance their interests and secure the continent. As Franklinite judge David Campbell idealistically pondered: "Is not the continent of America one day to become one consolidated government of the United States?" After much debate, US policymakers determined that the new trans-Appalachian states would be admitted into the union as coequal to the original thirteen states.

Many expansionists came to embrace the westerners' belief that Anglo-American settlers were destined to spread republican institutions across North America. Born in the state of Franklin in 1786, David Crockett resembled one of these settlers who followed in Sevier's footsteps. Yet, like Sevier, Crockett and his fellow antebellum adventurers would spread republicanism with or without the United States.[81]

The founders and Franklinites were not the only ones imagining the territorial, social, and political destiny of the West. The geopolitical turmoil spawned by the Atlantic revolutions motivated the diverse inhabitants of the Americas to articulate their own alternative destinies. Imagining the Great Lakes region free of white settlers, Shawnee brothers Tecumseh and Tenskwatawa drove US leaders to set their sights on the Canadian North.

## THREE

# THE MICHIGAN AND UPPER CANADA BORDERLANDS

As the United States struggled to expand westward in the early 1800s, Shawnee chief Tecumseh aimed to push the republic eastward. Born in 1768, a young Tecumseh witnessed waves of Anglo-Americans transform the Ohio Valley with homesteads and violence. He lost his father during Lord Dunmore's War (1774) and his temper after the signing of the Treaty of Greenville (1795), which ceded southern Ohio to the United States. Tecumseh channeled this frustration into forging a pan-Indigenous confederacy in 1808, building on the spiritual teachings of his prophet brother, Tenskwatawa. During the War of 1812, Tecumseh sought to remove white Americans and create an independent Indigenous state in the Great Lakes. Tecumseh appeared, British officer Isaac Brock remarked, "determined to continue the contest until they obtain the Ohio for a boundary." The War of 1812, however, crushed his confederacy and took his life. Nonetheless, the Native state imagined by Tecumseh and Tenskwatawa circumscribed the empire of liberty envisioned by Thomas Jefferson and James Madison.[1]

The Great Lakes region, particularly along the Michigan-Canadian borderlands, represented a battleground where these conflicting visions of nation-building clashed in the early nineteenth century. US territorial officials attempted to transform Michigan from a native ground—where Native peoples determined Indigenous-white relations—into a space where self-governing, independent farmers would secure republicanism. Jefferson's and his adherents' expansionist imagining of the Midwest hinged on the acquisition of land and the misguided belief that Native peoples would either assimilate or fade away.[2]

Michigan—where the two small forts of Detroit and Mackinac reflected the weakness of federal authority—contradicted the notion that Native peoples would disappear. The implications of Tecumseh's vision were most felt in Michigan, where proximity to Upper Canada and Anishinaabe hegemony undermined federal authority. Well into the 1800s, the Anishinaabe nations of Ojibwes, Odawas, and Potawatomis dominated the upper and lower peninsulas, vastly outnumbering the US population. During the War of 1812, Anishinaabe warriors overwhelmingly sided with Tecumseh and the British. Tecumseh and his Indigenous allies capitalized on Michigan's vast international border with Upper Canada, using ongoing tensions between the US republic and the British colony to dominate the borderlands. Native unity in and around Michigan undermined a core belief of Jeffersonian expansionism: North America was an unsettled continent waiting to be civilized by virtuous citizens.[3]

Tecumseh's vision drove and denied US expansion into Upper Canada. British officers dreamed of Upper Canada becoming a fortress for Loyalism, where the fertile fields between the Ottawa River and the Great Lakes and orderly British government would entice Americans away from their republican experiment. US policymakers certainly considered Upper Canada as a threat to their republican union. But Michigan territorial officials relayed to powerbrokers in Washington a more pressing motive for capturing Upper Canada. When the United States invaded Upper Canada during the War of 1812, these officials believed a decisive victory over the British would deliver a logistical, psychological, and military blow to Indigenous unity in the Great Lakes region. By extending northward into Canada, US policymakers would weaken Native unity's obstacle to Anglo-Americans' westward expansion. Ultimately, Tecumseh's short-lived confederacy and Canadian resistance dashed US expansion into the Canadian North and threatened the United States' tenuous hold over Michigan.[4]

The unpredictable course of the war in the contested Great Lakes region undermined any notion that US policymakers had imagined a clearsighted manifest destiny. Between the 1790s and 1810s, geopolitical actors articulated many unrealized destinies: a pan-Indigenous buffer state in Michigan,

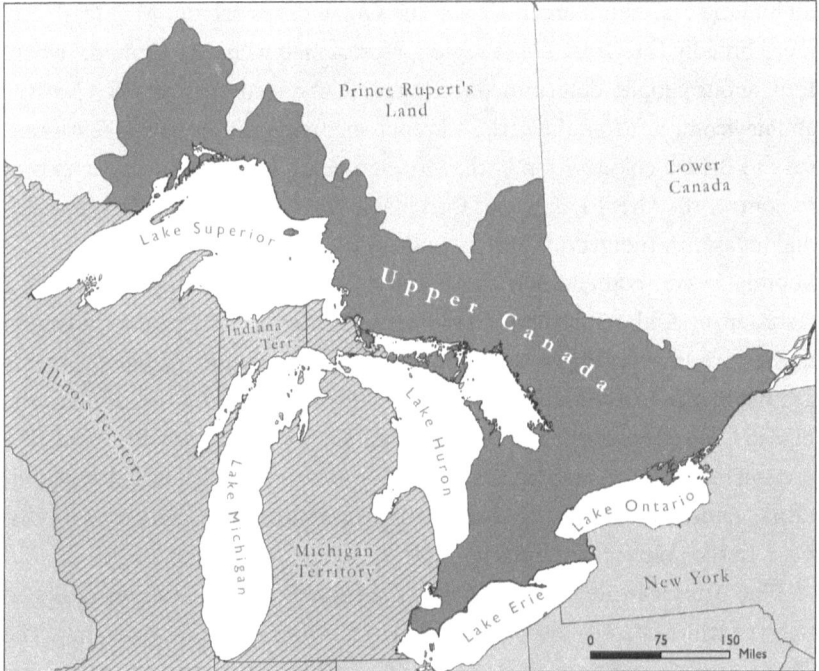

The Michigan Territory and Upper Canada, 1812.

an American Upper Canada, and a US republic halted south and east of the Ohio River. Indigenous, American, and British leaders in these contingent borderlands could not have predicted the Treaty of Ghent's restoration of prewar boundaries. Dread of a resurgent Indigenous confederacy pressured postwar policymakers to reconfigure their expansionist imaginings and remove Indigenous peoples near Michigan's international borders. By removing Native peoples along the US-Canadian border, territorial officials such as Lewis Cass rendered Upper Canada less of an existential threat to the republic's survival. While their destiny to the north was denied, US expansionists pursued removal to secure the West.[5]

## MICHIGAN: A NATIVE GROUND

Michigan hosted a complex history of Native unity and resistance to imperial intrusions long before the existence of the United States. The Anishinaabe nations of the Odawas, Ojibwes, and Potawatomis had been immersed in the diplomatic and commercial ties of the Great Lakes region. Michigan, and more broadly the Great Lakes region, represented a "native ground," where Indigenous peoples determined the outcome of encounters between Natives and newcomers. From the earliest French incursions in the seventeenth century to British colonization in the late eighteenth century, European efforts to control the Great Lakes met formidable resistance. Responding to colonial invasions, Indigenous nations such as the Wyandots, Anishinaabeg, and Miamis forged confederacies to reassert their regional hegemony. When Gen. Jeffrey Amherst attempted to impose British authority over the region in the early 1760s, Odawa chief Pontiac led a series of pan-Indigenous raids against British forts, including Detroit and Pitt. To avoid future conflicts, the British Crown issued the Royal Proclamation Line of 1763, which intended to prevent Anglo-American settler expansion beyond the Appalachian Mountains. These actions enraged eastern speculators and land-hungry colonists to the point of revolution.[6]

The American Revolution spawned a republican government designed to serve white citizens' needs, including securing access to Native lands. The Treaty of Paris (1783) granted the young republic a claim to the Great Lakes region, which US policymakers reorganized into the Northwest Territory and planned to divide into republican states. But as the Franklinites and other westerners had demonstrated in the early 1780s, a weak national government could not effectively address their regional interests, especially settlers' appetite for Native lands. The founders recognized that failure to acquire Native land and respond to Native warriors' retaliatory raids could invite Spanish or British intrigue. The adoption of the US Constitution empowered the federal government to raise sufficient funds and a military to handle westward expansion. Under the new US Constitution, President George Washington and his administration devoted 80 percent of the federal budget to their policy toward Native peoples in the trans-Appalachian West. With these funds, the Washington administration implemented a policy centered on acquiring Native lands by purchase, establishing solid boundaries, controlling trade, and assimilating Native peoples by means of Christianity, Euro-American gender norms, and Anglo-American agricultural practices. This "civilization" program, they hoped, would avoid war and ensure territorial expansion.[7]

US policy ran counter to the ambitions of Indigenous nations in the Northwest Territory. In the 1780s and 1790s, Indigenous peoples responded to unfair treaties, violent assaults, and unruly squatters by imagining a future for the Great Lakes that was free of the US republic. To realize this future, Native nations forged a loose military alliance of Miami, Shawnee, Kickapoo, Iroquois, Ojibwe, Odawa, and Potawatomi warriors. This confederacy, receiving supplies and arms from British officials stationed in Canada and at forts such as Detroit, waged a successful war against US forces from 1790 to 1792. Miami chief Little Turtle and Shawnee chief Blue Jacket won two decisive battles against the United States: the first against Gen. Josiah Harmar's army in northeastern Indiana in the fall of 1790, and the second against Arthur St. Clair's 1,400 troops at the Battle of the Wabash in November 1791. Emboldened by their victories, Northwest Indigenous leaders demanded that "no peace would take place, unless the Ohio river was established as a boundary, between the Indians & Americans." Their demands, supported by British agents bent on establishing an Indigenous buffer state between Canada and the American republic, raised doubts about the United States' long-term plans in the Great Lakes.[8]

The Battle of Fallen Timbers reversed the Native confederates' fortunes and revealed the cracks in Indigenous unity. After the defeats of Harmar and St. Clair, President Washington instructed Maj. Gen. "Mad" Anthony Wayne, a fiery and controversial leader, to instill professionalism and discipline in the US military. Wayne responded by creating the Legion of the United States—a standing army composed of professional soldiers rather than state militias. The drills and discipline paid off. In August 1794, the Legion of the United States decisively defeated the Native confederates at Fallen Timbers (present-day Maumee, Ohio). News of the victory and the subsequent Treaty of Greenville (1795) encouraged US settlers to inundate the fertile fields and hunting grounds of Ohio and Kentucky—at the expense of Native nations.[9]

The Battle of Fallen Timbers also signaled to US forces that pan-Native unity could be disrupted if a decisive victory could illustrate the might of US forces at the expense of the British. Wayne believed his victory at Fallen Timbers produced "a conviction to the Minds of the Savages that the British have neither the Power nor inclination to afford them that Protection they had been Taught to expect." Though US forces suffered greater casualties, the Native confederates retreated to Fort Miami, a British outpost in northeastern Ohio. British officer William Campbell closed the fort's gates to Native forces, damaging Indigenous morale and crushing their faith in their British allies. Wayne argued that Campbell's orders to close the gates represented a "Disgrace of the British" and an "Honour of the American Arms." Potawatomi chief Nanaume later reflected in 1807 that every time his people passed "the banks of the [Maumee]" it reminded them to never "place any dependence on [the British]." In flexing US authority, Wayne's American legion effectively disbanded the Native confederacy, leaving a blueprint for future territorial leaders in the Great Lakes.[10]

Wayne's victory weakened Indigenous control of the southern Great Lakes, but federal authority remained elusive in present-day Michigan. In the late eighteenth and early nineteenth centuries, Michigan had only a few sparse white settlements, including Detroit in the southeast and the small island outpost of Mackinac at the northernmost point of Lake Huron. US policymakers failed to encourage migration into the region and struggled to incorporate Michigan. Detroit, a small town immersed in the fur trade and protected by an even smaller fort, did not formally wave the American flag until 1796, when the British abided by the Jay Treaty and relocated across the Detroit River. Local Catholic priests and merchants, who had handled Detroit's judicial cases and political controversies under French and British rule, continued to exercise those powers until 1805, when Congress organized the Michigan Territory. While westward-bound settlers flocked into the fertile Ohio Valley in the 1790s and 1800s, the harsh winters and geopolitical climate of Michigan and the other Upper Lakes territories attracted few white Americans. By contrast, nations such as the Potawatomis, Odawas, and Ojibwes dominated Michigan. At the dawn of the nineteenth century, Michigan had an estimated Native population of 10,000, outnumbering the roughly 4,700 US citizens living along the Detroit River. Territorial officials floundered in transforming Michigan into a successful settler colony.[11]

Michigan's isolation from the rest of the United States bolstered Native hegemony. The fur trade incorporated Detroit into the Atlantic world, but poor transportation and communication left the city of straits out of the United States' orbit. Geographer William Darby observed that Detroit was "separated by an expanse of water, and by an uncultivated waste, from the other parts of the United States." The "isolated moral mass" had little in common but "a slight tie of interest to unite it to the sovereignty of which it forms a part." Beyond a land strip along the Detroit River, Michigan remained largely under Native rule, except for minor settlements such as Mackinac and Frenchtown (present-day Monroe, Michigan) along Lake Erie.[12]

Cultural differences and conflicting loyalties among white settlers hampered the United States' control over Michigan. Many French *habitants* remained in Detroit and other smaller settlements after France ceded New France in 1763. Differences in faith and language contributed to mutual distrust and even disgust between English Protestants and French Catholics. French men and women—who constituted four-fifths of the white population—often regarded Americans as unmannered brutes. Take, for instance, the failed efforts of lovestruck Frederick Bates to win the hearts of Detroit's Frenchwomen in the spring of 1799. The charmless territorial official complained that he made "little progress among the french Girls." "They are not very apt to think favorably of the Americans," Bates complained to his sister. "They think them a rough unpolished, brutal set of people." Conversely, Anglo-Americans usually considered the French Catholics idolatrous and consequently incapable of republican citizenship.[13]

National identities also divided Anglo-Americans in Michigan. As the United States took control of Detroit, American policymakers offered the town's white settlers US citizenship or allowed them to relocate to Upper Canada as British subjects. Some settlers stayed and accepted citizenship while others left for Canada. Nonetheless, US officials questioned the loyalties of many Michiganders, especially British and French-Canadian fur traders. Distance and distrust made, in the eyes of Michigan settlers, "every individual house ... a frontier."[14]

Conflicting loyalties invited a flurry of suspicion and schemes. In 1795, before British officers abandoned Detroit, several merchants purchased Odawa and Ojibwe lands in southern Michigan. Led by British merchant John Askin, the company attempted to bribe members of Congress into selling Michigan's lower peninsula for $500,000. Congress arrested the agents and then created a factory system to win the loyalty of Indigenous nations in the Great Lakes. US policymakers intended to use the factory system to control Indigenous peoples' trade and separate them from British fur traders. Even after Americans established factories in 1796, Canadian merchants continued dominating the fur trade in Michigan. Canadian fur traders operated out of Sandwich, Upper Canada (which Americans called "Smugglingburg"), appealing to Native peoples with better supplies and trust built on longstanding reliability. And, despite their failed plot, Canadian merchants asserted the validity of their land claims. Secretary of the Northwest Territory Winthrop Sargent warned that Englishmen in Detroit endeavored "to extend *their Claims* to the Indian Lands." The Canadians' control of the fur trade heightened US officials' distrust toward Native peoples and fed resentment of British agents in Canada.[15]

The Jay Treaty further solidified Michigan as a contested borderland and a native ground. The treaty's third article allowed Indigenous inhabitants, British subjects, and American citizens to freely "pass and repass by Land, or Inland Navigation" between the United States and Canada "to carry on trade and commerce." Michigan's upper and lower Peninsula shared a vast international border with Upper Canada; the US territory and British colony were separated only by navigable lakes and rivers. Michigan territorial governor William Hull emphasized that "the territory of Michigan" bordered "several hundred miles on the Canadas, and is only separated by an imaginary line, in the middle of the rivers and lakes." For territorial officials such as Hull, the treaty's third article undermined US security in Michigan. Anishinaabe and other Indigenous peoples crossed the Detroit River to reach Fort Malden in Canada, conjuring fear over the seemingly suspicious interactions between Native traders and British agents. The movements of Native warriors and British agents across an "imaginary" border, Hull argued, drew "the numerous, and powerful tribes of savages" closer to their British "allies and friends."[16]

Michigan's vast international border and small white population of questionable loyalty enabled Indigenous nations to dominate the upper Great Lakes region (such as present-day Michigan, Wisconsin, and Ontario). Native ascendancy terrified white settlers, soldiers, and territorial officials alike. When he learned that Fort Shelby, near Detroit, was his destination, US soldier Jeremiah Dubois Jr. considered "hiring a substitute or disserting" because "the idea of going where there is so many Indians [made] [his] very blood run cold." Like many newcomers, Dubois understood Native peoples through the lens of stereotypes, a set of misguided beliefs rooted in the English colonial experience. This hatred of Native peoples allowed white Americans to find a race-based common ground, justify violence and removal, and obscure Indigenous allies. Actual interactions with Native peoples often eased these anxieties. When he became the fort's gardener, Dubois traded with Anishinaabe merchants, who were "as friendly people as ever [he] saw." But many white Michiganders lacked Dubois's experience and instead relied on old tropes. Rumors, untethered from experience, convinced white settlers in Michigan that the "tenderest infant" and the "agonized mother" could not escape "the stroke of the relentless tomahawk." Ironically, these fears only served to bolster Native hegemony in Michigan in the early 1800s.[17]

Indigenous power, geopolitical isolation, borderland intrigue, and racial fears compelled Detroiters to request that the US Congress designate Michigan as an organized territory. In a memorial to Congress, Detroit judge Solomon Sibley requested that Wayne County be separated from the Indiana Territory because of the "inhospitable deserts" that lay between Detroit and Vincennes and Michigan's "contiguity to the Br[itish] Province of Upper Canada." In 1805, the United States placed Wayne County within the newly created Michigan Territory, which included the upper and lower peninsulas. The decision to organize the Michigan Territory developed in response to the clashing visions of US policymakers and Native leaders. Frustrated by their struggles to create republican states in the Northwest, US decision-makers feared Native nations' efforts to contain the US republic east of the Ohio River. By the early 1800s, these state actors identified their insignificant influence over Michigan and the continued British presence in Upper Canada as sources of Indigenous hegemony. To weaken Indigenous unity, territorial officials attempted to establish jurisdiction over Michigan. From Michigan, territorial and military leaders envisioned invading Upper Canada, believing its fall would crush Indigenous unity and British intrigue like Wayne's victory at Fallen Timbers. Such expansionist schemes surfaced when territorial governor William Hull arrived in Detroit.[18]

## TENSKWATAWA'S DREAM

When he reached Detroit in July 1805, Hull encountered a town recently destroyed by a fire and townsmen accustomed to local rule. Hull lacked credentials for a federal appointment in Anishinaabe country. However, for President Jefferson and his administration, Hull possessed two valuable traits: he was both a Democratic-Republican loyalist from New England and a Revolutionary War veteran. The Jefferson administration instructed Hull to transform the Michigan Territory from a native ground into a settler colony. His appointment as territorial governor meant he would also serve as Michigan's superintendent of Indian affairs. In his capacity as superintendent, the inexperienced Hull would be expected to protect Indigenous land rights, promote the settlement of US citizens, receive Native delegations, and handle hostilities between whites and Native peoples. Struggling to form a militia in a recently destroyed town, uncultured in diplomacy with Native peoples, and dreading the intentions of the British across the river, Hull headed the dysfunctional and underdeveloped Michigan Territory.[19]

In 1807, events outside the Michigan Territory exacerbated fears about a general war with Indigenous nations. A national crisis erupted after a British warship, the HMS *Leopard*, attacked the Mediterranean-bound USS *Chesapeake* off Virginia's coast on June 22. The *Chesapeake-Leopard* crisis reverberated far beyond the Atlantic Seaboard, as rumors of war with Great Britain coincided with the reality of a pan-Native religious revival in the Great Lakes. In the West, US policymakers worried that British agents conspired with an upstart Shawnee prophet, whose religious revival movement attracted Native peoples across the region. In 1805, Lalawethika received a vision from the Great Spirit that encouraged him to renounce alcohol, inspire Native unity, and reject Euro-American influence. This village outcast, overshadowed by his talented brother Tecumseh, was reborn as Tenskwatawa (Open Door). He assumed spiritual leadership of a broader grassroots religious revival that advocated for a complete separation from whites and Euro-American culture.[20]

Tenskwatawa reimagined the social and geopolitical order of the Great Lakes region. Like his contemporary revolutionaries throughout the Atlantic world, Tenskwatawa undermined traditional authority by offering a new political arrangement. He envisioned a common Native home that overlooked distinctions between nations. The Prophet created a religious community that purged witchcraft, critiqued accommodationist chiefs, and urged temperance. At the site where Indigenous confederates signed the Treaty of Greenville, Tenskwatawa resurrected their dream of securing the Ohio River as the boundary between a common Native state and the US republic. Such a boundary line was not unfamiliar to US policymakers. Though they rejected British attempts at establishing a proclamation line before the Revolution, US policymakers embraced an ever-shifting Indian boundary line that separated Indigenous peoples and white settlers—a line that continually moved westward. However, Tenskwatawa and Tecumseh sought to move the line eastward, which would inevitably breed animosity. The Prophet's teachings attracted flocks of Shawnees, Odawas, Mingoes, Wyandots, and other Native peoples to his settlement at Greenville, Ohio. US agent Thomas Forsyth claimed that "the Prophet had his Disciples among every Nation of Indians from Detroit in Michigan Territory, to the Indians on the Mississippi" and adherents from the Missouri River Valley and the Hudson Bay.[21]

Rather than reflecting on the faults of US policy, American policymakers used the uncertainty bred by the 1807 crisis to identify Tenskwatawa's movement as a British plot. From his post near Greenville and Upper Canada, Michigan governor Hull accepted the Prophet-British connection wholesale. Regarding the Michigan Territory, however, Hull worried more about a general war with Indigenous nations than a British invasion. In August 1807, his concerns gained credence when territorial judge Augustus Woodward reported that "the Indians on the head waters of the Huron River of Lake Erie had abandoned their settlements in an unusual matter." Woodward learned that the Native nations had "all gone on a visit to the prophet at Greeneville." A "pacific" visit to Greenville, in the eyes of Hull and Woodward, foreshadowed future conflicts between Native peoples and white Americans in the Great Lakes.[22]

Native peoples' movements in the Michigan Territory coincided with rumors of impending attacks on Mackinac and Detroit. "Letters, dispositions, and reports from Michillimackinac," Woodward cautioned, "shew that the conduct of the Indians was unusual." Woodward surmised that the Prophet's "bitter reproaches" had ignited "a little revolution" in northern Michigan. Two more reports in late summer 1807 suggested that a large body of Anishinaabe warriors from Amerherstburgh in Upper Canada and Saginaw in Michigan would descend on Detroit. While local French traders ridiculed "these silly apprehensions," the rumors confirmed for Hull the existence of a Native-British alliance. Indeed, with Native peoples and British agents separated only by rivers and lakes, Hull worried that these interactions could galvanize Indigenous warriors into forming a new military confederacy.[23]

Panicked by rumors of an impending raid in the early fall of 1807, Hull prepared to defend Detroit. He hastily fortified the town with a hodgepodge of "picquets, blockhouses, and batteries . . . in all directions." Augustus Woodward criticized the governor for giving "too much credit" to the rumors. Michigan would be calm, Woodward complained, "if it were not for another idle tale of an Indian war." "Our panic-struck inhabitants outrival the industry of the bee," Woodward lamented. Hull's preparations also "excited some sensibility among the Inhabitants living on the British Shore" of Upper Canada because he supported the formation of a Black militia. A leader of Detroit's African American community, Peter Denison, convinced Hull to support the creation of such a militia, which would protect the town from Native or British attacks. The Black militia of Detroit, which included both free and enslaved Black men, challenged generations of white lawmakers who had established restrictions on people of African descent from holding firearms. The prospects of a war with Native warriors and redcoats convinced Hull to overlook entrenched racial attitudes and race-based laws. In a letter to British officer Jasper Grant, Hull justified arming the Black militia because of Detroit's "local situation as a Frontier" and rumors of British agents conspiring with Native leaders. As war seemed inevitable in the summer and fall of 1807, white inhabitants on both sides of the Detroit River dreaded the prospects of armed nonwhites.[24]

Hull and Woodward devised a solution to prevent a general war with Native nations: invading Upper Canada. "If we are to have a war," Woodward informed Hull in August 1807, "I cannot believe that our government will neglect to authorize us to take immediately the British side of this strait." Woodward was far from the first to suggest an American invasion of Canada. Anglo-American expansionists had long coveted Canada. In the eighteenth century, Anglo-American colonists loathed French Quebec, believing that French traders fueled Indigenous resistance to their westward expansion. When they declared independence, revolutionary Americans considered British Canada a crucial component of their republic and allowed Canadians immediate admission into the union under the Articles of Confederation. After declaring independence, Americans feared British proximity to the north, viewing Canada as a base where British agents would disrupt republicanism and support Native warriors.[25]

Past experiences and current events convinced US policymakers that Upper Canada represented a major obstacle to US expansion. On the ground, Michigan officials recognized that the greatest threat to securing the empire of liberty stemmed from Indigenous unity. Territorial officials knew that a decisive victory akin to Wayne's triumph at Fallen Timbers could weaken Indigenous unity, prevent British intrigue, and help secure the Michigan Territory. Hull and Woodward believed that capturing Upper Canada would represent this decisive victory. Woodward reasoned that if US forces managed to capture "the lowest settlement [of Upper Canada] to the river Thames or aux Trenches," they would put "down forever all further Indian apprehensions." Hull relayed Woodward's suggestions to Secretary of War Henry Dearborn. Receiving reports that British officers collected "all the different nations of Indians at Amherstburgh," Hull believed that the "large number" who had already reached Upper Canada would join the British if war broke out. "*Prompt, decided* and *vigorous measures* ought to be taken,"

Hull continued, "for the security of the Frontier and the Reduction of the Canada's."[26]

Federal officials' fears about Upper Canada mirrored the hopes of British policymakers. In 1791, Parliament passed the Constitutional Act, which divided Canada into Upper and Lower Canada. Whereas Francophone colonists dominated Lower Canada, Upper Canada lay within lands controlled by Anishinaabe peoples and the Iroquois. Despite Indigenous dominance, Lt. Gov. John Graves Simcoe believed that Upper Canada would be "destined by Nature, sooner or later, to govern the interior World." Situated south of the Ottawa River, north of the St. Lawrence River, and along Lake Superior, Upper Canada was intended to be a haven for Loyalist refugees and the antithesis of American republicanism. Simcoe wanted Upper Canada—with its mixed constitution, its support of the Anglican Church, and its emphasis on order—to demonstrate "all the advantages of British Protection as a better Government than the United States." This vision, however, depended on Native resistance to US expansion. Indeed, into the nineteenth century, Upper Canada had only a few white settlements, including Sandwich (present-day Windsor) and York (present-day Toronto). Simcoe and his successors believed a Native buffer state would safeguard their Loyalist colony. In 1793, British agent Alexander McKee hoped that a Native state would "form an extensive Barrier between the British & American Territory." At the dawn of the nineteenth century, British colonial leaders identified Michigan as the site of this state. Whereas Indigenous unity threatened US influence in Michigan, pan-Native movements could secure Upper Canada.[27]

President Jefferson recognized Upper Canada's dependence on Native warriors and attempted to convey British weakness to the Native peoples of the Great Lakes. These nations included the Shawnee, Wyandot, Anishinaabeg, Ho-Chunk, Delaware, and Miami. In a letter to Secretary of War Henry Dearborn in August 1807, Jefferson devised a policy in response to reports from the territorial governors of Illinois, Indiana, and Michigan. With Tenskwatawa's anti-US rhetoric and the "assembly of the Indians" in Upper Canada, Jefferson believed that US officials needed to "immediately prepare for war" and aim for peace. Jefferson instructed territorial governors to prevent Indigenous nations from capitalizing on US-British tensions by raising militias, sending speeches and gifts to Native peoples, and increasing communications between the territories. In emphasizing the military might of the United States, territorial officials had to convey that the United

States was "strong enough to fight [their] own battles & therefore ask for no help." Jefferson wanted governors to stress that the British sought assistance because "it proceeds from a sense of their own weakness which would not augur success in the end." Accommodationist leaders such as Potawatomi chief Nanaume would rely on this rhetoric to avoid violence with the United States. "We believe [the President] is strong because he does not want any aid from us." Nanaume continued, "We believe the British are weak because they want us to assist them."[28]

Whether through speeches or proposed invasions of Upper Canada, US policymakers and territorial officials endeavored to "make a powerful impression" on the Great Lakes nations. Seeking to avoid war, Jefferson proposed another policy to assert federal authority in the Great Lakes: extermination or removal. "If ever we are constrained to lift the hatchet against any tribe," Jefferson warned, "we will never lay it down till that tribe is exterminated, or driven beyond the Misisipi." Jefferson's horrifying rhetoric of removal or extermination—built on fears of pan-Indigenous power—foreshadowed the removal policies of the antebellum era.[29]

Native peoples avoided conflict in the Great Lakes in 1807. But their neutrality likely resulted less from US threats and more from geopolitical considerations, a desire for independence from Euro-American wars, and memories of British betrayal. Nonetheless, the tensions that surfaced in 1807 revealed that the ambitions of Indigenous nativists, US policymakers, and British officials could not coexist. To prevent Indigenous unity in a native ground, territorial officials plotted invasions of Upper Canada and threatened Native communities with removal and extermination. These efforts, however, fueled Tecumseh and Tenskwatawa's movement.

## THE BATTLE OF PROPHETSTOWN: CLASHING VISIONS OF THE GREAT LAKES REGION'S FUTURE

In the fall of 1807, Hull negotiated a treaty with Indigenous nations in Michigan and Ohio that unknowingly jeopardized federal authority in the Great Lakes region. Instructed by Jefferson's administration, Hull convened with chiefs from the Wyandot, Odawa, Potawatomi, and Ojibwe nations at

Brownstown, a Native village in the Michigan Territory. Tecumseh vehemently opposed the meeting, believing that further land concessions disrupted his vision for an independent Indigenous nation in the Great Lakes region. Despite Tecumseh's obstructive measures, the meeting resulted in the Treaty of Detroit.[30]

The Treaty of Detroit secured southeastern Michigan and portions of northwest Ohio for the United States in exchange for $10,000 in money and supplies and promises of $2,400 in annual payments. Like most Native treaties, the Treaty of Detroit heavily favored the United States. The treaty system was premised on several ideological foundations. Policymakers believed that Native peoples were temporary occupants who did not permanently settle on North American lands. The treaty secured Native land along Lake Huron, which would fulfill Jefferson's agrarian vision for Michigan. But the Treaty of Detroit also represented a defensive measure against Indigenous unity. While early nineteenth-century US policy centered around the acquisition of land, the removal of Indigenous peoples in contested borderlands stemmed from a desire to achieve geopolitical security. Dividing Wyandot, Odawa, Potawatomi, and Ojibwe villages along Lake Huron disrupted pan-Indigenous communication and further separated these nations from Upper Canada. Determined to secure land in a native ground and along an international border, US policymakers lackadaisically adhered to the treaty's stipulations.[31]

Anishinaabe and Wyandot chiefs would be reminded how the US republic fell short of its promises. Indeed, dishonest agents often failed to deliver the promised annual payments to the Odawa, Wyandot, Potawatomi, and Ojibwe nations. In an 1811 speech, these nations' leaders urged President James Madison to remove agents that "appear fond of feathering their own nest" at the expense of Native men, women, and children. "It is a notorious fact in this country," Detroit merchant John R. Williams admitted, "that the indians have been greatly imposed on." Williams knew that Indigenous resistance resulted from settler violence and the practice "of creating new chiefs from amongst the most worthless of the tribes on the condition of their acquiescing to signing the Treaty which some of the principal chiefs refused to sanction." While treaties attempted to erase Native peoples from the region, Williams concluded that such efforts fueled Tecumseh's movement.[32]

Mismanaged and unfulfilled treaties drove many Native peoples closer to Tecumseh, Tenskwatawa, and their confederacy. In 1808, Tenskwatawa relocated his religious movement from Greenville to the Indiana Territory to avoid exacerbating tensions with white Ohioans. Upon arriving in Indiana, Tenskwatawa and his followers established Prophetstown (present-day Lafayette, Indiana) near the Wabash River. Like his brother, Tecumseh recognized the seriousness of US-British tensions and attempted to forge a large confederacy in alignment with Tenskwatawa's teachings. As US and British officials struggled to dominate the Great Lakes region, the Shawnee brothers conceived of a state composed of many Native nations that could resist settler colonialism—or even repel white settlers east of the Ohio River. Despite their unpopularity with accommodationists such as Miami chief Little Turtle, Tecumseh and Tenskwatawa promised to reject further treaties in favor of communal landownership among Native peoples, which appealed to younger warriors and chiefs.[33]

Their movement progressed after several accommodationist chiefs met with Indiana governor William Henry Harrison in September 1809. Worried that a potential land shortage would encourage Indiana's white settlers to migrate, Harrison convinced several Delaware, Potawatomi, Miami, and later Weas and Kickapoo chiefs to agree to the Treaty of Fort Dearborn (1809), which ceded roughly three million acres of Indiana and Illinois land to the United States in exchange for annuities and $5,250 in supplies. The land cession, however, would not be recognized by many Indigenous nations. Tecumseh's emerging confederacy declared the treaty illegitimate, but even nations friendly with the United States voiced their opposition. In the wake of the Treaty of Fort Wayne and other land cessions, many former accommodationist Miamis, Weas, Piankeshaws, and Wyandots gravitated towards Prophetstown. Indeed, Wyandot chiefs criticized "Our Great Father the President of the United States" for wanting "all the land on this Island."[34]

Tecumseh reminded US policymakers that if they wanted the entire continent, they would have to fight for it. For Tecumseh and Tenskwatawa, the Treaty of Fort Wayne challenged their vision of a pan-national state and their promotion of communal landholding for Native peoples. In a speech to Harrison, Tecumseh admonished the United States for driving Native peoples "into the great lake where they can't either stand or work." Tecumseh recognized that US policymakers aimed to disrupt Native unity through treaties, assimilationist tactics, and inciting tensions between nations. "You wish to prevent the Indians to do as we wish," Tecumseh continued, "to unite and let them consider their land as the common property." Countering US policy, Tecumseh traveled throughout the West to increase their movement's numbers. Tecumseh visited the Potawatomis and Kickapoos of the Illinois River, the Ho-Chunks of the Rock River (present-day Illinois and Wisconsin), and the Menominees near Green Bay (present-day Wisconsin). Thereafter, the Shawnee chief traveled southward to gain supporters from the Shawnees and Delawares of Missouri in the fall of 1810. By the spring of 1811, Tecumseh reached the Native communities of the Ohio Valley. Traveling across the West likely inspired Tecumseh to further dream of a world free of Anglo-American incursions.[35]

Harrison dampened the movement's spirits, however, during Tecumseh's absence. Following Secretary of War William Eustis's instructions, Harrison raised an army to destroy the Prophetstown if Tenskwatawa's adherents refused to disperse. On the evening of November 6, 1811, Tenskwatawa received a report that Harrison, whose forces had arrived near Prophetstown earlier that day, planned to strike the Native confederates. Before dawn on November 7, Tenskwatawa attacked Harrison and his forces only to retreat to Prophetstown. Tenskwatawa's forces—undersupplied and outnumbered—abandoned Prophetstown, which US forces razed the following night. The Battle of Tippecanoe, as it became known, convinced many Native and white Americans of an unavoidable war.[36]

News of the Battle of Tippecanoe terrified settlers when word reached Detroit in late November. From their position between Prophetstown and Upper Canada, Detroit officials immediately formed a night patrol and a committee of safety, recognizing that the ninety-four soldiers garrisoned at Detroit and seventy-nine stationed at Mackinac could not possibly protect the vast Michigan Territory. In December 1811, territorial judges Solomon Sibley and Woodward appealed to President James Madison and Congress for military support. "Dissatisfaction with the aboriginal inhabitants of these countries," they wrote, "[has] been kindled into an open flame, and their blood with that of the American citizen has stained the plains of the Wabash." Sibley and Woodward stressed that the Michigan Territory had a "double frontier," with the British "on one side" and Native warriors "on the other." Sparse settlements deepened the problem. The territory thus required federal military aid; militias could not defend the region. Michigan officials warned policymakers in Washington that settlers could not escape with their families because they could be intercepted by Indigenous warriors, who surrounded the territory to the north, west, and south. The 1811 appeal—written by influential and experienced men on the ground in Michigan—illustrated the weakness of the federal government and the intensity of racial anxiety in the upper Great Lakes region.[37]

Native peoples in the region, divided internally and externally in their response to Tippecanoe, prepared for the possibility of war in the early months of 1812. Some bands of Wyandots voiced their concerns to President Madison. Led by Myeerah (Walk-in-the-Water) and several other chiefs, Wyandots urged Madison to uphold the Treaties of Greenville and Detroit. Wyandots stressed that settlers' advances into their land undermined General Wayne's promises to respect their boundaries. "We are now told, that we and our children are not to be allowed to live on this land more than fifty years," Myeerah and other chiefs lamented. Recognizing the inevitability of war, these Wyandot chiefs pledged their loyalty to the United States. Nonetheless, US officials hoped Indigenous nations, including Wyandots, would remain neutral. For them, neutrality freed the United States from any postwar promises or alliances.[38]

While bands of Wyandots sought accommodation, the Indigenous confederates accumulated followers. In the spring of 1812, the population at Prophetstown and its environs swelled as more chiefs joined Tecumseh and Tenskwatawa in resisting US expansion. Tecumseh also traveled south to recruit warriors from—and secure alliances with—the Osages, Chickasaws, Choctaws, and Upper Creeks (Red Sticks). While the Chickasaws and Choctaws of Mississippi and the Osages of Missouri rejected the invite, Upper Creeks (in present-day central Alabama) supported the confederacy. Around the same time, US agent Thomas Forsyth reported that bands of Ho-Chunks reached Prophetstown in May. "There is every thing to fear from the Prophet," Forsyth warned. "His numbers are greater than they were before the battle last Nov and I should not be surprised if his numbers will increase daily." The confederates at Prophetstown also received renewed support from an influential Potawatomi chief and ardent resister of US expansion, Main Poc, who returned to Illinois to raid US settlements after a supply trip to Fort Malden. Forsyth worried Main Poc's presence would bolster the Native confederates' resistance. "I should not be the least surprised that on the arrival of the Main Poc," Forsyth continued, "the Indians will be prepared for mischief."[39]

The dreams of an independent Native state and an empire of liberty clashed at the Battle of Tippecanoe. Territorial officials' efforts to annex

Native lands in Michigan and the broader Great Lakes served to bolster the cause of the Shawnee brothers. Treaties might have convinced Native chiefs that the United States would absorb the continent. However, the Battle of Tippecanoe raised doubts about the inevitability of US expansion. Harrison warned that "the northern settlements . . . will be broken up, unless great exertions are made by the government." US officials anticipated a war with the ever-growing Native confederacy and a potential conflict with the British Empire. Faced with two enemies, Hull became convinced that a successful conquest of Upper Canada would become the means to secure federal authority in the Michigan Territory and the empire of liberty in the West.[40]

## WILLIAM HULL'S "WAR OF EXTERMINATION": THE FAILED INVASION OF UPPER CANADA

As war with Great Britain seemed possible in the spring of 1812, President Madison and Secretary of War William Eustis inquired with territorial officials about invading Upper and Lower Canada. Responding to their request, William Hull insisted on invading Upper Canada from Michigan. Hull argued that the safety of the republican union and the loyalty of the West hinged on invading Canada and protecting Michigan. Hull cautioned that the consequences of abandoning Michigan could be uncovered by "the history of the Campains in that very Country conducted by Generals, Harmer, St Clair & Wayne." If military commanders left Michigan to its own fate, Hull predicted that "Detroit, Michillmackanac, and Chicago, must fall [and] the Inhabitants must once more change their allegiance, and the Indians [will] become the exclusive friends and Allies of the King." The territorial governor argued that dispatching a military force to Michigan would allow them to easily take Canada and protect white settlers from raids by Native warriors. "If the conquest of the Canadas is the object of the government," Hull reasoned, "they will there have an Army, in a proper situation to commence the operations, and at the same time protect the defenceless Inhabitants, and controul the Indians within our Territory."[41]

Hull believed that capturing Upper Canada would end the Native hegemony of the Great Lakes region. He and his fellow Detroiters believed that

Indigenous peoples could, in the words of James Witherell, wage a "formidable war" even if the United States "should escape one with the English." But these formidable opponents received their supplies from Upper Canada. Deeply immersed in Anglophobia, Hull believed Fort Malden was "the great emporium, from which even the most distant Indians receive their Supplies." He estimated that "at least fifty thousand" Upper Canadians lived along the Detroit River and Lake Erie. Of this exaggerated estimate, Canadian fur traders swayed Native warriors in and around Michigan to aid the British cause. An invasion of Upper Canada, he boasted, "will do more to prevent a general Indian war, with the Indians as far West, & beyound the Mississippi, than any other measure."[42]

Hull's arguments convinced President Madison and Secretary Eustis. US policymakers, then, opted for a three-pronged invasion of Canada: attacks against Montreal, the Niagara frontier, and the Michigan–Upper Canada borderlands. The Madison administration was presented with two scenarios for the fate of Michigan and Upper Canada. If the United States raised a professional army, increased naval forces on the Great Lakes, and sent supplies to Michigan, the republic could secure federal authority over Michigan, erode Native hegemony, and rid the West of British influence. Conversely, failure to supply Michigan with arms, soldiers, and resources might yield a decisive defeat at the hands of Native confederates, which could undermine US efforts to maintain their republican states in the West. John R. Williams believed the seemingly impending war would determine the future of the Great Lakes region. "[The British and Native warriors] both consider this their last opportunity of contending against us in these parts," Williams remarked. Abandoning Michigan would force US soldiers to pass "thro' a wilderness, filled with Savages, under british controul, and devoted to british Interest." "It will not be in our power," Williams admitted, "to regain it easily afterwards."[43]

After years of plotting, Hull at last crossed the Detroit River to invade Upper Canada on July 12, 1812. Hull's forces surprised Sandwich's inhabitants and militiamen, who fled to Fort Malden. For white Michiganders, the occupation relieved concerns about attacks on their settlements. Williams experienced "nights & days without sleep or rest" because he expected "hourly to be attacked by the combined forces of British & Savages." But capturing Sandwich marked only the beginning, as Eustis had also instructed Hull to capture Malden and its surrounding environs without reinforcements.

Emboldened by the flight of the Canadian militia, Hull and other territorial officials decided their victory at Sandwich foreshadowed future conquests. "Though matters are yet unsettled," Williams continued, "we expect however that Malden must fall & our troubles will be at an end."[44]

Shortly after the conquest, Hull issued a proclamation to Upper Canadians. Like many US officials, the commander of the Army of the Northwest believed that Upper Canadians longed to become republican citizens. Considering this, he offered Canadians protection of their "persons, property and rights." To ensure their loyalty, Hull issued a harsh warning to any white settlers who supported Native warriors—including Catholic nuns. "No white nun found fighting by the side of an indian will be taken prisoner," Hull announced. "Instant death will be tis lot." Hull cautioned the inhabitants of Upper Canada that "if the barbarous and savage policy of Great Britain be pursued, and the savages let loose to murder our citizens and butcher our women and children, this war will be a war of extermination." Hull later explained that his use of the phrase "war of extermination" represented a consequence of wartime policy. But historians have stressed that it showcased American leaders' commitment to exterminating Native peoples for the benefit of white settlers—and such genocidal rhetoric indicated a total expulsion of Indigenous peoples. With an American army occupying Canadian soil, US efforts to control the Great Lakes region seemed more plausible. Hull's proclamation reached Canadian and Native circles in the following days, effectively discouraging opposition. Hull boasted that his proclamation could win the war in Canada.[45]

Hull contended that capturing Sandwich would prevent a general war with Indigenous nations. "I knew," he later reflected, "that it would have a great effect upon the Indians, to shew them the American flag flying on both shores." Moreover, Hull hoped that the occupation of the tiny hamlet might "facilitate and increase the defection from the British standard, which had manifested itself among the inhabitants and militia, and their Indian allies." He was initially correct. The capture of Sandwich convinced many chiefs to remain neutral or abandon their alliance with Great Britain. Accommodationist chiefs—including Myeerah of the Detroit Wyandots, Blackhoof of the Ohio Shawnees, and Tarhe of the Ohio Wyandots—"have made great exertions to detach the Indians from the British standard." As chiefs in Michigan and Ohio chose neutrality, Native peoples in Upper Canada such as the Ojibwes of Lake St. Clair and the Iroquois of the Grand River exchanged neutrality for the United States' protection. "Tecumseh and Marpot [Main Poc]," Hull bragged to Eustis, "are the only chiefs of consequence remaining with the British."[46]

The invasion of Upper Canada in July 1812 discouraged Tecumseh, Tenskwatawa, Main Poc, and their confederates. Like the chiefs who pledged neutrality, Tecumseh doubted the reliability of the British, worrying that Fort Malden would soon fall. Nonetheless, Tecumseh remained committed to securing the Ohio River as a boundary. Along with Main Poc, Tecumseh stationed warriors around Fort Malden to impede Hull's advance. At Malden, British Indian agent Col. Matthew Elliott reported that "the Indians with us are between 3 & 400 who have resisted every allurement which Gen' Hull laid before them." "Tech-Kum-thai has kept them faithful," Elliott wrote. "He has shewn himself to be a determined character and a great friend to our Government." Tecumseh, however, maintained his alliance with Great Britain because British arms and redcoats kept his dream of an independent Indigenous state in the Great Lakes alive.[47]

The momentum of Hull's swift capture of Sandwich stalled within a matter of days. The Army of the Northwest suffered from insubordination—a democratic trend that plagued most US armies—as Colonels Lewis Cass, James Findley, and Duncan McArthur questioned Hull's leadership and fought over their ranks. Despite Upper Canada's small detachment of troops, the army struggled to reach Fort Malden. Skirmishes with Native and British forces, fear over infrequent communication and unreliable supply lines, and an Indigenous-British raid on a supply caravan at Frenchtown paralyzed Hull. John R. Williams grumbled that Hull's hesitations gave "the British every opportunity of fortifying themselves." Although many Native peoples had abandoned the British "since the arrival of our army," Williams heard rumors that "great numbers are collecting above and are expected in the course of a few weeks." "We may yet have hard fighting," he warned.[48]

There would be no hard fighting on Mackinac Island. In mid-July 1812, British captain Charles Roberts mustered a force of British regulars, Canadian *métis* (people of Indigenous and European ancestry), three hundred Ojibwe and Odawa warriors, and roughly one hundred Ho-Chunks, Sioux, and Menominee warriors to invade Mackinac Island. This coalition of Indigenous and British forces vastly outnumbered US lieutenant Porter Hanks and his sixty-one men. Hanks surrendered Fort Mackinac without a fight.[49]

Mackinac's fall in mid-July 1812 escalated Hull's anxiety. The capitulation of Fort Mackinac convinced him that the powerful Northwest nations would unanimously side with Great Britain. Hull had long considered the "Indians about Michilimackinac, and to the Northward and westward" as "numerous and powerful." Indeed, bands of Ojibwes, Potawatomis, Odawas, Ho-Chunks, Kickapoos, and Sioux had a considerable number of highly skilled warriors and significant influence in the Great Lakes. Other US territorial officials shared Hull's belief. US agent Forsyth believed that the "very numerous nation[s] of Indians" found throughout northern Michigan were "the bravest and most warlike of any Indians that is known." Because the Odawas could muster "1000 to 1200 Warriours," and the Potawatomis could potentially raise "1000 warriors at least," the Anishinaabe peoples reminded US officials who held military superiority in the Upper Great Lakes. To make matters worse, Hull believed these nations would convince the Native peoples in the lower peninsula of Michigan and the wider Great Lakes region to ally with Great Britain. Hull reasoned that for at least five years, the chiefs of the lower peninsula Wyandots, Odawas, Potowatomis, and Ojibwes would "not join any Enemy . . . unless absolutely compelled by the more powerful tribes to the North & West."[50]

These fears convinced Hull to retreat from Upper Canada to defend Detroit, much to the chagrin of the Army of the Northwest. Although critical of Hull's leadership and retreat, Col. Lewis Cass shared Hull's fears about the consequences of Mackinac's fall. Convinced that "the capture of Michilimackinac has had a very injurious effect upon [US] interests," Cass had "no doubt" that the War of 1812 would "become a general indian war" that would draw in "almost all the nations East of the Mississippi." Cass shared Hull's prediction that the Northwest nations influenced the geopolitical considerations of Native peoples in Michigan's lower peninsula. "All the Brownstown Indians have gone over to the enemy," Cass grumbled. "There is not a friendly Indian in Territory." Indeed, Hull informed Eustis that "the Wyandots have become hostile, and other nations connected with them are following their example." Since the assault on Mackinac, Hull reported from Detroit that "the Indian force has been fast encreasing in this country." Once-neutral nations, including Wyandots in northern Ohio, sided against the United States to preserve their autonomy and rid the region of US settlers.[51]

Detroit became the next target. Tobacco dripped on his beard and uniform as Hull pondered his next step. He worried for his wife, his children, and all the citizens of Detroit, fearing an attack would claim many lives. The town lacked supplies to outlast the Indigenous warriors and British regulars that had surrounded Fort Detroit in the late summer of 1812. The British commanding officer, Maj. Gen. Isaac Brock, warned Hull in mid-August that "the numerous body of Indians who have attached themselves to my troops, will [move] beyond control the moment the contest commences." Tecumseh's commanding presence likely further troubled Northwest soldiers. Exaggerating the tropes of Native warfare, Brock convinced Hull to surrender Detroit without a fight—or even consulting his officers. Hull's surrender of Detroit on August 16, 1812, left the United States with even fewer neutral nations and Indigenous allies.[52]

The invasion of Upper Canada and the surrender of Mackinac and Detroit represented decisive moments in the War of 1812. But in many ways, these events were part of a protracted conflict over the future of the Great Lakes region. Hull had long coveted an invasion of Upper Canada, believing the downfall of the British province would discourage Indigenous unity and eliminate British intrigue. After the capture of Sandwich in July 1812, US forces appeared destined to prevail. But US impediments in Upper Canada and Native-British victories in Michigan shifted the tide of war. Hull's ineffective leadership and poor decision-making, culminating in the shocking surrender of Detroit, got him court-martialed near the war's end. Frustrated and vengeful officers under his command and eastern politicians enflamed public condemnation of his conduct. Hull stood trial in 1814 for cowardice, neglect of duty, and treason—the latter a capital offense. Hull avoided execution, but his surrender of Detroit sunk enthusiasm for the war and blasted hope that the United States would extend control over the Great Lakes region. "When the northwestern army, commanded by general Hull, marched, all western America were flattered with the hope of success," Kentucky governor Isaac Shelby wrote. After the fall of Detroit, Shelby mourned how "that hope ... [was] now followed by astonishment, by mortification, and anxiety." By the end of 1812, Tecumseh appeared closer to realizing his vision for the Great Lakes region than did the Jeffersonian Republicans.[53]

## THE UNCERTAIN FATE OF THE GREAT LAKES REGION, 1812-1813

The downfall of Detroit raised serious doubts about the future of the United States in the Great Lakes region. In the United States, many military and political officials believed that the capitulation of Detroit ruined any chance at preventing a general war and severing the Indigenous-British connection. The loss of Detroit, in the eyes of US leaders, would unleash waves of British-aided raids across western settlements. "The Indians, thus elated with success, encouraged and supported by the British from Canada," Shelby surmised, "will now endeavour to extend their savage and barbarous devastations, along the extensive frontier of the state of Ohio, and the several territories." For many white Americans, the subsequent capture of Fort Dearborn (present-day Chicago) on August 15 confirmed these fears. Under Hull's instructions, the fort's garrison evacuated, only to be killed by Potawatomi warriors. By the end of the summer of 1812, Native warriors and British troops had captured three US strongholds in the Great Lakes region: Mackinac, Detroit, and Dearborn.[54]

As US policymakers reeled over the loss of Michigan, Detroit's surrender revitalized Indigenous unity and Tecumseh's hopes to constrain the US republic to the Ohio River. Native warriors, including Odawa chief Nibakom and his men, celebrated the Union Jack waving on both sides of the Detroit River, exposing the weakness of the American republic. Indigenous warriors, Shelby noted, "are elated and will act with more vigor, and will be more determined than usual." Like US policymakers' objectives in the Great Lakes region, Native confederates aimed to demonstrate their superiority over the American republic and gain new followers. "Their partial success since the commencement of war," Forsyth continued, "occasions the Indians to believe that with the assistance of the British, they will be able, to drive the Americans across the Ohio River."[55]

Historians have dismissed the possibility of Tecumseh's vision, deeming it demographically and logistically impossible. But the actions of western settlers and the reactions of US leaders suggest that, in late 1812 and early 1813, Tecumseh's dream remained a postwar possibility. Many white Michiganders fled after successive Native-British victories. Escaping with his family from Detroit to Marietta, Solomon Sibley remarked that "the occupation of Detroit by the British and Indians became critical in the extreme and induced many of the inhabitants of the Territory to abandon it and seek safety in the states." Western settlers throughout the Great Lakes region followed white Michiganders' example. In the Upper Mississippi Valley, Forsyth reported that "many settlers are selling of their property and moving out of the Territory for fear of the British and Indians." Military setbacks and retreating settlers troubled Shelby, who worried that the United States "shall . . . for a time have the Ohio river for a barrier."[56]

Tecumseh knew his vision of a common Native state and an American republic restrained east and south of the Ohio River depended on British support. Fortunately for the Shawnee leader, British officials and Upper Canadians supported this vision in 1812. While those further from the western frontier boasted that Canadian militiamen repelled US expansion, Canadian settlers on the ground acknowledged the significance of Native contributions. "You may rely on it that without the Indians we never could keep this country," Canadian soldier and fur trader John Askin conceded. Recognizing this dependence, British officers such as Colonel (later Major-General) Henry Procter and Maj. Gen. Isaac Brock imagined transforming Michigan into an Indigenous-controlled buffer state that separated Upper Canada and the United States. After the surrender of Detroit, British commanders entertained such an idea, as Brock proclaimed that Michigan was "ceded to the Arms of His Britannic Majesty." Their support for an Indigenous state convinced many Native warriors to ally with the British. With memories of British abandonment at Fallen Timbers still fresh, Native confederates cautiously sided with the redcoats.[57]

Native nations controlled the geopolitical fate of Michigan and the broader Great Lakes region in 1812. To Native, US, and British participants and observers, the Ohio River boundary seemed plausible and at times more likely than a Michigan Territory controlled by federal officials. By the end of 1812, British soldiers occupied Forts Detroit and Mackinac and regained control of Sandwich in western Upper Canada—thanks in large part to Native warriors. By the end of 1812, William Henry Harrison commanded the Army of the Northwest, seeking to regain Michigan and conquer Upper Canada. Successful campaigns in 1813 and 1814 depended on the dismantling of the Indigenous confederacy and the subjugation of hostile Native nations.

## COLLAPSING VISIONS: WAR IN THE GREAT LAKES REGION, 1813–1815

The success of the Native-British alliance carried into early 1813. Despite Brock's tragic death at the Battle of Queenston Heights the previous fall, Michigan remained in Indigenous and British hands, primarily because of

Native warriors' commitment to expelling the United States. In mid-January 1813, the United States campaigned to reclaim Detroit. After an initial US victory at Frenchtown on January 18, Indigenous and British forces under the leadership of Henry Procter and Wyandot chiefs Myeerah and Roundhead successfully counterattacked Brig. Gen. James Winchester's forces on January 22. The next day, Indigenous warriors looted and burned Frenchtown and killed at least thirty American soldiers and Kentucky militiamen. The River Raisin massacre, as it became known, intensified the racial tensions that had already simmered in the Michigan Territory. The subsequent killing of already wounded soldiers enabled Americans to mask their atrocities and rally around a hatred toward Native peoples. Defending the actions of Native warriors and British troops after the war, Upper Canadian and Anglican rector John Strachan lambasted Thomas Jefferson because "Indian towns were burnt as an amusement or common place practice" by Americans.[58]

The momentum stalled, however, after a series of US victories in late 1813. Oliver Hazard Perry's victory at the Battle of Lake Erie in September 1813 gave the United States command of the southern Great Lakes. The early stages of the War of 1812 taught US policymakers that British success in the West depended on their access to the southern Great Lakes of Erie and Ontario, allowing British commanders to navigate between the Detroit and Niagara frontiers and coordinate attacks with Native nations. Following Perry's victory, President Madison boasted that "we command the Indians, can control the companies trading with them; and hold Canada."[59]

Perry's victory enabled Harrison to reclaim Michigan's lower peninsula and invade Upper Canada. After a successful defense of Fort Meigs, Harrison, the Army of the Northwest, and Kentucky militiamen scored a major victory over Native confederates and British forces at the Thames River on October 5, 1813. Amid the confusing array of gunfire and slashing steel, Kentuckian and future vice president Richard Mentor Johnson supposedly killed Tecumseh, handing a major and symbolic blow to the Native confederacy.[60]

Tecumseh's death collapsed the confederacy and dampened the crusade for an Indigenous state in the Great Lakes. US policymakers worked to crush the confederacy's remaining forces and seize Upper Canada at the end of the war. The United States, however, struggled to control Upper Canada and Michigan. After the Battle of Thames, Americans believed that the United States would hold onto key posts in Upper Canada. As such, many Kentucky militiamen resigned from service, leaving US outposts such as Detroit vulnerable. Disappointed by failed campaigns in the Upper Great

Lakes, Lewis Cass "anxiously looked ... for some brilliant operation ... well knowing the effect it would have upon the Indians."[61]

US officials and military officers continued to understand the conquest of the Canadas in terms of weakening Indigenous dominance—but failed to secure the British provinces. Secretary of War John Armstrong believed occupying Upper Canadian settlements would force Great Britain to abandon the Great Lakes nations. Indeed, he maintained that the occupation of York "interposes a barrier which completely protects Malden & Detroit" and "makes doubtful and hazardous the Enemies intercourse with the western Indians." At the same time, military officials such as Brig. Gen. Duncan McArthur considered requests to build forts at "the heads of the River St. Clair and on the River Thames" to provide "security for the inhabitants, who must be much anoyed by the Indians." At the war's end, the United States did not control any major strategic settlements, including Kingston or Montreal, making it difficult to acquire Canada in diplomatic negotiations. US military forces did, however, devastate the landscape of the Western District of Upper Canada.[62]

The War of 1812—a conflict intended to challenge Native hegemony and secure Canada in the West—also left the Michigan Territory in dire conditions. Michigan remained a native ground, US settlements were battle-ruined, and Upper Canada stayed a British colony. "The desolation of this Territory," Woodward lamented, "is beyond all conception." Woodward reported that the territory was beset with destroyed farms, houses, and lives. He even claimed that "inhabitants of the River Raisin have been obliged to resort to *chopp'd hay, boiled*, for subsistence." While Woodward and other officials blamed Native warriors' raids, Indigenous towns also suffered repeated attacks from US soldiers under Harrison's command. Such destruction persuaded military officer Duncan McArthur that the territory should be abandoned. "In case of an Indian War," he believed, "no part of it can be protected." Michigan's proximity to Upper Canada, moreover, enabled "hostile Indians" to "carry on the War." In a letter to Secretary of State James Monroe, McArthur suggested removing Michiganders "friendly disposed towards the United States ... into the interior" and "send a force into Canada next summer which would lay it Waste." Monroe rejected the proposal, but he and other officials agreed with McArthur's notion that "a desert" should be interposed between "us and the enemy."[63]

McArthur's plans for Michigan found strange bedfellows in British diplomats in Ghent. Throughout negotiations, British diplomats Lord Gambier,

Henry Goulburn, and William Adams demanded that the Americans let Michigan and the Great Lakes region "be a desert" so that the republic "cannot come upon us to attack us, without crossing it." They considered an "Indian Boundary" and "exclusive military possession of the Lakes by the British" to be necessary "for the security of Canada." Early in the negotiations, the British commissioners held several advantages over American diplomats John Quincy Adams, Henry Clay, Jonathan Russell, and Albert Gallatin: Washington, DC, had been burned by British forces in August 1814, and the American republic lacked a strategic victory over the British in the West. After word of the American victory at Plattsburgh, New York, in September 1814 reached the negotiation tables, the diplomatic playing field had been neutralized. With this news, British diplomats opted for peace rather than dragging out the negotiations. Once again, the British had abandoned their Indigenous allies in the Great Lakes region. The signing of the Treaty of Ghent on Christmas Eve 1814 ended the conflict between the United States and Great Britain.[64]

The Treaty of Ghent promised to restore prewar Indigenous boundaries but crushed any hope of British support for a Native state in the Great Lakes region. The dynamic territorial changes throughout the War of 1812 reminded US policymakers that the westward expansion of their republic was not inevitable. Indeed, the failure to annex Canada and the near loss of Michigan forced American officials to reimagine a path to regional control of the Great Lakes. To ease their fear of Indigenous unity and British intrigue, US policymakers strove to break apart Native nations by increasing removal efforts and encouraging new white settlements. While white settlements had been considered a way to obtain security throughout US history, the actions of powerful Native nations during the War of 1812 sharpened race-based removal and hardened borders in and around the Great Lakes region. White farmers not only safeguarded republicanism with their self-sufficiency and virtue; their presence could also divide Indigenous allies and prevent another Tecumseh.

## DRESS REHEARSAL FOR INDIGENOUS REMOVAL IN THE GREAT LAKES REGION

In the late 1810s and early 1820s, US policymakers worked to transform the Great Lakes region from a native ground into territories defined by exclusive and uncontestable US sovereignty. Well into the nineteenth century, however, the Anishinaabe peoples of Michigan managed to avoid relocation. By demanding that the federal government respect their treaty rights, Anishinaabe leaders ensured that Michigan would not only have an Indigenous past but a Native present and future, too. Their resistance countered the experiences of the Native nations of the Southeast—Cherokees, Choctaws, Seminoles, Creeks, and Chickasaws—whose efforts to adopt Anglo-American culture did not prevent removal. Despite Anishinaabe resistance, territorial officials such as Lewis Cass managed to remove Native peoples who resided near the US-Canadian border. Before becoming the secretary of war during the era of large-scale removal in the Southeast, Cass spent formative years fighting against Native confederates and contesting Indigenous power in Michigan. His efforts to remove Native nations along the border rendered Upper Canada less threatening in the minds of US policymakers and less of an obstacle to westward expansion in Native lands.[65]

From 1813 to 1831, Lewis Cass served as Michigan's territorial governor. Like many white Michiganders, Cass partook in the region's intensifying racial animosity, and he came to view all Native peoples as untrustworthy British allies. "I have reason to believe," Cass remarked, "that the professions of many of the Indian tribes are hollow & deceitful." Tasked with negotiating the Great Lakes region's postwar Native treaties, Cass acknowledged the threat of powerful Indigenous confederacies to US interests, especially in the aftermath of the War of 1812. Peace rendered Canada unobtainable, so Cass aimed to eliminate border-crossing through treaties and white settlements and by accusing Native peoples of using the border to steal from Americans (while ignoring the same crimes committed by white settlers). Secretary of State (and later president) James Monroe supported Cass's objectives. He instructed diplomats working with the British not to renew the "Article in the Treaty of 1794 which allows British Traders from Canada and the North West Company to carry on trade with the Indian Tribes within the limits of the United States."[66]

Cass assumed that the removal of Native peoples who lived near the Michigan-Canadian border would eliminate cross-border interactions. Writing to the War Department in 1816, Cass targeted Wyandots who held lands near the Detroit River. The Wyandots had two major settlements—Brownstown and Maguaga—near Upper Canada's Fort Malden. Their alliance with Great Britain, Cass continued, had provided an "example [that] was soon followed by the general disaffection of the Indians." The War of 1812 taught Cass how "important it is to us that this tract of country should be in our possession and that a white Settlement should be interposed between the British possessions on the opposite side and the Indians." In the eyes of Cass, if the Wyandots remained near the Detroit River and across from Malden, it would allow them to "preserve a continued communication almost equally dangerous to us in peace and war." However, Cass failed to understand that the Native-British alliance had begun to collapse after the Treaty of Ghent. Nonetheless, Native power, confederacies, and alliances with Great Britain increasingly rendered "a white population" as a "measure to the security of the Country."[67]

Unlike the Jeffersonian vision, which argued that Native peoples could potentially assimilate and hold on to their land if they adopted European norms, US leaders' newfound view further excluded nonwhite inhabitants. The efforts to remove the Wyandots of Michigan illustrate this evolution in thought. The Wyandots, Mohawk chief and British major John Norton observed, had their morals "firmly established by the precepts of Christianity." Though the Wyandots' "progress in the arts of civilized life has been great," Cass argued that their lands mattered to the prosperity and security of Michigan and the United States. Even after the passage of the Rush-Bagot Treaty (signed in 1817 and ratified in 1818) limited the naval presence of both the United States and Great Britain in the Great Lakes, Cass abandoned any rationales to allow the Wyandots to retain land along the Detroit River. In September 1818, Cass pressured the Wyandots to agree to a treaty that removed them from Brownstown and Maguaga. Advocates for removal in the 1830s and 1840s would later follow Cass in ignoring the efforts of Indigenous people to adopt Euro-American culture to avoid removal.[68]

The promotion of white settlement and removal of Native peoples along international borders informed how territorial officials negotiated with Native chiefs. In 1815, US territorial officials negotiated peace with the nations of the Great Lakes. During the summer, Illinois governor Ninian Edwards and Missouri governor William Clark arranged peace with Native peoples including Potawatomis, Sauks, and Sioux at Portage Des Sioux, Missouri. At Spring Wells (near Detroit) later in the year, Tenskwatawa and Anishinaabe, Delaware, Shawnee, Wyandot, Miami, and Seneca chiefs agreed to peace and protection under the United States. Thereafter, territorial officials, including Cass and McArthur, aimed to separate Native nations from each other and the British. Cass and McArthur pressed Wyandot, Delaware, Seneca, Shawnee, and Anishinaabe leaders to sell northwestern Ohio and parts of Michigan and Indiana. Cass and McArthur particularly sought a valuable strip of land in northwestern Ohio that separated southeast Michigan from the rest of the United States and lay near Upper Canada.[69]

On September 29, 1817, these nations agreed to the Treaty at the Foot of the Rapids (also known as the Treaty of Fort Meigs or the Treaty of Maumee Rapids), one of the largest land cessions in Ohio's history. The treaty ceded northwestern Ohio in exchange for an annual payment in perpetuity of $4,000 to the Wyandots, $500 to the Seneca, and $2,000 to the Shawnee. The *Detroit Gazette* celebrated the treaty because the acquired territory would be "highly important in the event of another conflict on this frontier." In his presidential message, James Monroe boasted that land purchases provided "a strong barrier, consisting of our own people, planted on the Lakes, the Mississippi, and the Mobile." With the presence of troops and settlers, Monroe believed that "Indian hostilities, if they do not altogether cease, will henceforth lose their terror." In the eyes of policymakers, poor communications and sparse white settlements threatened US sovereignty. In reality, however, the violence wrought by settler colonialism endangered the stability of the Great Lakes region, not Native peoples.[70]

Land purchases encouraged the already growing settler populations in the Great Lakes region. The *Detroit Gazette* celebrated the Treaty at the Foot of the Rapids for making Michigan's "agricultural and commercial advantages" more apparent. The treaty, the paper announced in November 1817, "completely unites" southeast Michigan to "the southern states," which would encourage regional growth through land purchases. Farmers, missionaries, fur traders, and soldiers flocked into southeastern Michigan and the Great Lakes region. In 1816, Detroiter James Witherell saw that "the population seems to [belong] more to Americans" as "there are several making purchases of lands at the River Raisin, and at the Rapids of the Miami of Lake Erie." Other newcomers began purchasing farms around Detroit and on former Native lands. Native peoples persisted, of course. Equating white settlements to security, Witherell believed that it would take "many years before people will feel their scalps quite as safe as in Vermont." And in 1819, US soldier Jeremiah Dubois reported that "there is not more than Five or six families of white People in twenty miles of [Fort Gratiot] but there is plenty of Indians." Nonetheless, soldiers at new forts such as Gratiot (1814) ensured the loyalty of Native nations while missionaries and fur traders also eroded Native dominion in Michigan and the upper Lakes. As Catholic and Protestant missionaries continued to flock to the Great Lakes, John Jacob Astor's American Fur Company worked for profits and to eliminate British competition.[71]

By 1820, Indigenous nations still largely controlled and occupied Michigan, but US efforts to expand were eroding native power in the broader region. Tecumseh's dream of an independent, pan-Indigenous nation withered in the face of treaties and settlers. To encourage further removal, Cass recruited Tenskwatawa to establish a temporary village near Detroit to encourage local Indigenous people to relocate west of the Mississippi River. By 1826, Tenskwatawa—the prophet of a former pan-Indigenous movement aimed to remove Euro-American settlers and customs from the Great Lakes—convinced 250 Shawnees to resettle in present-day Kansas. The removal of Native peoples along the US-Canadian border contributed to the easing of US-British relations. Expansionists would continue to covet Canada for decades, viewing the northern British colony as vital to the republic's security. But by practicing dress rehearsal for the removal of Native peoples along the border, territorial officials such as Cass made Upper Canada less dangerous to the republic's survival and expansion to the West.[72]

Tecumseh's vision for a pan-Indigenous state prevented the United States from extending northward and nearly stopped westward expansion. He and his brother Tenskwatawa imagined this new pan-Indigenous realm within the context of the revolutionary Atlantic's geopolitical turmoil. This vision countered the ambitions of US policymakers, who sought to undermine Indigenous hegemony and secure republican state-making in the West. Far from dreaming of a clearsighted manifest destiny, US policymakers feared that Indigenous unity and British proximity undermined their weak hold over Michigan and the broader Great Lakes. To secure the West, territorial and military officials attempted to invade Upper Canada to disrupt Native hegemony. The United States failed to conquer Upper Canada during the War of 1812 largely because of the contributions of British-allied Indigenous confederates. By repelling US invasions alongside Canadian soldiers, Native confederates helped solidify the permanent borders between the republic and the British colony. The successful defense of Canada inspired

Canadian nationalism and convinced many Americans to accept their northern neighbors as distinctive peoples.[73]

The failure to capture Upper Canada and fear of a resurgent Native confederacy urged policymakers to rework their expansionist imaginings. Before the war, US leaders believed that securing western Native lands meant annexing northern territory in Canada; the former appeared impossible without achieving the latter. After all, Canadian merchants had supplied Native confederacies in their resistance against Anglo-American expansion for decades. Yet the Treaty of Ghent closed the possibility of annexing Upper Canada—at least in the 1810s. Territorial officials responded by removing Native peoples near the US-Canadian border and encouraging white settlements to separate Native peoples throughout the Midwest. By working to prevent the rise of a Tecumseh imitator, US policymakers made Upper Canada appear less dangerous to the republic's stability.

Two events in the 1830s illustrate how these efforts changed these border dynamics. When Sauk chief Black Hawk attempted to rally resistance against the United States, he received no support from the British. An ally to the British during the War of 1812, Black Hawk imagined relying on British support and forming a coalition of Native nations. Americans continued to fear a Native-British connection, even calling Black Hawk's warriors the "British Band." However, when Black Hawk visited Fort Malden in Upper Canada on several occasions, the British officers urged him to pursue peace with the United States. Britons' refusal to aid Black Hawk mirrored the objectives of US policymakers a few years later in 1837. That year, Canadian rebels declared the creation of the Republic of Canada on Navy Island—a small island between New York and Upper Canada. While some Americans formed secret militias called "Hunters' Lodges" to support these Canadian republicans, President Martin Van Buren supported the restoration of British rule. While antebellum advocates of manifest destiny clamored for Canada, such schemes held little sway in the minds of government officials. The failed Native war and Patriot rebellion reflected the growing acceptance that Americans and Canadians could coexist.[74]

The thwarted destinies for the contested Great Lakes region transformed how policymakers imagined and pursued expansion. Indeed, several national politicians—William Henry Harrison, Lewis Cass, and Richard Mentor Johnson—fought Native confederates in Michigan, Upper Canada, and the wider Great Lakes region. Others, such as James Madison and James Monroe, led the young country through wars with Indigenous nations in the Midwest. Nineteenth-century politicians recalled their experiences fighting Native confederates when crafting and implementing the Indian Removal Act of 1830. Echoing the sentiments of Cass, President Andrew Jackson remarked that the act would "incalculably strengthen the southwestern frontier" by removing the Native nations of the Southeast. For men like Jackson, however, racial fears about the stability of the South extended beyond the presence of independent Native peoples. As they worried about Native confederacies to the North, fears of free Black republics to the South also reconstructed the expansionist imaginings of US policymakers.[75]

# FOUR
# CUBA

What first seemed a small uprising on a French landowner's plantation turned out to be a coordinated revolt led primarily by enslaved Africans who had recently been transported to Cuba in the summer of 1825. Versed in traditional African warfare, Lorenzo Lucumí and his followers destroyed plantations, murdered enslavers, and marched toward Matanzas—a port city named after a massacre that occurred during early Spanish colonization. The Guamacaro Revolt of 1825, as this uprising became known, lasted for ten days until quashed by Cuban forces. The unsuccessful revolt horrified white Americans. After all, US citizens had close ties with Matanzas. US merchants clogged the port at Matanzas to acquire sugar, and New England expatriates established sugar plantations on the city's outskirts. But Americans' fears of a slave revolt superseded their commercial interests in the island. Slave revolts on Cuba conjured images of another Haitian Revolution—a possibility that US leaders fervently hoped to avoid.[1]

The fear of a second Haitian Revolution had increasingly informed US policymakers' pursuit of Cuba. US expansionists had long believed that Cuba's economy and strategic location in the Gulf of Mexico mattered to US security and interests. Between the 1790s and 1820s, US merchants and diplomats established deep commercial ties that gave the republic an informal influence over Cuban affairs. Cuba's significance to the United States changed, however, as its plantation economy and growing enslaved population increasingly resembled the conditions of prerevolutionary Haiti. The dread of a slave revolt in Cuba led US policymakers to imagine encirclement by revolutionary, free Black populations. Located one hundred miles from Florida, a free Black Cuba could spread insurrection to plantations across the South.[2]

US policymakers sought to prevent this possibility by either annexing Cuba or maintaining Spanish rule. But they were not the only ones who articulated visions for the island. Capitalizing on the collapse of French Saint-Domingue, Cuban planters maximized sugar production by rapidly expanding slavery on the island. Consequently, these planters sought independence or union with the slaveholding United States. Cuba's destiny as an American state was also challenged by the budding rivalry between the United States and Great Britain in the Caribbean and by the Spanish American Wars for Independence. British policymakers desired Cuba to halt US southward expansion while Mexican and Gran Colombian politicians hoped to remove Spain from the hemisphere. Real and imagined resistance by Cubans of African descent intensified this tense diplomatic situation and thwarted the realization of these visions. Unable to annex the island, US policymakers sought to ensure Spanish rule rather than a transfer of power that might ignite a revolt by enslaved Cubans.[3]

The thwarted expansion into the Caribbean South in the 1810s and 1820s upends any notion that US policymakers pursued aggrandizement with an uncompromising drive to free the hemisphere of European powers. Nor does it portray a slaveholding republic capable of dominating its Caribbean and Spanish American neighbors. Rather, the un-manifest contest for Cuba illustrates the early republic's weak influence over Caribbean geopolitics. Certainly, influential Americans such as Thomas Jefferson believed Cuba was destined to join the union. In 1809, Jefferson boasted that he "would immediately erect a column on the Southernmost limit of Cuba & inscribe on it a Ne plus ultra as to us in that direction." But this belief did not constitute a straightforward, clearsighted manifest destiny. Instead, US policymakers had to consistently adjust their ambitions for Cuba, fearing the prospects of a slave insurrection within a hundred miles of US shores. These possibilities further racialized US fears about geopolitical neighborhoods. Rather than liberating the hemisphere of European empires, US policymakers sought to maintain Spanish colonialism to prevent a Cuban Toussaint. This racialized

The United States, Cuba, and the Caribbean in the 1820s.

neighborhood policy, crystalized over the contest for Cuba, would shape antebellum aggrandizement in the decades to come.[4]

## "THE INFLUENCE OF THEIR EXAMPLE": HAITI TRANSFORMS THE GREATER CARIBBEAN

The Haitian Revolution (1791–1804) rocked the dynamics of slave societies across the Atlantic world. The cries for liberty and equality in France spread to Hispaniola, where a staggeringly cruel slave regime producing sugar for global markets turned French Saint-Domingue into one of the world's wealthiest colonies. The enlightened rhetoric of France's revolutionaries initially appealed to colonial planters, but in August 1791 enslaved people of African descent turned the calls for *liberté* into resistance against enslavement.[5]

Haitian revolutionaries began pushing for political independence after Napoleon aimed to revive the French empire in the Americas. In the early 1800s, the First Consul of France coveted the former French colony of Louisiana—from the fertile fields of the Missouri Valley to the trading outposts along the Mississippi River—to feed his armies. After Spain exchanged Louisiana for territories in the Italian peninsula with the Treaty of San Ildefonso of 1800 (ratified 1801), Napoleon focused on restoring slavery, sugar profits, and French order in Saint-Domingue. In early 1802, Gen. Charles Victor Emmanuel Leclerc, Napoleon's brother-in-law, launched a campaign to seize authority from Haitian commanders, including Toussaint Louverture and Henri Christophe. But, as President Jefferson predicted, "the conquest of St. Domingo will not be a short work." Driven by the wealth and allure of the tropical Caribbean, a yellow-fever-ridden French force of sixty thousand soldiers underestimated the prowess of Black soldiers, who razed towns and fields to secure liberty. After thirteen years of destroying plantations and defeating European armies, Haitians secured independence in 1804.[6]

Haitian policymakers, however, sought to contain the revolutionary spirit within their half of Hispaniola. Soon-to-be-emperor Jean-Jacques Dessalines wanted to establish commercial connections and secure international recognition with neighboring nations. He feared that a zealous "spirit of proselytism" in the name of Black emancipation would compel neighboring powers to retaliate and further isolate Haiti. Thus, in the Haitian Declaration of Independence, Dessalines urged his fellow Haitians to allow the British, Spanish, and Americans to "breathe in peace."[7]

Neither people of African descent nor white policymakers and slaveholders heeded Dessalines's declaration. The Haitian Revolution fueled abolitionism, contributed to the downfall of the transatlantic slave trade, and galvanized people of African descent across the Atlantic world. The revolution also served as a guiding vision for Black nationhood, freedom, and respectability in an Atlantic world of white supremacy. Enslaved people did not require republican ideology or the Haitian Revolution to desire freedom. However, Haiti provided an inspiring, successful example of Black resistance. News of slave revolts traveled through the "common wind"—a loose information network fueled by the movement of people of African descent and ideas across imperial boundaries. Word of Haiti's success quickly spread to plantations and ports, including in the United States and Cuba. In 1812, free Black Cubans Juan Barbier and José Antonio Aponte sought to galvanize enslaved people in the Cuban countryside. Barbier, disguised in uniform as Haitian general Jean-François, rallied enslaved people to secure their freedom. Cuban authorities foiled this plot and traced it back to Aponte, a carpenter in Havana. Havana police raided his house, where they discovered a book of drawings reportedly depicting "a black king of Haiti with others of Generals Lauvertú, Juan Fransuá, and Tusen [Toussaint]." For Barbier and Aponte, Haiti represented a vision of Black freedom and equality.[8]

This resistance terrified slaveholders. Ignoring the brutality of slavery that lay at the heart of the revolts, American, Spanish, and British slaveholders fixated on murdered white families, exiled planters, and plummeting profits. Slaveholders feared that the words and actions of Haitian revolutionaries would reach enslaved circles throughout the Greater Caribbean. Virginia slaveholder Thomas Jefferson considered Haiti as an infectious "contagion," and he worried the presence of "black crews, supercargoes & missionaries" from Haiti might encourage insurrection in port cities or rural plantations. When he assumed the presidency in 1801, Jefferson joined other Atlantic world leaders in refusing to engage in diplomatic and commercial relations with Haiti.[9]

Spanish officials immediately acted to prevent the common wind of neighboring Haiti from reaching Cuba's shores. In 1791, Cuban planter Francisco de Arango y Parreño worried that "even if the insurgents do not cross over and the doctrine of rebellion is not spread by those infernal apostles, we might suffer from the influence of their example." Cuba's colonial policies, population, and geography frustrated colonial administrators' attempts to avoid a slave revolt. Between 44,000 and 50,000 inhabitants resided in Havana in 1791, with free people of color representing roughly 22 percent of that population. Spanish commercial reforms and diplomatic settlements throughout the eighteenth century meant that Havana welcomed a flurry of economic activity, including British slave ships. These reforms created a bustling atmosphere in Havana and Santiago de Cuba—ideal hideouts for runaway slaves escaping the cruelties of sugar cultivation. Other freedom seekers avoided the risks and economic rewards of colonial towns for maroon communities (*cobreros*) in the Sierra Maestra. Seeking to safeguard their island from revolution, colonial officials intercepted contact with the French-speaking world by searching incoming merchandise for revolutionary pamphlets. Spanish officers also monitored the movements and conversations of people of African descent. Indeed, when Jean-François reached Cuba in 1795,

Gov. Luis de Las Casas wanted to keep the Haitian revolutionary's presence hidden from "a population composed primarily of people of color oppressed by a smaller number of whites."[10]

While colonial officials dreaded the consequences of Saint-Domingue, some Cuban planters responded to the collapse of the wealthiest sugar-producing colony with cautious optimism. Arango spearheaded the efforts. Cuba's wealthiest planter had already compelled the Spanish monarchy to temporarily lift the monopoly on the slave trade for two years beginning in 1788. In the early 1790s, in a series of reports to the Spanish government, Arango stressed that Cuba's large garrison at Havana, sizeable white population, and fertile fields would enable planters a chance to reap the "well-founded advantages" created by France's misfortune on Saint-Domingue. Arango hoped to accelerate the growth of Cuba's sugar and coffee industries by learning from Saint-Domingue's white refugees, encouraging liberal economic reforms such as free trade, promoting an unrestricted slave trade, and funding militarization.[11]

His strategy worked: Cuban sugar mills and coffee plantations expanded at unprecedented rates, with sugar production doubling from 16,731 metric tons in 1790 to 32,586 metric tons in 1799. The expansion of the cash-crop industries spurred the rapid importation of enslaved Africans. By 1792, nonwhite inhabitants outnumbered white settlers for the first time since colonization. Though the rising nonwhite population conjured images of another Haiti, Arango boasted as early as 1793 that "the era of our good fortune has begun."[12]

Arango had few counterparts in the United States. Most white Americans regarded the slave revolt in Saint-Domingue as a threat—not an opportunity. President John Adams and the Federalists briefly, tepidly, supported the Haitian revolutionaries in a bid to punish France during the Quasi-War (1798–1800). The beginning of the Jefferson administration in 1801 spelled the end of all economic and political support for the rebellion. Southern Republicans—led by the Virginian dynasty of Jefferson, James Madison, and James Monroe—sought to contain the revolutionary effects of Saint-Domingue. Nevertheless, the events on Hispaniola raised debates about the future of US slavery. Political economist Tench Coxe advocated for the diffusion of slavery in the wake of Gabriel's Rebellion (1801)—a revolt by Virginia slaves that many believed had connections to Haiti. Diffusing slavery would simultaneously prevent slave revolts and strengthen the economy, he reasoned. In an 1802 letter to Jefferson, Coxe argued that every effort should "be made to subserve *the great end of checking, counterbalancing, and diffusing the blacks.*"[13]

Coxe also urged Jefferson to monitor Cuba. Anglo-Americans had long marveled at the geopolitical and commercial value of Cuba. British and Anglo-American leaders recognized Cuba's commanding position in the Gulf of Mexico, which motivated British commanders to invade Havana during the Seven Years' War. The growing trade between the United States and Cuba—which surpassed the island's trade with Spain in 1798—linked Philadelphians, New Yorkers, Bostonians, and Charlestonians to the merchants and planters of Havana and Santiago de Cuba. These commercial ties laid the foundations for the United States' "informal empire" in Cuba, whereby the republic's economic influence shaped Cuban politics and society.[14]

Haiti altered US interest in Cuba. Coxe observed how the Black population on the Spanish island "daily increased by importations" and feared that Haitians might infiltrate and "excite an insurrection in Cuba." A slave revolt in Cuba would disrupt slavery in the US South and Spain's control of West and East Florida. "Should any turn of affairs put Cuba into the Situation of St. Domingo," Coxe cautioned, "we are to remember that it is but 30 or 40 leagues from our continent." He speculated further that "enterprizing and enthusiastic men might be disposed to introduce mischief among the black & red . . . in our Southern ports." Coxe warned Jefferson to consider "possible events in Florida & Louisiana" with "prudence & forethought."[15]

The Haitian Revolution transformed Cuba's economy and demography. Seeking to supplant Saint-Domingue's sugar production, Cuban planters worked to expand and protect slavery on their island. As the enslaved population swelled in Cuba, Spanish and American officials feared a revolt akin to the Haitian Revolution. Early nineteenth-century Americans also recognized the threat posed by Black revolutionaries to the stability of slavery in the US South. While proximity and profitable trades sustained US interest in the island, people of African descent throughout the Greater Caribbean transformed the nature of US-Cuba relations. Indeed, the Haitian Revolution also helped Jefferson and his administration secure the Louisiana Territory in 1803. But, in doing so, US policymakers gained another reason to fret over Cuba's fate.

## DRAWING CLOSER TO THE CARIBBEAN: THE US ACQUISITION OF LOUISIANA

The success of the Haitian revolutionaries altered the imperial fortunes of Napoleon Bonaparte and Thomas Jefferson. When French colonial officials closed the port of New Orleans to American merchants and settlers, Jefferson and his political allies practiced patience that paid off when Haitian forces and yellow fever unnerved an impatient Napoleon into selling the vast Louisiana Territory. The acquisition of Louisiana in 1803 doubled the size of the American republic. But the purchase also introduced US policymakers to the complex racial dynamics of the Spanish and French Caribbean. New Orleans simultaneously complemented and contradicted Jefferson's empire of liberty. The bustling port town offered yeoman farmers unabated access to the Mississippi River and markets in the Caribbean, ensuring their loyalty to the United States. New Orleans also gave the republic a foothold in the Gulf of Mexico, which provided greater protection for American commerce and abundant maritime resources. At the same time, however, the city's diverse population of Catholic creoles, free people of African descent, mixed-race residents, Indigenous peoples, Europeans, and Americans complicated the binary, black-and-white racial categories of the early republic. The commercial ships and diverse populations that entered New Orleans's port immersed the slaveholding republic in the unstable geopolitics of the revolutionary Caribbean.[16]

New Orleans gave US policymakers an entry into the realm of Caribbean geopolitics. As newcomers, Jefferson and his administration quickly learned how their nation was at the mercy of European powers. When Napoleon invaded the Iberian Peninsula in 1808, royal authority deteriorated in Spanish America. Jefferson and his administration feared that Great Britain or France might capitalize on Spain's instability by capturing Cuba. "We shall be well satisfied to see Cuba & Mexico remain in their present dependance," Jefferson commented, "but very unwilling to see them in that of either France or England." US policymakers preferred a feeble neighbor like Spain over France or Great Britain. Cuba's reliance on Spain meant continued trade relations and stability on the island. US agent William Shaler agreed with this assessment after observing the island's political conditions. He hoped Cuba would "remain in the hands of its present possessors" because Spain's "torpid character and weak government would never excite our apprehension." By contrast, a British or French Cuba might serve as a base to impress sailors and disturb the United States' western territories along the Mississippi River. Despite seeking to "exclude all European influence" in the Americas, Jefferson hoped in 1808 "to avoid the necessity of going to war" over Cuba and Mexico.[17]

Orleans territorial governor William C. C. Claiborne also recognized Cuba's significance to the stability of the American West. Throughout his stay in New Orleans, Claiborne consistently warned Jefferson and Madison that Cuba could determine US commerce and expansion in the West. In a letter to Jefferson in 1810, Claiborne insisted that "Cuba is the real Mouth of the Mississippi, and the nation possessing it, may possibly at a future day command the western Country." Claiborne believed that should the United States annex the island, or at least support Cuban independence, the western territories would remain firmly attached to the United States. "Let that Island be ours," he remarked, "and the American Union is placed beyond the reach of change."[18]

Instability in Cuba validated Claiborne's belief that the island could destabilize the American republic. Refugees fled revolutionary Saint-Domingue for New Orleans, Havana, and other port towns in the Atlantic world. Many French-speaking exiles flocked to Cuba, where their cultivating expertise and market connections helped spark the island's sugar boom. However, Napoleon's invasion of Iberia cooled the Cubans' warm reception of the refugees. In the spring of 1809, anti-French riots consumed Cuba, leading to the exile of thousands of Saint-Domingue refugees to New Orleans and other port towns in the United States. American newspaper editors blamed Black Cubans for the island's turmoil and drew parallels between the riots in Cuba and the revolution in Haiti. The *Philadelphia Aurora* reported that "negroes rose and plundered all the French houses . . . and committed some murders." As refugees inundated the port of New Orleans, Claiborne heard rumors that "at Havannah, the state of things is approaching to Anarchy" because "robberies and assassinations are frequent" and "life and property [are] insecure." Claiborne feared that soon "the fate of the Island of Cuba may be as wretched, as has been that of St. Domingo."[19]

Cuba transported the specter of Haiti to American shores. The waves of refugees introduced roughly three thousand free Black immigrants to the Orleans Territory's already sizeable free Black population, while white planters brought around three thousand enslaved people of Caribbean and African origin. "We are in a fair way of being over run with french people & Negroes from St. Iago, Havana & other ports in Cuba," complained New Orleans resident James Sterrett. Governor Claiborne initially stopped refugees of African descent from disembarking their ships but eventually allowed them to enter the territory, anticipating they would disperse throughout the countryside. The arrival of foreign free and enslaved Black immigrants stoked fears of slave revolts and Black violence in the minds of white Americans. Claiborne worried that the refugees of African descent—versed in Haitian revolutionary ideals—could influence free Black Americans or even infiltrate plantations in the Orleans Territory. These concerns seemed plausible when the German Coast Uprising of 1811, the largest slave revolt in North American history, occurred roughly thirty-six miles from New Orleans. Ultimately, however, the refugees contributed to transforming the Mississippi River Valley into a deeply entrenched slave society, providing knowledge on sugar cultivation in lower Louisiana and joining American planters in the cotton business.[20]

By the end of the first decade of the nineteenth century, Cuba proved a troublesome neighbor. The Louisiana Purchase rendered Cuba increasingly valuable to the United States' geopolitical and commercial footing in the Gulf of Mexico. Whether in Washington or New Orleans, US officials, including Jefferson and Claiborne, embraced the no-transfer policy, hoping Cuba would remain Spanish if not American. However, US policymakers could not control the course of Caribbean geopolitics; they could only be exposed to it. Indeed, events in the Caribbean from 1803 to 1810 showed how Cuba could upset racial slavery in the US South. Cuba, as Virginia representative Thomas Newton Jr. exclaimed, "almost witnessed the same scenes as St. Domingo." Mirroring scenes from Saint-Domingue, the disorder in Cuba relocated nonwhite and white refugees to the racially diverse Orleans Territory, potentially transferring insurrectionists to the United States. In the 1810s, warfare in the Gulf would further racialize US interest in Cuba.[21]

## INVASIONS FROM CUBA: WAR AND RESISTANCE IN THE GULF, 1812–1818

President James Madison shared Jefferson's convictions about Cuba's significance to the United States. In the early years of his presidency, Madison inquired about the island's condition and instructed agents to assess Cubans' sentiments toward the United States. After Napoleon invaded the Iberian Peninsula, US agent Maurice Rogers reported that Cubans feared a French conquest of their island. But France's rumored ambitions offered an opportunity for the United States. "I am persuaded," Rogers reasoned, "that soon than the Island should fall into the hands of the French Government, it would be cheerfully placed under the protection of the United States even in preference to Great Britain." In 1811, Madison instructed US agent William Shaler to collect information about Cuba and Mexico. Shaler argued that Cuban independence threatened US interests by leaving the island vulnerable to a British or French invasion. Misguided tropes about Spanish colonialism—which emphasized cultural and economic backwardness—informed Shaler's assessment that "pride, indolence or prejudice" stunted Cuban creoles from achieving independence. Mutually beneficial commercial ties and cultural contacts convinced Shaler that the republic would continue to "be regarded in Cuba almost as their Metropolis."[22]

The War of 1812 distracted the Madison administration from further inquiries about Cuba. However, Cuba factored into the exacerbating racial anxieties that sharpened during the United States' second war for independence. US policymakers worried that the common cause that Britons and Spaniards found in their resistance against Napoleon would extend to the Americas. After all, border disputes over Louisiana and unruly settlers fed hostilities between the United States and Spain. Throughout the War of 1812, southerners feared Spanish officials would enable British forces—including large contingents of Black troops—to station at Cuba and Florida. Black soldiers, southerners argued, would inspire the enslaved people of African descent to revolt. In early September 1812, the *Tennessee Herald* reported that "black troops, under the command of British officers, have arrived from Cuba, and taken possession of [Pensacola]." Stationing troops "of that description" so close to US territory, would, the article continued, "renew upon the Mobile and Lower Mississippi the tragedy of St. Domingo."[23]

These fears motivated American agent George Mathews to invade Spanish East Florida with US forces in the spring of 1812. Mathews's unauthorized invasion initially embarrassed President Madison, who viewed the occupation of East Florida as a threat to the federal government's authority and a breach of diplomatic norms. However, Madison ultimately supported the stationing of US troops and Georgia militiamen in Florida after declaring war on Great Britain in June. The invasion that became known as the Patriot War underscored the racial complexities and animosities that defined the

Gulf region. As westerners accused British agents in Canada of supplying Native peoples, southerners complained that Spanish officials in Florida armed Creeks and Seminoles during their wars against the United States.[24]

Spanish Florida also had a sizeable population of individuals of African descent, free and enslaved, whose greater freedoms frightened planters in Georgia and South Carolina. Since the early eighteenth century, Anglo-Americans had fumed over Spanish officials arming runaway slaves and recruiting Black soldiers for their colonial armies. Opponents of the invasion of East Florida, such as Rhode Islander William Hunter, warned that war with Spain would draw Black soldiers to the Southeast. "The Spaniards," Hunter contended, "intend to employ black troops." Desiring to protect the interests of Rhode Islanders invested in Cuban slavery, Hunter added that African Americans would be "aroused to reflection by the sight of black soldiers, and black officers, may suspect themselves to be fellow-men, and fondly dream they likewise could be soldiers and officers." Hunter's warnings that the "bloody tragedy of St. Domingo, may be acted over again, in this devoted country" may have been on the minds of the Patriot invaders of East Florida, who encountered volunteers from the Cuban Disciplined Black Militia. Indeed, in late June 1812, Lieutenant Colonel Smith notified Georgia governor Mitchell that "a hundred Black Troops have actually been landed, which are only a part of the force brought from the Havanna."[25]

Spain's willingness to employ Black troops and support nonwhite resistance continued to concern US policymakers after the War of 1812. Multiethnic, multiracial, and multi-imperial, Florida remained a haven where people of color could resist US expansion and escape the horrors of plantation slavery. As John Quincy Adams later reflected: "For many years the territory of Florida had been at the mercy of foreign nations, of Indians, and of negroes, and had been used by all for purposes of annoyance to the United States." Between 1814 and 1816, "Negro Fort" on Prospect Bluff—an armed maroon community established around an abandoned British fort—attracted almost a thousand Black residents. In the eyes of US officials, the fort threatened southern security, demonstrated British aggression, and proved Spain's cooperation with the Union Jack. In 1816, Gen. Andrew Jackson—in his crusade against the Seminoles and their runaway allies—destroyed the fort at Prospect Bluff and helped pave the way for the US acquisition of Florida in 1819.[26]

Some military officials derided Cuba as a source of the Deep South's postwar unrest. Influenced by the anti-Spanish merchants and lawyers known as the New Orleans Associates, Col. Thomas S. Jesup coveted Cuba. When

Jesup and the New Orleans Associates received word in late summer 1816 that Spanish ships had attacked the USS *Firebrand*, the colonel awaited a response from the Madison administration and General Jackson. Ironically, Secretary of War William Crawford instructed Jackson, who had illegally invaded Spanish Florida, to keep Jesup within the boundaries of the United States. Although Jackson considered Jesup's "project against Cuba ... a good one," he nevertheless persuaded the colonel to remain stationary.[27]

Jesup instead took to stationery to press for an invasion of Cuba. In a letter to Secretary of State James Monroe, Jesup wrote that the Spanish island controlled the fate of western commerce. "The productions of the West will, in a few years, perhaps double those of the Atlantic," Jesup remarked. "Those productions must pass to a market almost under the guns of Havana." Sharing Claiborne's sentiments, Jesup stressed that "Cuba is . . . the key of all Western America, whether we consider it in a military, a commercial, or a political point of view." As Great Britain coveted Florida, Jesup reasoned that the next hostile movement from Spain warranted a conquest of Cuba. In his mind, the United States already had endless reasons to invade Cuba, including Spanish and British agents storing arms at the fort at Prospect Bluff, which "could have been intended for and be used only by the hostile Indians and their adherents." With the "increased and increasing Spanish force at the Havana," Jesup argued that Spain mobilized for war. He promised Monroe that with four thousand men and naval assistance, the Stars and Stripes would wave atop Castle Morro in Havana. If the United States did not act, Great Britain might seize Florida and Cuba, using the colonies as launchpads to capture New Orleans.[28]

Jesup's plans never materialized. Nonetheless, policymakers adopted his belief that Cuba controlled the fate of western North America. As the expansionist republic battled in the Gulf of Mexico in the 1810s, US officials feared that Black soldiers and Spanish agents from Havana could provoke slave revolts and other nonwhite resistance. Once again, American policymakers saw in Cuba the makings of a Haitian-style revolution on American soil. The Transcontinental Treaty of 1819 (ratified in 1821) relieved white Georgians and Carolinians because the acquisition of Florida paved the way for extending white supremacy and plantation slavery to the peninsula. But planters in the lower Deep South now channeled racial anxieties about Florida toward Cuba. As Cuba became increasingly visible from US shores, the economic ambitions of New England slavers and planters placed Cuba closer to the republic and social disorder.[29]

## PIRATES OF THE CARIBBEAN

Despite ongoing tensions in the Gulf region, Americans claimed that the Treaty of Ghent (1814) heralded an era of political unity and economic opportunity. This "Era of Good Feelings," which masked simmering sectional tensions, inspired economic development at home and abroad. Internal improvements conquered distance by linking the expansive union with canals and roads, while merchants endeavored to penetrate new markets. Ambitious New England merchants saw in Cuba an opportunity to amass a fortune. Rhode Island merchants, in particular, participated in Cuba's skyrocketing sugar production as expatriate planters and slave traders. While southerners expanded the cotton kingdom in the lower Mississippi Valley, New England slaveholders and traders in Cuba made sugarcane king.[30]

After the War of 1812, New England slavers increased their activities in Cuba, formed connections with elites, and even held political offices. Through their connections, these slavers circumvented the 1807 ban on the transatlantic slave trade. And they also evaded the flowery, humanitarian commitments in the Treaty of Ghent to prevent the illegal slave trade in the Atlantic world. "This infamous traffic," "Philanthropos" complained to Madison, "is carried on by unprincipled interested Americans from the Ports of Cuba." Despite participating in illicit human trafficking, many of these slave traders were stalwarts of their communities—most notably Bristol, Rhode Island, merchant and politician James DeWolf. Philanthropos warned that the "famous Privateer Yanke has made three Voyages to Africa, and brought each time over 300 Slaves." Upon becoming a senator in 1821, DeWolf befriended Secretary of State John Quincy Adams, ensuring New England's Cuba interests would be protected diplomatically.[31]

In the late 1810s, liberal and economic reforms transformed Cuba, and New Englanders contributed to the ongoing social and economic changes. In 1817, Spanish monarch Ferdinand VII naturalized all white immigrants and allowed unrestricted foreign trade to enter Cuba's ports. As a result, Cuba's revenue from foreign trade rose 75 percent between 1794 and 1817, while the earnings of Matanzas, a region dominated by American planters, spiked 4,000 percent. Cuba's exports to the United States witnessed substantial growth in the early 1820s. Cuba sent nearly half of its coffee exports, over half of its sugar exports, and roughly 90 percent of its cigar exports to the United States. Cuban creoles' desire for economic liberalization and the efforts of US merchants rendered the island the world's largest sugar producer by the early 1820s.[32]

Cuba's profitable sugar industry depended on the exponential growth of slavery. Between 1780 and 1830, the population of enslaved people in the Caribbean doubled, mostly through human trafficking. Of all the cash crops cultivated by enslaved people, none was crueler than sugar. Harsh overseers used gang labor systems to guarantee high profits. Planting and cutting sugarcane proved gruesome, and those workers who survived to harvest endured endless workdays. Upon harvest, sugarcane demanded immediate processing, which meant that enslaved laborers experienced unrelentingly strenuous conditions and met early deaths. Cruel working conditions, the torrid Caribbean climate, and the gruesome nature of sugar cultivation led Cuban planters to demand the constant illegal importation of enslaved Africans. US citizens willingly participated in the illegal slave trade in Cuba, contributing to the increasing population of African descent on the island. US diplomat Joel Roberts Poinsett estimated that slave traders illegally trafficked at least 172,054 enslaved Africans to Havana between 1810 and 1820.[33]

Slave traders and planters in Cuba created a conundrum for US policymakers and Cuban officials. As American slavers expanded slavery on the island, they simultaneously increased the odds of a slave insurrection. Relying on data from an 1817 report, Poinsett noted how nonwhite inhabitants (45,713) outnumbered the white population (37,885) in Havana. Poinsett also remarked that the able-bodied, arms-bearing nonwhite residents (8,111 free and 9,427 enslaved) outnumbered their white counterparts (13,530) in Havana. Amid the Spanish American revolutions, Spain or an invading army might arm Cubans of African descent. Thus, by the early 1820s, US policymakers shared Poinsett's fears that any rupture to the island's stability would enable Black Cubans to gain "an ascendancy."[34]

The growth of sugar production in Cuba and the instability of the revolutionary Caribbean enticed Cuban and Puerto Rican pirates to raid trade in the 1810s and 1820s. The Spanish American wars for independence in Mexico and Central and South America overstretched Spain's naval forces and encouraged privateering in the Caribbean, posing perilous traveling conditions for merchant vessels. Between 1815 and 1823, nearly three thousand piratical raids targeted merchant vessels in the Caribbean. When pirates sold stolen goods at markets in Havana and Matanzas, Cuban officials looked the other way. But Americans watched. To suppress piracy in the Caribbean, some Americans even "dream[ed] of a conquest of the island of Cuba [so] that our ships may navigate the Gulf in safety." In an 1823 letter to Poinsett, one American justified occupying "some of her territory" to counter the pirates' "lawless depredations." Privateers and pirates also imperiled the commercial interests of slave traders. Although several nations denounced their trade as piracy, James DeWolf and New England slave traders recognized that pirates threatened their interests. As such, they called for at least five or six more US warships in the Caribbean.[35]

Captured slave-trading vessels not only undercut profits but also freed more people of African descent, who occasionally joined pirate crews. Multiracial and multinational pirate crews terrified the unstable Caribbean plantation societies. Stationed in Cuba, US agent John Warner noted how one crew was "composed of all nations, and many Blacks." But what proved most troubling to white Americans was the movement of unregulated people of African descent. From St. Jago, Cuba, US agent Thomas Wilcock reported that "negroes & mulattoes" served as members of the "Carthagenian Privateer[s]" that roamed around the Caribbean.[36]

The practice of piracy against human traffickers and other commercial undertakings stoked both hopes and fears for Cuba among US interests. On the one hand, the postwar years opened new economic avenues for ambitious Americans who sought to profit from Cuba's growing sugar industry. On the other hand, such economic activity conjured images of a second Haitian Revolution. Multiracial pirate and privateering crews from Cuba and Puerto Rico heightened the anxieties of slaveholders and policymakers. US policymakers could no longer ignore the skin color of Cuba's inhabitants. As independence movements grew in Cuba and some Cubans weighed joining the American republic, leaders in the United States contemplated annexing the slaveholding island.

## NO-TRANSFER GEOPOLITICS IN THE 1820S

Republicanism, revolution, and reform in the late eighteenth and early nineteenth centuries besieged the ideologies and palaces of the *ancien régime*. Napoleon's armies marched across Europe, spreading ideals of incipient nationalism and human rights to discontented inhabitants and ambitious elites. Across the Atlantic Ocean, Spanish American revolutionaries touted republicanism and anticolonialism at the expense of monarchical authority. The wars for independence in the Spanish colonies spelled consequences in Spain after King Ferdinand VII rejected the liberal Cadiz Constitution of 1812. As such, by the spring of 1820, liberal Spanish forces pressured the absolutist monarch to recognize the constitution, eventually imprisoning Ferdinand later that year. Ferdinand appealed to the Holy Alliance—a coalition of European monarchies bent on shielding absolutism from the onslaught of republicanism—to help restore royalism in Spain and America. "God grant that our part of our continent may remain safe," Richard Rush warned. "All that is South of us I fear is in jeopardy."[37]

As revolutionary and antirevolutionary forces waged war, Cuba remained comparatively stagnant. Though they remained Spanish colonists, many liberal Cubans envisioned the island's independence while simultaneously fearing colonial occupation by another power. Independence-seeking Cubans formed masonic affiliations called Soles y Rayos de Bolívar, which conspired against the island's colonial government. A member of Caballeros Racionales, a branch of the Soles, José María Heredia claimed that these Masonic groups "endeavored peacefully to prepare public opinion for independence" and dabbled in "overheated theories of social improvement." Whereas some Cubans favored independence, others sought statehood within the United States. Faced with the possibility of a British occupation in the spring of 1822, Cuban planters determined that the survival of slavery and their commercial connections depended on close relations with the United States. In the fall of 1822, Cuban elites contemplated declaring independence and requesting admittance as a state into the United States. Led by Barnabé Sanchez, the Cuban elites formed "the strongest party in *Cuba*," at least according to President Monroe. Sanchez and like-minded Cubans desired "admission at once . . . as one State, with full interior sovereignty of its own." Upon receiving this secret request, Monroe and his cabinet debated how to respond to Sanchez's proposal. Secretary of War John C. Calhoun and Secretary of State John Quincy Adams split over the question of Cuban annexation, but not over sectional differences. Indeed, both the New Englander and the southerner sought to annex the island, but they anticipated different consequences for accepting the proposals of the creole elites.[38]

Calhoun supported the annexation of Cuba to prevent the island from falling "into the hands of Great Britain." Calhoun was not the only American who feared a British Cuba. In US information networks, rumors circulated about British diplomats pressuring their Spanish counterparts to give up their crown jewel colony of the Caribbean. A contributor to the *Columbian Centinel* feared that the British would block US citizens from "participating in the commerce of the island" and would station their Royal Navy at Havana in the event of a future war with the United States. The presence of the Royal Navy would also disrupt the island's illegal slave trade. Great Britain had long meddled in Cuban slavery, from importing enslaved Africans under the *asiento* to encouraging Spain to ban the transatlantic slave trade with the Anglo-Spanish Treaty of 1817. Despite Cubans' willingness to expand the institution of slavery, the island could harbor the British Navy, whose ships impeded the illegal trafficking of enslaved Africans.[39]

Adams shared Calhoun's sentiments but cautioned that annexation of Cuba might unnerve Great Britain. In his voluminous diary, Adams recorded that the cabinet discussed a potential war with Great Britain over Cuba. Adams recognized that Great Britain had long coveted Cuba and would not accept an American annexation. "A war with Great Britain for Cuba would result in her possession of that island, and not ours," Adams warned. "In the present situation of our maritime forces," he added, "we could not maintain a war against Great Britain for Cuba." Reminiscent of his father's interest in Nova Scotia and Bermuda during the War for Independence, the threat of the Royal Navy tempered John Quincy Adams's desire for Cuba. Adams believed that openly supporting Spanish colonialism in Cuba would ease British and Spanish anxieties and allow American merchants to continue to trade with the island. Adams persuaded Monroe and the cabinet to decline to respond to the Cuban liberals' pleas.[40]

These private conversations between members of Monroe's cabinet did not reach British policymakers. Rather, British secretary of state for foreign affairs George Canning feared an American occupation of Cuba. In the eyes of British policymakers, Cuba appeared to be a logical target for the United States, especially given the republic's close commercial ties with the island. In the wake of increased piracy, Canning feared that the United States would invade Cuba. Canning worried in 1822 that Americans "shall make the military occupation of Cuba a part of [their] security" against piratical raids. Along with their recent acquisition of Florida, the United States would use Cuba as a launchpad to expand into the Antilles. An American Cuba, Canning worried, would endanger Jamaica and Britain's "West Indian interests" in the event of a future war. Rumors about American interest in Cuba erased any assurances from the Monroe administration. Political and diplomatic circles in London likely heard whispers out of Madrid that Cuban Freemasons had direct ties with their ideological brethren in Philadelphia. British policymakers responded to ongoing piracy and rumors of an American invasion by increasing their naval presence in the Caribbean in 1822 and by voicing their support for continued Spanish colonialism in Cuba.[41]

American and British diplomats thus preferred Spanish colonialism over Cuban independence. Spanish colonial officers agreed. In late 1822 and early 1823, the forces of absolutism struck back. The Congress of Verona tasked France with restoring royalism in Spain while the Holy Alliance strategized to reimpose European rule over the Americas. Meanwhile, in Cuba, newly arrived Spanish governor Francisco Dionisio Vives eliminated prorepublican threats by banning books, crushing a Masonic conspiracy, and establishing a military court. Under Vives's reign, Spanish officials imprisoned and silenced members of the Soles. US consul John Mountain intimated Vives's strategy to ensure Cubans' loyalty to Spain. When Havana's *cabildo* (municipal council) openly discussed independence in the summer of 1823, Vives arrived at a meeting with "city police, and one company of regular soldiers," forcing the *cabildo* to retire early. Vives also cooperated with local "mulatto chiefs," recognizing that Cuban planters feared a potential independence movement could replicate events on Saint-Domingue. At the same time, Spanish officers and loyal Cubans attempted to convince colonists that members of the Soles attempted to prepare "a scene of horror" akin to the Haitian Revolution. Rejected by the United States, Cuban liberals and planters instead incurred the wrath of Spain.[42]

These renewed attacks on republicanism alarmed US policymakers. Monroe and his cabinet feared that the counterattacks on republican movements would bolster European colonialism in the Western Hemisphere. Calhoun warned Andrew Jackson that this effort to quell republicanism "will probably approach our shores, as Cuba will be involved in all likelyhood in the course of events." John Quincy Adams imagined a bleak future. Whereas France would conquer Mexico and Buenos Aires, Russia would consume the Pacific coast. Amid this chaos, Adams reasoned, Great Britain would seize Cuba while France occupied Spain. In this imagined scenario, the United States would be surrounded by powerful antirepublican empires.[43]

The Monroe Doctrine responded to this possibility by declaring that the Western Hemisphere must be free of *future* European colonialism. Delivered to Congress in late December 1823 during Monroe's State of the Union address, the doctrine espoused the principles of anticolonialism and nonintervention in the Western Hemisphere by European powers. The relatively weak United States, in other words, would not tolerate any future European colonies or influence in the Americas. Adams, the architect of the doctrine, hoped to keep foreign powers not only out of the Pacific Northwest but also away from Cuba. Less threatened by Russia in the Pacific Northwest than by Great Britain in Cuba, Adams rejected Monroe and Canning's desire for a bilateral declaration. Instead, Adams argued that the United States could unilaterally issue a declaration without Great Britain. In doing so, Adams intended to protect the interests of US merchants who participated in the slave trade with Cuban merchants.[44]

By seeking to preserve Spanish colonialism, US policymakers did not abandon hope that Cuba was destined to join the republic. Like many of his contemporaries, Adams believed that geography determined the course of nations. In a letter to a future US minister to Spain, Hugh Nelson, Adams boasted that should Cuba separate from Spain, the island "can gravitate only towards the North American Union, which by the same law of nature cannot cast her off from its bosom." Commerce and geography made Cuba's admission into the United States seem inevitable. No wonder Calhoun claimed that "our confederacy is not complete" without Cuba.[45]

But this destiny was delayed by a factor beyond the British: the island's growing population of inhabitants of African descent. Calhoun argued that US annexation would prevent Cuba from being "revolutionized by the negroes." However, Adams argued that Cuba's population complicated any effort at independence and annexation. Adams claimed that "were the population of the island of one blood and color," Cubans would likely have declared independence upon the French invasion of Spain. Adams also argued that "the character of its population" and "its situation midway between our southern coast and the island of San Domingo" mattered to "national interests." With the increasing population of African descent in the Gulf region, he asserted that racial demographics added to Cuba's geographical significance. If in the wrong hands or independent, Cuba, with its midway position in the Gulf between the United States and Haiti, could potentially destroy "the continuance and integrity of the Union itself." By keeping the island under the formal control of Spain and the informal influence of the United States, American policymakers could prevent an external threat to slavery in the Gulf of Mexico.[46]

Adams and Calhoun were not the only white Americans who contemplated the geopolitics of race. US citizens debated whether annexing or protecting the island from outside influence would buttress the racial structure of the Caribbean. Southerners and New Englanders shared a similar interest in annexing the island, even after sectional tensions flared following the controversy surrounding the admission of Missouri as a slave state in 1821. Though retired at Monticello, Jefferson advised Monroe about Cuba. He considered Cuba's "addition to our confederacy is exactly what is wanting to round our power as a nation, to the point of its utmost interest." Monroe agreed with Jefferson that acquiring Cuba "was of the highest importance to our internal tranquility" because the island would enable the republic to command the Gulf of Mexico and prevent any invasion into the Deep South. He warned, however, that white Cubans "think that they cannot maintain their independence themselves, for even if foreign powers would not molest them, they fear, that if separated from Spain, the superiority of the black population would secure the gov't to them." As such, Monroe and his administration advised white Cubans "to cling to Spain, for the present." Likewise, in addition to provoking a war with Great Britain or Spain, New Englander W. H. Sumner recognized that the United States had to be "willing to add to its black population, by taking the island into its confederacy." Cuba's population of African descent shaped foreign policy agendas.[47]

Unable to annex the island, US policymakers sought to maintain Spanish rule over Cuba. Despite the lofty rhetoric of the Monroe Doctrine, the threats of a British occupation or the creation of a free Black nation reminded members of the Monroe administration how little control they had over Caribbean geopolitics. While they rejected European colonialism, in reality US policymakers remained restricted by Great Britain and the Royal Navy. Wanting the "suppression of piracy," Pennsylvania politician Jonathan Roberts complained in 1825 that "the Cuba war does not flourish in Senate." Roberts conceded that "a mere pitch to occupy Cuba" would have resulted in a "collision with Britain." US leaders also considered Spanish Cuba a preferable neighbor over an independent island. US policymakers feared that independence from Spain would guarantee the creation of a sister republic to Haiti near US shores. The Monroe Doctrine, however, did not preclude other powers in the Western Hemisphere from intervening in Cuba. As Sanchez contemplated annexation by the United States, independence-seeking Cubans turned to the antislavery powers of Mexico and Gran Colombia (composed mainly of present-day Colombia, Ecuador, Panama, and Venezuela).[48]

## PREVENTING THE "SHOCKING SCENES" OF HAITI

Longstanding fears about Cuba were confirmed when the Guamacaro Revolt erupted on the eastern side of Matanzas on June 15, 1825. Roughly twenty-three plantations crumbled as freedom seekers killed their enslavers. Commanded by a West African military leader, Lorenzo Lucumí, the rebels resisted local Cuban forces for ten days. Expatriate overseers reported the destruction to their American investors and employers. S. A. Rainey informed New York investor N. Talcott that "the Negroes were . . . about from 200 to 250 strong" and destroyed "every thing on the way for a league." The 1825 uprising compelled the governor of Matanzas and other Spanish officials to initiate reforms. Spanish authorities partially blamed the presence of foreign-born planters whom they had previously courted—namely the American planters who dominated Matanzas. But upon further inspection, Governor Vives determined that France's recognition of Haiti compelled the rebels to revolt. In all likelihood, the Guamacaro rebels neither drew inspiration from the Haitian Revolution nor relied on the support of people of African descent living in Cuban towns—as Lucumí and other leaders were born in West Africa. To slaveholders, however, the rebellion resembled a prologue for the second Haitian Revolution. Cuban policymakers worked to militarize the region while ensuring that larger walls blocked enslaved people from contact outside their plantations.[49]

When word arrived on US shores, newspapers emphasized racial animosity in their coverage of the Guamacaro Revolt. One paper reported that "about 300" enslaved people of African descent "killed about fifteen or twenty whites including one female." "Whole families were flocking into Matanzas for safety," the *Maryland Gazette* stressed, as the insurrectionists "revolted and murdered . . . in the most shocking and cruel manner." In a letter sent to the *New York Daily Advertiser*, an anonymous American writing from Matanzas informed US audiences that "Negroes from estates at some little distance joined the insurgents, which evinces a premeditated scheme of revolt." While the letter reassured southern planters that Cubans "were in themselves sufficiently powerful to put an immediate stop to these concerted operations of the negroes," American readers encountered new tales of insurrection in the wake of the Guamacaro Revolt. In mid-August 1825, Rainey noted that an enslaved man confessed to plotting to "kill all the male whites." After nine rebels had "been executed and their hands cut off and stuck up in various parts of the country," planter Ephron William Webster argued that Cuba "was never so safe in regard to a negro revolt." Nonetheless, word quickly reached the United States. Though local officials prevented this potential revolt, the *Providence Patriot* claimed that this "plan of an insurrection" was "of more consequence" than the Guamacaro Revolt, likely because of the intended goals to "destroy all the whites they could, and to promote a general insurrection." These reports confirmed US fears of the precarious nature of Cuba's slaveholding society.[50]

US anxiety over Cuba's stability was exacerbated when rumors of Mexico's and Gran Colombia's supposed plans to invade Cuba reached US audiences in the mid-1820s. Receiving reports from his diplomatic agents, Secretary of State Henry Clay believed that the United States of Mexico and Gran Colombia shared similar motives for conquering Cuba and Puerto Rico—ones not unlike earlier US justifications to invade Canada. "[Mexico and Colombia] will be stimulated to attack by the double motive arising from the richness of the prize," Clay wrote, "and from the fact that those islands constitute the rendezvous of Spain." Mexican and Colombian policymakers also felt pressured by Cuban emigrants to invade the island. As minister to Mexico, Poinsett noted how "emigrants have . . . made an application to this government to assist them to realise their project." British diplomat Patrick Mackie also reported how Cuban commissioners ascertained in 1823 whether Mexico would support "in establishing their Independence" and allow Cuba "to join and become a component part of the Mexican Empire."[51]

Such rumored expeditions terrified US policymakers. But in fact, Simón Bolívar expressed reservations about an invasion of Cuba. Military officers such as Gen. Antonio José de Sucre, Cuban emigrants, and Gran Colombian diplomats all pressured El Libertador. Bolívar supposedly received a commitment of "6,000 men and ships" from Mexico should he "head an expedition to Havana." He certainly understood the justifications for conquering Cuba. After all, Bolívar long believed that Gran Colombia's "first concern is the Atlantic" and therefore considered Spanish Cuba to be a critical threat to the nation's geopolitical security and commercial prosperity. However, the Gran Colombian president identified two potential dangers of capturing Cuba. Similar to John Quincy Adams, Bolívar feared that capturing Cuba would upset Great Britain. "The Spanish are no longer a danger to us," he wrote, "but the English are very much so." And, like most US policymakers,

Bolívar feared that an "attempt to liberate Havana" would result in "creating another Republic of Haiti."[52]

Bolívar's reluctance to invade Cuba did not reach US audiences. Instead, the antislavery rhetoric of Bolívar and other Spanish American revolutionaries alarmed US policymakers, who dreaded that Colombia's and Mexico's incipient armies would incite a slave revolt in Cuba. In particular, they worried that Bolívar's desire to end slavery in Gran Colombia along with his efforts to encourage social reform might lead to the creation of another free Black nation. Although Bolívar also sought to avoid such revolutionary tumult, American policymakers regarded the revolutionary hero's antislavery beliefs as evidence otherwise. If not Colombia, then Mexico. Indeed, Mexico's 1824 constitution marked the abolition of slavery in most states, paving the way for President Vicente Guerrero (of African descent) to decree in 1829 the end of slavery except in Texas. Representative John Floyd of Virginia thought a British occupation less threatening than a Mexican or Colombian invasion because Cuba "has from six to seven hundred thousand slaves" in the Caribbean. Mexico and Colombia, Floyd argued, "by their provision in their Constitution, have abolished slavery, and placed every color on an equal footing."[53]

Dread over a Mexican or Colombian invasion of Cuba spilled into congressional debates over the Panama congress in 1826. Proposed by Bolívar, the Congress of Panama intended to bridge differences between the American republics, formulate a policy toward Spain, and address the liberation of Cuba and Puerto Rico. Before the Panama congress, US citizens had celebrated the Spanish American wars for independence as a continuation of their republican revolution. President John Quincy Adams and Secretary of State Henry Clay decided to send two delegates to the congress, hoping to address the issue of Cuba and capitalize on the Pan-American solidarity that had captivated Americans. However, they failed to anticipate the vehement opposition from southern politicians.[54]

Both proponents and opponents of the Congress of Panama despised Spanish Americans' proposed invasions of Cuba. Southern congressmen, however, channeled their distrust toward the Adams administration in their racialization of foreign relations with Spanish America. Frustrated by the "corrupt bargain of 1824," which propelled Adams to the presidency at the expense of Andrew Jackson, southern congressmen rallied by tapping into white Americans' fears of powerful national governments and extending rights and equality to nonwhites. In their tirade against the Congress of

Panama, southern politicians solidified decades of concerns about Cuba—the island's proximity, its potential to disrupt US nationhood and commerce, and its military value as a base to invade the mainland—under the banner of race. These longstanding issues had become solidly racialized to safeguard slavery in the US South. Southerners framed their argument by claiming that should Cuba change hands, the slaveholding island should be under the guidance of Anglo-Americans. In June 1826, *Niles' Weekly Register* hinted at the changing priorities in US policy toward the Spanish island: "Cuba to us, as the key of the gulf or as a place of trade is greatly important to the United States, but it is far more important, on another account, that the sovereignty over the island should remain where it is."[55]

Southern politicians denigrated Spanish Americans, arguing that their "weak" character and military forces would enable nonwhite Cubans to take over the island. They revived the language of the Black Legend during the debates over the Panama mission. Catholic Spanish Americans, southern congressmen contended, would be incapable of handling their newfound liberty and practicing republicanism. Indeed, Georgia senator John M. Berrien worried that an invasion of Cuba by *"buccaniers, drunk with their new born, liberty"* would imperil the *"safety of the southern states."* Bankruptcy, shifting borders, collapsed republics, short-reigned monarchs, military dictatorships, and revenge-seeking Europeans seemingly destabilized the Spanish American nations. In the 1810s and 1820s, military leaders rose and fell in Spanish America. Emperor of Mexico Agustín Iturbide (r. 1821–23) and Supreme Director of Chile Bernardo O'Higgins (r. 1817–23) exemplified Spanish America's authoritarian problem.[56]

Bolívar commanded attention because of his plans to invade Cuba using soldiers of African descent. Prorevolutionary Americans blurred this knowledge and instead lionized Bolívar as a republican hero. However, Bolívar increasingly became villainized as a military despot as his perceived plans for Cuba threatened US interests. Bolívar, who emancipated his slaves in return for their military service, had Black soldiers and commanders within Gran Colombia's ranks. US opposition to his ambitions and tactics crossed party lines. Even New Englander Alexander H. Everett maintained that Bolívar's invasion plans endangered the United States' stability. As early as 1825, Everett feared that changes to Cuba's "present condition"—whether brought on by a failed invasion by either Mexico or Colombia—might transform the island into "an independent principality of blacks." To prevent this possibility, Everett believed that "it is the policy and duty of the United States to endeavor to obtain possession of the island immediately in a peaceable way." Annexation would provide "complete security from the danger of any change in the position of the island in consequence of the present danger." In his eyes, Bolívar's conquest of Cuba would place Black soldiers—committed to emancipation and liberty—near US territories in the Gulf of Mexico. "A military despot of talent and experience at the head of a black army," Everett wrote Secretary of State Clay, "is certainly not the sort of neighbor whom we should naturally wish, if we had the choice, to place upon our Southern frontier."[57]

White Americans worried that Gran Colombia's soldiers of African descent would not be the only nonwhites armed if a war erupted on Cuba. As southerners learned during the Patriot invasion of East Florida in 1812, Spain willingly armed people of African descent, including enslaved Blacks. In late 1825, the *Weekly Raleigh Register* reported rumors that 12,000 or 13,000 Mexican troops would invade Cuba and rely on the support of revolutionary creoles. Spain, the *Register* noted with loathing, "would seek revenge on the Creoles by arming the blacks." If Mexico failed, such an act "would probably lead to the independence of the island under a government similar to that of Hayti." Other US observers contended that Mexico's and Gran Colombia's success depended on arming the enslaved population of Cuba. Bolívar and his soldiers, Poinsett argued, "could [find] their hopes of success only upon arming the negroes."[58]

The possibility of Cuban independence produced by an invasion also disquieted southerners in favor of the Panama mission and the Adams administration. An ally of Adams, Louisiana senator William Leigh Brent argued that sending representatives to the Congress of Panama would enable the United States to convince Bolívar and Mexican president Guadalupe Victoria to end their bids for Cuba. On the floor of the US Congress, Brent reminded his fellow southerners that "the condition of the islands of Cuba" greatly impacted "the state of Louisiana," which excited his "most liveliest anxieties." Brent dreaded the prospect of sizeable free Black populations surrounding Louisiana. "Is it not reasonable for us to suppose that part of its population . . . would all be declared free," Brent wondered, "and, if so with the black population of Mexico, on the frontier of Louisiana, and Hayti and Cuba for neighbors, what would be the condition of the southern planters?" Like his political opponents, Brent hoped to avert an invasion of Cuba by a

Spanish American power. But for Brent, sending representatives to the Panama congress seemed the best means to prevent free Blacks from encircling the United States.[59]

The British shared the same concerns as US policymakers. British policymakers worried that a revolution in Cuba would threaten their Caribbean colonies and disrupt cotton production (and therefore the British textile industry) in the US Deep South. British diplomats frequently discouraged Mexican and Gran Colombian officials from pursuing the invasion, stressing that an occupation of Cuba would embroil them "with the Powers of Europe." Canning also believed that the inflammatory rhetoric of US officials indicated that the United States intended to "interfere directly, and by force, to prevent or repress such an operation." Canning encouraged his observer to the Panama congress, Edward J. Dawkins, to warn Spanish Americans that an invasion might result in either a slave revolt or a US occupation of Cuba.[60]

The Adams administration (1825–29) also sent officials to Panama to discourage Spanish American schemes to seize Cuba. Despite opposition from southerners, the administration sent two ministers to the congress in the summer of 1826: Richard Clough Anderson Jr. and John Sergeant. Anderson passed away en route to Panama City, and Sergeant did not arrive in time for the congressional sessions. Though unable to reach Panama in time for the congress, US policymakers did not need to discourage Spanish American leaders from invading Cuba. By the late 1820s and early 1830s, as tensions between Spain and its former colonies eased, most Spanish Americans abandoned their zeal for conquest. Occasional plots surfaced but quickly subsided. In 1829, Mexican colonel and minister to Haiti José Ignacio Basadre attempted to recruit Haitian soldiers to "excite the slaves in the Island of Cuba to revolt." However, the Mexican government quickly recalled Basadre after US envoy Anthony Butler raised concerns about the colonel's schemes.[61]

By the end of the 1820s, many powers coveted Cuba but none pursued action. US politicians, Mexican military officers, Gran Colombian leaders, British diplomats, and Cuban planters and expatriates all articulated grand plans for the island once freed from Spanish rule. At the same time, these geopolitical schemers all feared the consequences of Cuba falling into the hands of their rivals—afraid that the island's strategic location endangered their respective empires. Americans worried about war with the British and rumored invasions by the upstart Spanish American nations. Britons dreaded US expansion in the Caribbean. Spanish Americans feared proximity to Spain and US aggression. Despite these rival visions, all participants in the contest for Cuba shared a common concern that any convulsion on the island would result in a massive slave revolt that mirrored the tumult of Haiti. Spanish diplomats and colonial officers frequently reminded these nations and Cuban colonists of this possibility. The outcome of the Haitian Revolution ensured that Cuba would remain a Spanish colony until the end of the nineteenth century.

Though their plans to expand into the Caribbean South were thwarted, US policymakers emerged from the acute international squabble over Cuba with a highly racialized policy of neighborhood relations. Regardless of political or regional affiliation, US policymakers and publishers believed that Cuba, unless an American territory or Spanish colony, would fall under the sway of nonwhite leaders. Entrenched in the longstanding belief that Cuba controlled the fate of the American union, Virginia senator John Randolph painted a bleak image for southern slaveholders: "Cuba lies in such a position in reference to the United States, and especially to the whole country on the Gulf of Mexico, as that the country may be invaded from Cuba in rowboats." Because Cuba possessed a large Black population, Randolph warned, if Spanish Americans invaded Cuba, they would unleash "this genius of universal emancipation—this sweeping anathema against the white population." He beseeched his fellow congressmen to ask themselves, "What is the situation of the South States?" Congressman Floyd answered: "Cuba is scarcely more than eighty miles from Florida and that was a distance often passed in a few hours, in open boats; leaving the whole of Louisiana, Florida, and Georgia, open to the sudden invasion from these black Republics at any time." In early 1827, New Englander William Tudor shared these southerners' concerns, equating the downfall of Cuba with the destruction of slavery. Tudor told Clay to "look at Hayti now, & at Cuba (inevitably) a short [time] hence, & at the infallible success of the English abolitionists . . . calculate the census of our slaves in 1830 . . . observe the confines of black, triumphant liberty, & of black, sullen slavery, & how many days or hours sail they are from each other." Tudor believed that the United States needed "a steady, systematic harmonious plan of relief" supported with "the surplus of the national income" over a twenty- or thirty-year period. Otherwise, the republic "at no remote period will be desolated with all the honours of a servile war."[62]

The tensions over the fate of Cuba would not be lost to US expansionists. The racial anxieties that drove the United States' racialized neighborhood policy sharpened expansionist arguments for the entire Gulf region. In an 1829 letter to the *Nashville Republican*, a "Patriot" argued that British interest in Texas mirrored Cuba's geopolitical situation. "Our Government has manifested its policy in relation to Cuba, namely that it shall not change hands," the Patriot stressed. "The same policy will certainly extend to Texas," the writer continued, "a similar country, communicating with us by land and water." If Great Britain neighbored Louisiana, the British would "encourage the insurrection and elopement of slaves." Attempting to disrupt British intrigue, the Patriot also contended that the United States should annex Texas. Indeed, slaveholders argued that Texas could serve "as an outlet" to address "the great and increasing disproportion of the white to the slave population of Louisiana." Seeking security from potential Black revolutionaries and Britons, proslavery southerners applied their logic about Cuba to Texas to secure the racial order of the Gulf.[63]

The United States formally admitted Texas into the union on December 29, 1845, which precipitated the US-Mexico War. Slaveholding politicians celebrated the annexation of Texas as a security measure against abolitionists in the North and Great Britain, slave revolts, and the rising number of free Blacks throughout the Western Hemisphere. Adding Texas to the union convinced proslavery advocates to press for the conquest of Cuba. Throughout the 1840s, US presidents, politicians, publishers, and proslavery filibusters sought to add Cuba to the union. New York editor John O'Sullivan, one of manifest destiny's mouthpieces, worked with the Club de la Habana (composed of wealthy Cuban planters) to pressure President James K. Polk to purchase the island from Spain for $100 million. Meanwhile, secretaries of state including Abel P. Upshur (1843–44) and John C. Calhoun (1844–45) promised Spain that the United States would protect Cuba from foreign invasion. Despite these assurances, proslavery filibusters and diplomats attempted to pry Cuba from Spain. In 1850 and 1851, American filibusters joined Venezuelan adventurer Narciso López's thwarted invasion of Cuba. A few years later, in 1854, US diplomats Pierre Soulé, James Buchanan, and John Mason conspired to craft the Ostend Manifesto, which called for the United States to war with Spain should the latter refuse to sell Cuba. This simultaneous desire to protect and annex Cuba grew out of proslavery politicians' determination to shield the remaining slave societies (including Brazil) from abolitionism.[64]

The failure of the United States to annex Cuba in the antebellum era has often been attributed to increasingly bitter sectional politics. This view assumes that Cuba's incorporation was thwarted primarily by northern opposition. Before the antebellum era, however, policymakers from both the North and South coveted Cuba but proved incapable of altering Caribbean geopolitics. Far from representing a clearsighted vision of manifest destiny, US interest in Cuba evolved in response to an entanglement of ambitions expressed by enslaved and free Cubans, American and Cuban expatriates, European officials, and Spanish American revolutionaries. In the wake of the Haitian Revolution, politicians, merchants, planters, and newspaper editors monitored the growing population of African descent in Cuba and throughout the Caribbean. Into the 1810s, however, Americans thought about Cuba primarily in commercial and geopolitical terms. As slave traders and Cuban and American planters worked to expand the sugar industry, the enslaved population in Cuba expanded. For white Americans and Cubans, the transformation of slavery on the island triggered the specter of Haiti. By the mid-1820s, American leaders trembled at the thought that a Spanish American invasion of Cuba would result in slave resistance or emancipation.[65]

Ultimately, the un-manifest contest for Cuba and the possibility of a second Haitian Revolution buttressed Spanish rule over the island. The Haitian Revolution has often been credited for contributing to US expansion by pressuring Napoleon to sell Louisiana to the Jefferson administration. However, the long-term consequences of Haiti also ensured that Cuba remained a Spanish colony. Despite losing its mainland colonies, Spain managed to maintain political and military rule over Cuba and Puerto Rico. But Spain was not the primary obstacle preventing US, British, Cuban, and Spanish American actors from realizing ambitions for Cuba. Rather, these revolutionary and diplomatic actors believed that the growing population of African descent, with their aspirations for freedom and equality, proved the greatest impediment to accomplishing their plans for Cuba. Fearing antislavery nations would disrupt the racial order of the island and thus threaten the security of the American South, US policymakers stressed the necessity of Cuba remaining a Spanish colony or becoming an American state. However, federal officials and diplomats recognized that any attempt to acquire the Spanish colony would likely provoke a war with Great Britain and its powerful navy.

The United States would not expand into the Caribbean South. But Cuba was far from an afterthought for expansionists. In the first three decades of the nineteenth century, influential Americans focused on Cuba as much as, if not more than, Texas and the Pacific coast. Indeed, in the wake of the Transcontinental Treaty of 1819, Thomas Jefferson believed that, in addition to Texas, "Cuba will join us & give us sugar." Cuba's supposed destiny to enter the union and the inability of US policymakers to realize that destiny helped racialize their apprehensions about stable geopolitical neighborhoods. Throughout the mid-nineteenth century, US expansionists idealized territorial expansion as a remedy for ongoing social and racial tensions in and around the United States. Wary about Cuba's growing population of African descent, US officials strove to maintain Cuban social structures through annexation or the no-transfer policy. By the 1820s, the maintenance of slavery was the driving force for US interest in Cuba—as the creation of a free Black government on the island might spark a slave revolt in the United States. The constant fear of repeating the scenes of revolutionary Haiti in Cuba had undoubtedly shaped antebellum anxious aggrandizement, crystallizing earlier racist arguments for expansion.[66]

Unbeknownst to them, free and enslaved people of African descent shaped the policies and visions of diplomats, generals, and presidents throughout the Greater Caribbean region. Unfortunately for these unintentional shapers of US expansionism, slavery continued to expand on the island of Cuba. Cuba's sugar production doubled between 1827 and 1840, generating over a fifth of the world's supply. This massive production owed much to the roughly 180,000 enslaved Africans illegally trafficked by the 1840s, the introduction of internal improvements, and emancipation in the British Caribbean. By 1840, a railroad connected Havana to the sugar-producing countryside, which was now dotted with steam-powered mills. In a world increasingly pushing toward emancipation, slavery prevailed in Cuba until 1886, twenty-one years after the United States and two years before Brazil abolished slaveholding.[67]

Cuba—its location, slaveholding policies, inhabitants, and geopolitical value—shaped the expansionist imaginings of early US policymakers. Cuba and the United States remained intertwined after the 1820s. The United States imposed three military occupations in Cuba between 1898 and 1922, formalizing its longstanding informal imperialism. By the 1960s, conditions in Cuba once again threatened the stability of the United States. A concern over Cuban communism replaced the dread of slave revolts—and geopolitical tensions again reminded Americans of their republic's proximity to the island. The Cuban Missile Crisis of 1962 and the persistence of the US Guantanamo Bay detention camp suggest the prescience of Thomas Jefferson, who in 1808 considered "their interests & ours as the same."[68]

FIVE

# THE PACIFIC NORTHWEST

I n an 1825 proclamation to his fellow citizens, a North American president celebrated his republic's transcontinental destiny. This president, Guadalupe Victoria, reminded Mexicans that their newfound independence would empower them to reap Mexico's bountiful resources, precious metals, and strategic geography. "Mexico," Victoria stressed, "presenting one aspect to Europe, and another to Asia, offers the riches of her virgin bosom for the reciprocal commerce, relations, and utility of mankind." Before US citizens and Canadian subjects secured a foothold on the Pacific coast, Mexicans had long enjoyed access to the Atlantic and Pacific Oceans. In the age of revolutions, Spanish Americans believed that their newly independent nations such as Mexico and Gran Colombia (present-day Colombia, Ecuador, Panama, and Venezuela) would transform the commercial world with free trade and interoceanic canals. Translated and published in the London-based *American Monitor*, Victoria's proclamation was one of countless pieces touting the national futures of Spanish America that reached US and European audiences. In the 1810s and 1820s, these visions captivated US citizens, who imagined how Spanish America's commercial liberation would facilitate their nation's territorial and commercial expansion on the Pacific coast of North America.[1]

The belief that Spanish America's prosperity would facilitate US expansion gets obscured when manifest destiny is read back into earlier decades. The narrative of manifest destiny portrays the United States heading toward an inevitable clash with Mexico, Indigenous nations, and Great Britain en route to the Pacific coast. However, in the 1810s and 1820s, few Americans expected that a distant settlement on the Pacific coast would remain attached to the republic. The Transcontinental Treaty with Spain of 1819 provided a claim to justify the US fur-trading outpost of Astoria on the Columbia River (present-day Oregon). US expansionists had hoped that Astoria and other future settlements would ensure their republic's commercial growth in the Pacific Ocean. But these aspirations had to reconcile realities on the ground. The Astorians adapted their ambitions to the economic and kinship structures of the Chinookan-speaking peoples, who had established deep commercial networks in the Columbia River basin. The Pacific Northwest was not only an Indigenous space but also a faraway battleground for imperial powers such as Great Britain and Russia. Between 1813 and the mid-1820s, Astoria—the American republic's greatest claim to the Pacific coast—was occupied by Canadian traders. As they met the limits of empire to the Canadian North and Caribbean South, few US policymakers believed that their republic was manifestly destined to reach the distant Pacific coast.[2]

US expansionists envisaged how inter-American commerce and cooperation could remove the obstacles to colonizing the Pacific coast in the 1810s and 1820s. The collapse of the Spanish Empire has long been understood as a pivotal event that contributed to US expansion across North America. But before the antebellum United States seized northern Mexico, US policymakers dreamed of expanding to the Pacific coast amid an era of Pan-American unity—a moment when Anglo-Americans and Spanish Americans believed they shared a commitment to republicanism and anticolonialism. During their wars for independence, Spanish Americans produced countless writings articulating how their new nations would transform global commerce with free trade and canals linking the Atlantic and Pacific Oceans. Editorialists, adventurers, and expatriates exported these writings to US audiences. Optimists including Missouri politician Thomas Hart Benton and diplomat Theodorick Bland drew on this discourse to envision securing Astoria's attachment to the union and accelerating its development. As mainland Spanish America gained independence in the early 1820s, Spanish

The United States following the passage of the Transcontinental Treaty in 1821.

Americans and Anglo-Americans imagined how interoceanic canals could help them overcome geographical and spatial obstacles to consolidating their nations' boundaries. Engaging with this discourse, US expansionists envisioned maintaining a planned pacific policy toward the Spanish American republics while rooting out European empires and implicitly removing Indigenous nations.[3]

By the mid-1820s, this fantasizing had increasingly descended into disillusionment. US efforts to establish a greater territorial presence on the Pacific coast remained elusive. US merchants expressed disappointment about their trade with the new nations, especially as canal projects failed and their British counterparts found greater success in Spanish American markets. Consequently, this unrealized vision of expanding to the Pacific coast through Pan-American cooperation progressively gave way to aggressive justifications to annex northern Mexico. By the end of the 1820s, US policymakers claimed that Mexicans could not capitalize on their northern provinces' natural resources and ports on the Pacific coast. The economic and transcontinental arguments of antebellum expansion proved in great part a corruption of this earlier inter-American dialogue.[4]

## FOUNDING ASTORIA

Anglo-Americans had marveled at the Pacific coast of North America since the earliest colonial projects of the seventeenth century. Visions of expansion to the western coast of North America had always been tied to commercial expansion in the Pacific world. Uncertain about western North America, Anglo-Americans hoped to discover a Northwest Passage that would shrink the distance between the Atlantic and Pacific Oceans. Finding a secret sea route would bring New England merchants closer to Canton—the sole Chinese port open to western merchants—and other East Asian markets. By the early nineteenth century, the United States surpassed Great Britain in trade with China. To maintain this growth, US policymakers sought to establish a presence on the Pacific coast of North America. This desire intensified after Scottish explorer Alexander Mackenzie trekked across North America in 1793. Fearing the prospect of British forts on the Pacific coast, in 1803 President Jefferson instructed Meriwether Lewis, William Clark, and the Corps of Discovery to explore the interior of North America and chart a path to the Pacific coast.[5]

Consequently, the Corps of Discovery expedition inspired ambitious adventurers to establish a fur-trading outpost along the Columbia River. Immersed in the Great Lakes fur trade, German-born New York merchant John Jacob Astor formed the Pacific Fur Company, whose members established Fort Astoria in the spring of 1811. Astor held commercial ambitions for himself and expansionist aspirations for the United States. He envisioned Astoria becoming a key component of the China trade, whereby American merchants could acquire coveted sea otter pelts and furs from Native hunters and ship them west to Canton. Seeking to block the Canadian North West Company (NWC) and the Hudson's Bay Company (HBC), Astor hoped to establish a permanent US settlement on the Pacific coast. The lower Columbia River seemed like the ideal location. Astor boasted to Jefferson that the Columbia River basin proved "abound with fish & game" and had a "quantity of valuable furrs fare exceeding our most Sangguine exspectations." Sharing these sentiments, Astorian Alexander Ross also believed that the nearby Willamette Valley would one day become "the garden of the Columbia." Optimistic Americans hoped that Astoria would serve as a permanent base for territorial and commercial expansion in the Pacific world. Ironically, the crew that would establish the republic's greatest claim to the Pacific coast was composed of Canadians, Iroquois, Hawaiians, Europeans, and a few Americans.[6]

This imperial and commercial venture floundered in the face of well-established Indigenous political and commercial structures in Oregon Country (modern-day British Columbia in Canada and the US states of Oregon, Washington, Idaho, and parts of Montana and Wyoming). For Chinookan-speaking peoples, the Columbia River basin was *Illahee*—or land, earth, ground. Kinship and trade networks created a complex of villages that bound together *Illahee*. Marriages cemented familial, economic, and political ties between villages along the Columbia River. Though removed from the Euro-American populations, these Chinookan-speaking peoples had been exposed to the Columbian Exchange, enduring a smallpox epidemic and profiting from the budding commercial networks. Nations such as the Clatsops and Kathlamets established deep commercial ties with Indigenous peoples in the continent's interior. One Astorian noticed how Chinookan peoples' horses "had been marked with a hot iron by Spaniards" and likely came from "New Mexico." As American and European merchants increased their whaling and hunt for sea otter pelts in the 1790s, Chinookan traders received goods from China, the United States, and Europe. These Chinookan villages confounded Euro-Americans, who understood *Illahee* as a collection of "so many little sovereignties." Any attempt to impose a vision for the region had to reconcile this complex world.[7]

Powerful Chinookan leader Comcomly considered the Astorians as one of these little sovereignties. Comcomly believed that the Astorians could enhance his commercial and political influence, and even married off his daughter Ilchee to Fort Astoria's chief factor, Duncan McDougall. McDougall's marriage aligned with the customary economic- and kinship-building practices of *Illahee*. Far from a romantic, McDougall described his marriage as "the means of securing to us [Comcomly's] friendship more effectually than any other measure that could be adopted." Far from the United States and ready supply lines, the Astorians depended on this alliance as well as connections with other Chinookan villages to receive enough salmon and other resources to survive.[8]

The budding Euro-American competition in the Pacific Northwest magnified the Astorians' struggle for survival. In the late eighteenth and early nineteenth centuries, British and Russian merchants attempted to increase their commercial and territorial presence in the Pacific Northwest, transforming the region into a faraway battleground for European empires. This imperial contest intensified amid the Nootka Dispute of the 1790s, when Great Britain challenged Spain's centuries-old claims to Vancouver Island. Though the powers avoided war, the Nootka Conventions established the belief among Europeans and Euro-Americans that colonial settlement was necessary to justify land claims. A few decades later, Astoria stood as the United States' only claim to the Pacific Northwest. In 1813, however, that claim was lost. Fearing a British attack during the War of 1812, Astorians sold Fort Astoria to the Canadian North West Company, which renamed the outpost Fort George.[9]

The Treaty of Ghent promised to restore prewar boundaries. However, McDougall's sale of Fort Astoria to the North West Company complicated its return to the United States. The postwar fate of Astoria exemplified the un-manifest nature of the early republic's expansion to the Pacific coast. The United States' future on the Pacific coast seemed uncertain or improbable to even the most imaginative expansionists. Astorian Alexander Ross believed that the distance between the Columbia River basin and the eastern United States ensured that "colonization" would occur in "a period far beyond the present generation." Jefferson assumed that an Anglo-American population would establish a permanent settlement over time, but he doubted that these settlers would seek union with the distant United States. In a letter to Astor, Jefferson anticipated the Pacific coast being covered "with free and independant Americans, unconnected with us but by the ties of blood & interest, and enjoying like us the rights of self-government." At the end of the War of 1812, however, the Columbia River basin seemed destined to remain *Illahee*—a region of Chinookan-speaking villages tied by kinship and commerce. Distance and rival ambitions thwarted the Astorians' aspirations to secure the Columbia River basin and expand their trade in the Pacific world. In the two decades that followed Astoria's founding, US expansionists would search for a remedy to overcome these obstacles.[10]

## VISIONS OF SPANISH AMERICAN INDEPENDENCE

Spanish American creoles shared Astorians' desire to remake the commercial world. On the eve of revolution, Spanish Americans boasted that nature destined them to direct the world's commerce. Whether in New Spain, New Granada, Peru, or Chile, Spanish Americans argued their geographic location and abundant natural resources enabled them to transform the commercial world. Their claims were solid, as Spanish America already fueled the global economy. After all, silver mined in Peru and the Bajío region of Mexico sparked trade with China, while products from the Atlantic and Pacific worlds reached the markets of Panama City. But Spanish Americans felt that their colonies had even greater commercial potential. Geographer and scientist Francisco José de Caldas believed that nature gifted "the trade of the universe" to transcontinental New Granada (present-day Colombia, Ecuador, Panama, and western Venezuela). Surpassing the Tyrians and Alexandrians of the ancient Mediterranean world, New Granadans would export gold and cash crops such as sugar and cacao in exchange for "perfumes" from Asia, "ivory" from Africa, manufactured goods from Europe, and "furs" from North America. With access to the Atlantic and Pacific Oceans, colonists could engage in "mercantile speculations from the sun's birth to its sunset."[11]

Spanish Americans reasoned that their colonies' capacity to revolutionize global commerce lay in their access to the Pacific world. Since the sixteenth century, Spain had immersed New Spain and Peru into its Pacific Ocean networks, sending Manila galleons laden with luxuries to Acapulco in exchange for silver and gold. However, Spanish policies limited Chile's exports of surplus wheat flour to Peru. Chilean Jesuit Juan Ignacio Molina noted his homeland's potential to transform trade with the East Indies in his *Ensayo sobre la historia natural de Chile* (1782). Living in exile in the Papal States following the suppression of his order in 1767, Molina argued that "the trade of East India ... would attract ... Chileans" because the colony's "products [were] scarce, or not found at all in that abundant portion of Asia." Chile's resources could be easily transported across the Pacific by the southern winds, Molina contended, making the trade with Asia both convenient and profitable.[12]

Bourbon policies, however, stymied these aspirations. The eighteenth-century Bourbon reforms intensified the colonies' dependence on Spain by limiting agricultural exports and allowing European manufactured products to overwhelm markets and ruin local industries. These policies reinforced Iberian-born *peninsulares*' monopoly of trans-Atlantic trade. In New Granada, for example, Cartagena *peninsulares* commanded the overseas trade by exploiting creoles' desire for European manufactures in return for gold extracted from the interior. Disgruntled creoles complained that the *peninsulares'* control of overseas commerce provided Spain with little incentive to develop the agricultural interior or improve internal transportation. Caldas lambasted Spain's reluctance to construct an interoceanic canal in New Granada. "We have not taken a single step on this matter," he lamented in 1808, "one capable of changing America's ideas of commerce." In the eyes of the colonists, the Bourbon reforms revealed Spain's intention to reduce them to consumers of European manufactured goods and suppliers of precious metals and cash crops.[13]

Spanish American revolutionaries maintained that independence would empower them to realize the dreams of Caldas and Molina. Napoleon's invasion of Iberia in 1808 sparked a series of political reforms and revolts that rocked the Spanish Empire from Mexican Texas to Cape Horn. To legitimatize their republican revolutions, Spanish American rebels crafted "colonial legacies," arguing that Spanish rule stunted economic and political progress. In 1815, revolutionary Venezuelan leader Simón Bolívar imagined the political and economic progress that would follow the Spanish Empire's collapse. Repudiating mercantilism, Bolívar imagined Spanish American citizens constructing an interoceanic canal in Panama—the future "emporium of the world." "Their canals will shorten distances throughout the world," Bolívar boasted, "strengthen commercial ties between Europe, America, and Asia, and bring to that happy area tribute from the four quarters of the globe." Before, during, and after the revolution, creoles embraced the notion that independence signaled a new commercial epoch.[14]

Expatriates, adventurers, and publishers disseminated Spanish Americans' ideas to US and international audiences by the early 1810s. Settling in cities such as Philadelphia, London, and Paris, Spanish American expatriates galvanized Europeans and US citizens by promising that supporting independence would be rewarded with access to their homelands' lucrative markets. Ambitious adventurers pledged themselves to revolution and riches, recounting their experiences in memoirs. Newspaper editors reprinted these writings to captivate their audiences. These multinational writers expanded on the ideas of Spanish American revolutionaries to underscore how the destruction of the Spanish Empire would alter global trade to the benefit of the United States.[15]

These writings found an eager audience in the United States. Anglo-Americans had fantasized about Mexico and South America since the colonial era. The legendary gold and silver extracted from Mexican and South American mines enthralled Europeans and North Americans, who sought to find precious metals in their earliest colonial projects. This view of Spanish America persisted for centuries. New Englander Samuel Gilman hoped in 1824 that US consul to Peru William Tudor had "found a mine of gold at that far-off place of metallic memory," won over "the daughter of a noble Incas," and gained access to "some vice-royal library full of Mss. & other rich treasures of literature." Americans also celebrated the revolutions in Mexico and South America as continuations of their republican experiment. These misguided fantasies and prorevolutionary sentiments led Americans to readily believe hyperbolic projections for their sister republics. Jared Sparks, editor of the *North American Review*, lamented his countrymen's ignorance of Spanish America. "Our newspaper editors are mostly ignorant of Spanish and give only obscure and broken hints, and these often erroneous," Sparks grumbled, "and yet all our knowledge comes through the newspapers."[16]

American readers encountered passages in newspapers and pamphlets that celebrated the transcontinental form of Spanish America. Well before the United States had become a transcontinental nation, New Granada and New Spain stretched from the Atlantic to the Pacific. Longstanding animosities between the colonies ensured that South America and New Spain would remain divided into several nations. However, optimistic expatriates such as Manuel Torres still hoped that Spanish America would capitalize on its transcontinental form. Banished from New Granada and reestablished in Philadelphia, Torres wrote *An Exposition of the Commerce of Spanish America* (1816) to entice American audiences to support independence. Capitalizing on his popularity, Torres argued that Spanish America's "situation between Asia Europe and the United States" and "its excellent harbours opening on the Pacific and the Atlantic Oceans" made it "destined by the Author of Nature to become the centre of the commerce of the whole world." Even cranky skeptics such as John Adams maintained in 1815 that "an independent free Government in South America" would have "greater advantages for Commerce" than any other country. Spanish Americans such as Torres allowed American readers to imagine the possibilities of a nation that extended from the Atlantic to the Pacific.[17]

Transcontinental New Spain seemingly held the greatest commercial promise. New Spain had been shrouded in mystery for Anglo-Americans and Europeans, who, for centuries, had constructed an image of the province based on legends of abundant riches, cruel Spaniards, and conquered Aztecs. While liberal Spanish policies enabled US merchants to trade with Cuba and South America beginning in the 1790s, New Spain remained shut to the world. Prussian explorer Alexander von Humboldt, however, provided a clearer picture of the once-blurry colony. On a journey through New Spain in 1803–4, Humboldt recorded a bevy of commercial, demographical, and geographical data for his *Political Essay on the Kingdom of New Spain* (1811). The essay's boastful claims about Mexico's potential gained widespread praise from literary circles and inspired Mexican revolutionaries to imagine the economic possibilities of independence. Humboldt reasoned that Mexico boasted the best geographical position in the Western Hemisphere. Mexico possessed these advantages because it was "placed on an isthmus" and "washed by the South Sea and Atlantic Ocean." Humboldt hinted that New Spain under "careful cultivation" would "alone produce all that commerce collects together from the rest of the globe."[18]

For Protestant Americans, "careful cultivation" meant political independence from Catholic Spain. Viewing monarchies and colonial rule as obstacles to commercial progress, Americans theorized that independent republics would embrace free trade. The mercantilist and allegedly cruel policies of Spain, they professed, undermined Spanish America's commerce and exploited its inhabitants. Spanish colonialism evoked tales of religious persecution and outdated economics carried out by clergymen and unrestrained conquistadors at the behest of a tyrannical king. Such beliefs convinced international observers that Spanish America's treasures remained locked away. In fact, Spanish America already contributed 90 percent of the total world production of silver in 1800 and had made recent strides to increase exports. Between 1762 and 1804, the minting of silver pesos in Mexico increased from 5 million to 27 million. Nonetheless, international observers made bold speculations. Drawing from the "Journal of General Pike" and the "Travels of Humboldt," the *Providence Patriot, Columbian Phenix* reported that "the immense wealth centered in the hands of a few individuals in Mexico" equaled "the whole expences of the civil government of the U. States." Independence would allow Mexicans to sell the "bars of gold and silver" piled away "in their cellars."[19]

Revolutionary expatriates convinced Americans that their nations' tremendous riches would benefit the United States' Pacific commerce. Visions of Spanish metals revolutionizing trade with China and India contributed to the imperial conflict of the mid-eighteenth century. Spanish American revolutionaries revived these fantasies in the nineteenth century. Appealing to US merchants and politicians, Torres stressed that the United States, "more than other nations" would benefit from Spanish America's "precious metals," which could be used to "trade throughout the world, and particularly with Asia." Vicente Pazos Kanki, a Bolivian agent of Aymara descent, agreed with Torres. In a series of published letters, Kanki informed US readers that "they will be able to procure from Peru all the specie which they may want... to carry on, upon a more profitable and extended scale, their commerce with the East."[20]

These speculations alluded to the reality that metals mined in Spanish America had facilitated US trade with China for decades. To trade with merchants at Canton, Americans relied heavily on Spanish specie (*pesos fuertes*), which functioned as the world's currency. Between 1807 and 1813, US merchants traded with Spanish American ports to supply 98 percent of the western silver specie that entered China. To receive Spanish specie, US merchants traded, in the words of Connecticut politician Timothy Pitkin, "the manufactures of Europe, particularly Great Britain, as well as the manufactures and produce of the East-Indies and China." US traders also reexported British goods to Spanish America that remained unaccounted for in official US ledgers. Between the late 1800s and early 1810s, these British "ghost" exports were roughly twice as large as US official reexports to Spanish America. These murky exchanges help explain how US silver payments at Canton totaled $29.4 million, but US trade with Spanish America (where they received most of their specie) only reached $18.7 million between 1799 and 1810. No wonder many Americans assumed that the independence of Spanish America would increase their already profitable trade with Canton. Grounded in a Puritan tradition of criticizing Catholics, John Adams nevertheless envisioned how Spanish American Independence might redraw imperial boundaries and flood the Pacific Ocean with streams of silver-carrying ships. "What would Soon happen in Indostan and in China," Adams asked in 1815, "if a Communication of Commerce, Navigation and Naval Power was opened between South America and the East Indies? What is to become of the East India Company and the British Possessions?"[21]

Not every US citizen embraced this belief. Amid the French Revolution and the Napoleonic Wars, Spanish officials opened ports in the Caribbean and South America to exchange silver and sugar for American flour and lumber. By 1798, Cuba's trade with the United States surpassed its trade with Spain. By supporting independence, however, the United States endangered its invaluable trade with the Spanish Caribbean for speculative trade with newly independent nations. The Cuba trade, Philadelphia merchant James Yard exclaimed, "is of more value to the United States, in one year, than that with Mexico could be in ten!" Yard also eschewed the idea that Spanish America would strengthen Pacific commerce. As Yard put it, "On a general survey of the extensive line of the western coast of America, we see but little either in the present or prospective means of the commerce of its numerous ports, that can be essentially beneficial to our own."[22]

Yard's predictions, however, could not overwhelm the widespread support for Spanish American Independence. Spanish American expatriates had convinced many Americans that their republic stood to benefit most from the liberation of Mexico and South America. Recognizing the popularity of Spanish America, House Speaker Henry Clay championed sending a diplomat to Buenos Aires in 1818. In front of Congress, Clay argued that "no nation offers higher inducements to commercial enterprise" than an independent Spanish America. "Washed on the one side by the Pacific, on the other by the south Atlantic," Clay emphasized, "her commerce must, when free from the restraints of despotism, be immensely important." These beliefs compelled expansionists to imagine how a settlement on the Pacific coast would develop and remain attached to the United States.[23]

## SPANISH AMERICA AND US EXPANSION TO THE PACIFIC NORTHWEST

The diplomatic activities of the Monroe administration allowed US expansionists to confront their longstanding fears about Pacific expansion. Boundary disputes with Spain over their northernmost province (Texas), the Floridas, and the Pacific Northwest prevented the Monroe administration from publicly supporting Spanish American independence in the 1810s. Nonetheless, the popularity of Spanish American independence pressured Monroe to send agents to observe the rebellious colonies. In December 1817, his administration assigned commissioners Caesar A. Rodney, John Graham, and Theodorick Bland to assess South America's political and economic conditions. The administration instructed the commissioners to review "the principal articles of commerce" and uncover "what articles from the United States [will] find the best market." Acting Secretary of State Richard Rush also stressed that "the President is desirous of availing himself of your services in Chili and Peru." Before departing, Bland agreed with Monroe that "the public interest would be much promoted by correct information on the state of affairs on the coast of the Pacific." Monroe ordered the commissioner to travel from Buenos Aires to Chile. Reaching Secretary of State John Quincy Adams in November 1818, Bland's report on Chile illustrated how US officials connected Spanish America's potential to future US settlement on the Pacific coast.[24]

In his report, Bland presented Chile as a hidden treasure of overflowing silver mines and endless wheat fields sealed off by Spanish rule. Declared independent in February 1818, Chile appeared poised to benefit the United States' commerce in the Pacific Ocean. "The free access to that great bread country of the other hemisphere lays open channels of trade hitherto closed against us," Bland proclaimed, "and cherishes and sustains every other branch of all our rich, profitable, and increasing commerce of the Pacific." Like the Spanish American creoles, Bland argued that the metals of Chile would "enable [US citizens] to extend their enterprise" in the "China and India trade" to a "greater advantage than ever."[25]

Bland's predictions contributed to the well-established discourse about Chile's potential. His ideas received support from US agent John Bartow Prevost, who visited Valparaíso in early March 1818. Building on Molina's "work on this Province," Prevost argued that the Chilean Jesuit "might have added to give to the observation its full weight, that the taste of the Natives is decided for India Goods and that the consumption is immense both in Chile and Peru." Prevost informed Secretary of State Adams that Chile received most of its imports from Great Britain and the United States, including goods from China. Prevost stressed that the East India Company's monopoly stymied British merchants, but American traders could "supply the wants of this country at a cheaper rate than the Purchasers of the same wares in a European port." According to Bland and Prevost, US merchants could bring spices and teas from Canton and receive Chilean and Peruvian gold, silver, and wheat to boost their Pacific commerce.[26]

These expectations convinced Bland that Chile's independence would accelerate Astoria's growth. Bland learned that the United States had secured "unquestioned possession of Columbia river" when Adams sent the USS *Ontario* to reclaim Astoria from the British in late 1817. He boasted to Adams that Chile would "furnish the means of cherishing the growth of that settlement." Bland stressed that "the settlement at Columbia river will have a ready and unrivalled market on the southern Spanish coast, particularly in Chili" because of the Pacific Northwest's abundant wood for shipbuilding, furs for trade, and salmon for Chilean consumption. Bland estimated an annual average of $6 million in trade with Chile. The *Philadelphia Gazette* reported that this paragraph of Bland's report "particularly engaged attention." The *Raleigh Register* expressed a similar belief that trade with Spanish America would foster US settlement in the Pacific Northwest. "No event will tend more to extend our settlements towards the Pacific Ocean," the paper continued, "than the independence of the colonies." Chile's open markets would entice US merchants and adventurers to settle along the Columbia River and challenge the widespread assertion that Pacific expansion would occur in the distant future.[27]

Amid these discussions, Adams secured a claim to the Pacific Northwest with the Transcontinental Treaty (also known as the Adams-Onís Treaty, ratified in 1821). The treaty conceded Texas to Spain but granted Florida to the republic and recognized American claims to the Pacific Northwest between the forty-second parallel to the forty-ninth parallel. Several factors influenced the Monroe administration's demands, including the Yellowstone expedition (1819), the growing presence of Britons and Russians in the Pacific Northwest, improved relations with Great Britain, and pressure from politicians and private citizens. One can speculate whether Adams was influenced by the reports about Chile and Pacific expansion and the newspapers touting Spanish America's capacity to alter the East India trade. After the treaty, however, Adams openly appreciated the transcontinental potential of emerging Spanish American nations. In 1823, Adams contended that Gran Colombia's "central position upon the surface of the globe, directly communicating at once with the Pacific and Atlantic Oceans" rendered it "destined by the author of nature, as the center and the EMPIRE of the human family."[28]

Adams's treaty with Spain intensified the connection between Spanish American independence and Pacific expansion. Expansionists relied on this transnational discourse to counter concerns that a settler colony on the Pacific coast would break away from the republic. Influential Missouri politician Thomas Hart Benton was convinced that a free-trading Mexico would strengthen Astoria's attachment to the United States. In his *St. Louis*

*Enquirer,* he promoted St. Louis as the central connection between the corners of the American republic, integrating the economies of Philadelphia, New Orleans, and the Columbia River basin. Benton argued that Mexican independence and the Pacific Ocean trade would link these disparate regions. Dispelling naysayers' claims that US settlements along the Columbia River would struggle to establish an "active commerce" due to their distance from "any white settlement," Benton declared that "the mines of Mexico" would provide the "requisite means of carrying on this intercourse." Disregarding Mexico's immersion in the networks of the Pacific world, he suggested that the topography of Mexico rendered "it impossible for them ever to become a maritime nation." As such, US merchants would serve as the country's "carriers and factors on the Pacific ocean." Mexican metals would reach the markets of St. Louis via the Gulf of Mexico and the Mississippi River, solidifying the city's role as "the medium of exchange between the mouths of the Columbia and the Mississippi." The Missourian boasted that this scheme would "not only advance [St. Louis's] prosperity, but that of the United States."[29]

Other publishers shared Benton's confidence that inter-American trade would strengthen the common interests between the United States and the Pacific Northwest as well as between North and South America. In a circulated report to President Monroe published in the *Daily National Journal*, an "intelligent citizen" reasoned that the commercial interests of Mexico, South America, and the United States were "natural and reciprocal." This natural connection proved especially true along the Pacific coast, where US traders would carry the trade "of the whole western coast of the continent, commerce with China and other parts of Asia." For this anonymous author, southern cotton, western agriculture, northern capital, far western furs, and South American metals would strengthen regional economic ties and fuel development in the Pacific Northwest. "*Western and Southern section* of the United States, and the *North-West territory,*" the *Daily National Journal* reported, "are the natural links in the political chain." The report argued that those links would "indissolubly bind the prosperity and interests of North and South America together, at least so far as relates to the intercourse of the inhabitants of countries bordering on the Pacific."[30]

Expansionists relied on revolutionary Spanish Americans' aspirations to imagine their future in the Columbia River basin before and after the signing of the Transcontinental Treaty. Spanish American revolutionaries envisioned transforming commerce with East Asia with open markets and precious metals—ambitions that garnered US and international attention. Whether Benton or Bland, US expansionists reasoned that proximity to Chile and Mexico would allow US citizens to develop prosperous and loyal settlements on the Pacific coast.

Regardless of these fantasies, however, the treaty only provided a claim to the territory around the Columbia River: Astoria remained a British outpost surrounded by Chinookan villages. When the USS *Ontario* arrived to reclaim Astoria from the British in 1817, Captain James Biddle raised an American flag in Fort George, declaring the Pacific Northwest for the American republic. In October 1818, Prevost followed Biddle's footsteps by raising another American flag in front of the North West Company at Fort George. Prevost allowed chief trader James Keith and the North West Company to continue occupying the fort. The Union Jack flag continued to wave above Fort George. But the North West Company recognized its occupation of Fort George was tenuous. After all, the United States could reclaim the fort at any point. Both the United States and Great Britain shared a claim to the Columbia River basin under the terms of the Treaty of 1818, which allowed both nations to occupy Oregon Country. Realistically, the survival of Fort George depended on continued support from Comcomly and other Chinookan-speaking leaders. These on-the-ground realities did not indicate that US citizens would settle at Astoria and trade for precious metals with Spanish Americans. Instead, Oregon Country seemed likely to remain *Illahee* well into the nineteenth century. Many Americans felt expansion into the Pacific Northwest would be a thwarted endeavor given the vast distance between US populations and the Columbian River basin. Several politicians, as Adams suggested in 1824, still feared a "territorial settlement on the Pacific" because it would inevitably "separate from the Union." As Spanish America secured independence in the 1820s, expansionists challenged these arguments about distance and overextension with promises of interoceanic canals.[31]

## CANAL FEVER AND SETTLER COLONIALISM IN THE AGE OF SPANISH AMERICAN INDEPENDENCE

By the early 1820s, Spanish American revolutionaries had crushed most of the royalist forces on the American continents. As the Spanish Empire collapsed, Spanish American revolutionaries, US citizens, and European subjects attempted to realize the commercial vision of Spanish American independence. American and European policymakers scrambled to capitalize on these nations' independence. In an 1822 letter to Lord Castlereagh, Briton John Lowe begged the secretary of state for foreign affairs to recognize Gran Colombia's independence or risk being "deprived of the riches and the abundance" of this new republic. Because "the ports of Colombia command an intercourse with the Atlantic and Pacific Oceans," Lowe argued that "a freedom of trade and a liberal policy will enable them to draw the riches of India and offer their own." Spanish American leaders and international actors attempted to transform fantasy into reality.[32]

The establishment of new nations such as Mexico and Gran Colombia heated up canal fever in the 1820s. Schemes to carve a path through Central America to connect the Atlantic and Pacific Oceans had been theorized since at least the mid-sixteenth century, but discussions intensified amid the Spanish American wars for independence. It is easy to dismiss these schemes as impossible in hindsight, especially given the Panama Canal was not completed until 1914. However, the success of projects such as the Erie Canal (1817–25) and the possibilities of Spanish American independence inspired Spanish Americans, Europeans, and Americans to realize the promise of an interoceanic canal. Humboldt identified nine isthmuses for this "communication," including the Isthmus of Panama. "Should a canal of communication be opened between the two oceans," Humboldt boasted, "the productions of *Nootka Sound* and of *China* will be brought more than 2000 leagues nearer to Europe and the United States." US merchant-adventurer William Davis Robinson argued that the emancipation of Spanish America offered an ideal moment to carve out a canal. Robinson wrote his popular *Memoirs of the Mexican Revolution* (1820) to recount his experiences fighting for Mexican independence; he also used it to propose a canal between the Gulf of Mexico and the Pacific Ocean. Relying on Robinson's *Memoirs*, the *National Advocate* argued that "the prospect of a valuable trade between the Pacific and Atlantic Oceans is of the first importance to this country, and our government will not fail to cultivate very project having in view its beneficial promotion."[33]

US citizens recognized that a canal to the south would overcome the vast expanse of North America. In the early to mid-nineteenth century, US citizens had three options to reach the Pacific Ocean: an inland route from the Missouri River to the Columbia River, a voyage around Cape Horn, or an inland journey across Panama. The Corps of Discovery had taken roughly seventeen months to travel from St. Charles, Missouri, to the Pacific Ocean, but the journey around Cape Horn was also arduous. Capt. James Biddle warned John Quincy Adams that traveling to "the Pacific Ocean and the Columbia River" proved "a long and distant voyage" that required "additional preparations & inquiries." Departing from Rio de Janeiro, Biddle achieved his fifty-five-day voyage to Valparaíso, Chile, by sailing around Cape Horn, which was not "a very small affair." By contrast, Robinson claimed that a canal would shorten the voyage from the United States to China to *"sixty-three* days."[34]

Whereas a vast continental interior separated the United States from the Pacific world, Mexican policymakers believed a canal could conquer topographical challenges and secure national boundaries. Mountainous terrain and unnavigable rivers separated Acapulco—Mexico's main port on the Pacific coast—from the populous and wealthy central plateau. Mexican policymakers argued that an interoceanic canal could help them conquer geographical barriers and consolidate their settlements in sparsely populated, Indigenous-controlled regions. Similar to the United States' weak settler presence in the Columbia River basin, Mexico lacked a significant creole population on the Isthmus of Tehuantepec. Inspired by Humboldt, Mexican politician Tadeo Ortiz viewed settlements and canal projects as mutually reinforcing elements of Mexico's future prosperity. A canal carved through the isthmus would compel the Mexican government to encourage creoles to consolidate authority in Tehuantepec—a region occupied by the Zapotec Mayas. A settler population, Ortiz reasoned, would protect the isthmus from invasion by a European power and provide the necessary labor force to maintain the canal and develop the region's agriculture. These colonists would export "all the productions of the Pacific coast" and the coffee and sugar of Central America for Atlantic and Pacific markets. As a consequence, the Isthmus of Tehuantepec would "change the face of the commerce of China and India."[35]

Bolívar believed that a canal across the Isthmus of Panama would allow Gran Colombia to realize its transcontinental destiny. In 1819, he imagined Gran Colombia "as the very heart of the universe, its far-flung shores spreading between those oceans which Nature kept apart but which our country will have joined by imposing a system of extensive canals." But to become the "emporium of the human race," Gran Colombia would have to secure its presence on the Pacific coast. Mountains, jungles, and rivers divided Gran

Colombia, making the Pacific lowlands difficult to reach. In the colonial era, Spaniards and creoles forced enslaved miners to extract the lowland's gold and spent little of their earnings on internal improvements and permanent settlements. Bolívar had reasons to sponsor a canal project beyond commerce. During the war for independence, El Libertador transported his armies across Panama to shrink "the immense distance" between the Atlantic and Pacific regions of South America. Bolívar also struggled to control the republic's westernmost regions when Guayaquil (present-day Ecuador) overthrew Spanish rule in October 1820. An invaluable port and naval base in the Pacific, Guayaquil was formerly part of colonial New Granada and coveted by Peru. Minister of Foreign Affairs Pedro Gual stressed in an 1822 letter to Bolívar that the republic had "no effective outlets in the Pacific other than those of Panamá and Guayaquil." No wonder, then, Bolívar recruited British army captain John Augustus Lloyd and Swede Maurice Falmarc to survey the Isthmus of Panama for a canal in 1827.[36]

Spanish American expatriates recognized that an interoceanic canal would help the United States overcome the obstacle of distance. Vicente Pazos Kanki suggested to US readers in 1819 that an interoceanic canal would foster the growth of a US settlement in the Columbia River basin. "Next to Peru and Mexico," Kanki commented, "the United States are more interested in this splendid project than any other nation, on account of their proximity to South America, their commerce with the East Indies, and precious metals of Peru and Mexico, the furs of Nootka Sound, and their establishment at the Columbia river, on the Pacific ocean." Agreeing with Kanki, "A Native of Cusco" argued that "the northwestern territory of the *United States* . . . has a deep stake" in a canal because "the fatigues of the journey might be diminished."[37]

Spanish American expatriates' arguments addressed the concerns about distance and settlement that had deterred US policymakers from supporting expansion to the Pacific coast. As Spanish Americans achieved independence in the early 1820s, Congress debated the establishment of a permanent military outpost in the Columbia River basin. Beginning in 1821, Virginia representative John Floyd and like-minded expansionists attempted on several occasions to pass a bill in the House to occupy and fortify the Columbia River basin. Floyd viewed the Pacific Northwest as a means to command the entire Pacific Ocean trade. However, Floyd encountered fierce opposition to his proposal. In early 1823, Kentucky representative James Breckinridge warned Floyd that "the wholesome blood which flowed from the heart of this confederacy cannot reach the confines of Oregon." Believing the republic's resources and populations were already too overstretched, he asked his fellow congressmen if the United States was "prepared to protect the territorial or commercial rights of the people of Oregon?" Distance, he warned, made any journey arduous. Whereas a seabound trip to the Columbia River would "be worse than a voyage to the East Indies," Breckinridge claimed that the members of the overland Corps of Discovery Expedition "would have starved, had they not made food of their own dogs!"[38]

US expansionists employed the discourse about interoceanic canals to conquer these fears. For US expansionists, a canal would allow settlers to avoid the arduous journey around Cape Horn or across the North American continent to reach the Columbian River basin. Indeed, the *Scioto Gazette* predicted in 1825 that a canal through the "Isthmus of Tehuantepec" would save "12,000 miles . . . in a voyage from the Metropolis of the Republic to its infant colony at Astoria." A supporter of Floyd's proposals, Massachusetts representative Francis Baylies argued in 1826 that a canal in Central America rendered a settler colony invaluable and realistic. A fortified settlement in the Pacific Northwest, Baylies stressed, would already benefit from its proximity to countries "filled with precious metals, and with the richest articles of commerce." However, Baylies understood how "these advantages . . . will be trifling in comparison to what will be, whenever a water communication between the Atlantic and Pacific oceans . . . shall have been effected."[39]

Spanish American and US policymakers reasoned that an interoceanic canal would help safeguard their national boundaries and ward off rival powers from encroaching on their claimed territories. However, the commercial prospects of independent Spanish America also enticed Russia and Great Britain. In 1821, Russia issued an infamous ukase (proclamation) that declared its hegemony in the Pacific Northwest as far south as 51 degrees, threatening the United States' claims to the Columbia River basin and challenging Mexico's control over Upper California. The Russians, Tadeo Ortiz observed in 1822, likely found their way to California because of its "rich productions and excellent ports for the Mexican trade between Lima and China." Spanish American and US policymakers regarded Russia's advance in the Pacific Northwest as an aspect of the Holy Alliance's crusade against republicanism. A coalition of European monarchies, the Holy Alliance sought to reimpose colonial rule over Spanish America. At the same time,

Americans worried about British designs for the Pacific Northwest. The Treaty of 1818 promised joint occupation of Oregon by the United States and Great Britain—an agreement that did not reflect reality for Chinookan-speaking peoples on the ground. Nonetheless, the *Louisville Public Advertiser* regarded the Transcontinental Treaty as "a great national event" because it allowed the United States to halt Great Britain, who endeavored "to weave herself into the affairs of . . . Chili and Peru, whence she may give us . . . trouble on the Columbia River."[40]

Responding to European threats, US citizens and policymakers issued declarations and doctrines of their own. And, in doing so, Americans continued to imagine how cooperation with Spanish America would secure their future on the Pacific coast. Many Americans embraced Clay's call for Pan-American resistance against European monarchies. In a letter to Jefferson, Hugh White of the "Columbian Union Society"—composed of rural Pennsylvanians with hemispheric ambitions—proposed "a grand Convention" between the "Southern New Born Sons of Liberty" and the "Northern Republic" to respond to the "falsely so Calld" Holy Alliance. The Society's "Select Brothers" urged Jefferson to support "the First Real union of the immense Collumbian Nation," which would meet either "in the City of—Mexico (or Cusko)." White considered Pan-Americanism as a means not only to resist encroaching Europeans but also to promote US territorial expansion. "Incalculable advantages Can be Aquired by this meeting," White continued, "especially the Long Contemplated Canal To unite the Waters of the Atlantic & pacific oceans; & More Especialy Wher a permanant Settlement is to be Established on the Collumbia River." White concluded that addressing the canal and settlement questions "Would Immediately consolidate a Wester nation settlement" by encouraging "the annual Swarms of opressed uropeans" to flock to the Pacific coast instead of the Atlantic. The audacious proposal of the Collumbian Union Society illustrated how Americans imagined pacific cooperation with Spanish America in their efforts to expand to the Pacific coast.[41]

The Monroe administration captured the sentiments of Americans such as the Collumbian Union Society members in the Monroe Doctrine. In his 1823 message to Congress, Monroe asserted the nation's intolerance toward *future* European colonization of the Americas. Instead, the Western Hemisphere—still largely under the control of independent Indigenous nations—would be reserved for settlement by the American republics of North and South America. The Monroe Doctrine signaled a foreign policy that advocated cooperation with Spanish America; took an anticolonial stance toward Europe; and implicitly promoted imperial expansion into lands controlled by Indigenous nations. The doctrine's architect, John Quincy Adams, also eschewed Russia's claims to the Pacific Northwest. "Independence meant," Adams wrote, "the Pacific Ocean, in every part of it, will remain open to the Navigation of all nations, in like manner with the Atlantic." As their struggles to control the fate of Cuba suggest, US policymakers could not enforce the doctrine's principles. The United States nevertheless convinced Tsar Alexander I to revoke the ukase and accept US claims to the Pacific Northwest south of 54'40 degrees latitude in 1824.[42]

As Spanish Americans secured their independence and European powers sought to reimpose colonial rule, US expansionists further connected their future in the Pacific Northwest with the new republics. In the early 1820s, American, Colombian, and Mexican politicians imagined how an interoceanic canal could help them overcome the geographic and spatial barriers that prevented them from consolidating their national boundaries. Rival powers—European, Euro-American, or Indigenous—had ambitions for the contested spaces of Oregon, Guayaquil, and Tehuantepec. Whether members of Monroe's cabinet or the Collumbian Union Society, US citizens connected anticolonialism, canals, and Spanish America with their future on the Pacific coast. This Pan-American unity, however, did not last. When Bolívar proposed a congress be held in Panama in 1826, Americans were less enthusiastic about their southern neighbors than ever before.[43]

## SEIZING SPANISH AMERICA'S DESTINY

Despite their expectations for Spanish America, US expansionists had become increasingly anxious about their republic's future in the Pacific Northwest by the mid-1820s. Oregon appeared far from destined to join the United States. Instead, except for a few forts, the Columbia River basin remained controlled by Chinookan-speaking peoples, who dominated the region's extensive trade networks. In 1823, Jedidiah Smith and his fellow American trappers reached the lower Snake River, which fed into the Columbia River. Smith encountered a British Hudson's Bay Company (HBC) trapping brigade led by former Astorian Alexander Ross, who boasted about the fertility and productivity of the Snake River country. Ross excited US adventurers about the potential of the Snake River country, which resulted in his transfer. But this interaction also underscored the growing imperial competition in the Pacific Northwest. British forts in the Columbia River basin convinced Lewis A. Tarascon to galvanize support for establishing a wagon road that connected the Missouri River to the Columbia River. His 1824 circular encapsulated all the arguments for the potential of Spanish America to consolidate US authority over the Pacific Northwest. Tarascon believed that the "Bay of Columbia" would be the base to "prevent any European or Asiatic power from colonizing the western coasts of America"; a point from which they could "best protect our friends—the Chilians, Peruvians, Colombians, Guatimalians and Mexicans, on the Pacific"; and "an important mart for Asiatic and American goods" where they could "obtain specie" from the Spanish Americans. Tarascon tied the United States' future on the Pacific coast with Pan-American fervor. He warned Americans that the republic needed to shore up the Columbia River basin to be "well secured against all possible contingencies" in the event of another war.[44]

Louisianian James Bradford also urged US policymakers to seize the Pacific Northwest. In late 1824, he requested that US senator Josiah Stoddard Johnston rally congressional support for his plans to erect "a collonial establishment on the Pacific" north of California. "If that is not done," Bradford warned, "depend upon it an effort will be made to purchase the country between the northern settlement of California and our limits on the Pacific and the advantages our country would derive from such an establishment will be transferred to Mexico."[45]

US policymakers, however, remained less concerned about Mexico and more worried about the presence of Great Britain. Though the United States and Great Britain agreed to jointly occupy the Oregon Country, HBC fur traders increased their activity in the Pacific Northwest in the mid-1820s. Britons established new forts near the Pacific coast and in the continental interior. These forts would allow them to control the fur trade and check US expansion. Indeed, in the 1820s, the HBC sought to create "a fur desert" in the Snake River basin to deter US fur traders from making overland journeys. British policymakers sought to use the activities of the HBC to shore up trade with Chinookan-speaking merchants as well as to block US expansion. Secretary of State for Foreign Affairs George Canning worried about US expansion in the Pacific Northwest and regretted the "return" of

Astoria to the United States. Though Astoria remained occupied by British fur traders, Canning lamented the joint occupation. He believed that Astoria's location would allow British merchants to directly influence the budding trade between "China and Mexico." In 1825, the HBC eliminated any contingencies by establishing Fort Vancouver roughly one hundred miles north of Astoria. From this fort, HBC merchants launched expeditions to monopolize the trade of the interior and southern Columbia River basin—hoping to secure the river as Canada's southwestern boundary. In 1826 or 1827, Indigenous peoples, most likely members of the Clatsops or Chinooks, burned Fort George down. Largely occupied by British and French Canadians, Fort George (formerly Astoria) had served as the United States' primary claim to a transcontinental republic.[46]

The destruction of Fort George complemented US policymakers' and citizens' disillusionment with expansion to the Pacific coast. In 1825, the bill to establish a military outpost on the Columbia River basin passed in the House but was not voted on in the Senate. North Carolina representative Lewis Williams did not vote in favor of a military post on the Pacific coast. Williams regurgitated many conventional arguments against expansion to the coast in a circular letter to his constituents. He believed it would be roughly "fifty or a hundred years" before Euro-Americans could properly settle the region. Even then, he doubted the "policy of going beyond the Rocky mountains[;] for it seems . . . the people who may inhabit that region, never can be included within the body of this Union." Unable to predict the rapid US migrations to the Pacific Northwest over the next two decades, US expansionist R. L. Colt argued in 1829 that "a great majority of the good people of this Country . . . are very anxious to get rid of the Oregon territory." Colt believed that securing the "Rio del Nord" as a southern border and the "East Summit of the Rocky Mountains" as a western boundary would be "a great gain" for the United States. Even as US settlers flocked to Oregon in the wake of the Panic of 1837, the fate of the Pacific Northwest remained murky until President James Polk secured the 49th parallel.[47]

Disappointment with early commercial interactions with Peru and Chile exacerbated US policymakers' anxiety over their presence in the Pacific world. In the 1810s and early 1820s, US citizens relied on Spanish Americans' optimistic plans to remake commerce in the Pacific world. While some merchants and expansionists held out hope, Americans pointed to the disappointing trade with Chileans and Peruvians in the mid-1820s. Blockades and political instability convinced US policymakers to maintain the Pacific squadron's presence near the shores of Peru and Chile. For such reasons, merchants and diplomats frequently warned about the risks of establishing commercial enterprises in those countries.

Peruvians had won their long, destructive war for independence in 1824 (though some Spanish forces remained until 1826). This lengthy conflict rendered Peru an unattractive market for US merchants. In 1824, US consul William Tudor cautioned Boston merchant Thomas Handasyd Perkins that "commerce has been almost extinct" in Lima and that "it must be some time before the [quicksilver] mines can be put into full operation." In another letter to Perkins, Tudor advised against "connecting... with any establishment here for the present" given the "distracted and uncertain state of the country." Perkins still hoped that if royalists or patriots seized control of Peru, "something brilliant" could be done "to the fabricks of this country" and that Lima might become a market for traders bound for Canton. As late as 1826, Connecticut merchant Daniel Wadsworth Coit complained that instability prevented Peru from realizing its commercial potential. If peace could be had there, Coit stressed, "trade might flourish and prosper." But overall, Tudor concluded in 1827 that trade in Lima "is not brilliant."[48]

Americans also tempered their hopes for Chile. In the 1810s, Americans such as Theodorick Bland boasted that Chile's independence would benefit American commerce and territorial expansion. In 1817 and mid-1818, Bland's prediction seemed plausible, given that twenty-seven American ships entered Valparaíso and Coquimbo compared to twenty-three British ships. Several of these ship crews docked at Chilean ports to acquire specie and wheat en route to Canton, the Marquesas Islands, and the Columbia River basin. However, Supreme Director Bernardo O'Higgins favored monarchical Britons over US merchants, fearing their republican ideals undermined his authority in Chile. Consequently, British ships outnumbered American vessels at Chilean ports by 1819.[49]

American merchants employed racism and old tropes about Spanish colonialism to explain their lackluster trade with Chileans. In Valparaíso, New Englander Isaac Foster Coffin complained in the early 1820s that Chileans had "all the pride & prejudice of old Spaniards, but are infinitely less enlightened & of course infinitely less susceptible of the improvements of commerce." A champion of free trade, Coffin also grumbled that government officials proved "extremely inexperienced in the great, fundamental and reciprocal principles of commerce" and therefore placed "duties upon foreign merchandise." Not all the blame could be placed on O'Higgins and Chileans, however. In 1827, US Consul Michael Hogan wrote to US diplomat Joel Roberts Poinsett that "our nation three years ago stood highest of any in intercourse with this coast." Hogan lamented that there "were no gentlemen amongst us North Americans" in Chile, as US merchants possessed "a penury & poverty of mind and ignorance of the common courtesies of life."[50]

Faith in Spanish America's capacity to alter the Pacific world weakened after canal speculation simmered by the late 1820s. Throughout the decade, multinational enterprises vied to identify the ideal canal location and subsequently control the interoceanic flow of commerce. Such hopes inspired policymakers in the Central American Republic, who sought to carve a canal through Lake Nicaragua. In an 1825 letter to Secretary of State Adams, Central American Republic minister Antonio José Cañaz proposed a "foreign co-operation" to build a canal that would produce "the general prosperity of the two worlds." Fearing British involvement, Adams and later Clay rejected these proposals, arguing that no nation should take over the canal project. As such, the Central American Republic turned to a company bidding process. In 1826, President Manuel José Arce and his congress selected the bid of US citizen Aaron H. Palmer to construct a canal. But Palmer's efforts quickly collapsed due to topographical obstacles and instability spurred by a civil war that began when Arce refused to accept electoral defeat. US diplomat John Williams attributed Central America's inability to capitalize on its "rich land" to Acre's dictatorship. "The failure here at Representative Government," Williams decried, "has grieved me to the heart." Palmer's shortcomings and the instability of Central America dampened canal fever by 1827.[51]

Williams's comments conveyed a broader disillusionment with Spanish America. Increasingly, Americans labeled Spanish America as unstable and antirepublican. This sentiment was most apparent in southern politicians' rejection of sending ministers to the Panama congress of 1826. When the Adams administration intended to send Richard Anderson Jr. and John Sergeant to Panama City, Adams and Secretary of State Henry Clay received vitriol from Andrew Jackson's supporters in Congress. Politically, Senators John M. Berrien and John Randolph of Roanoke channeled opposition to the congress to assail Adams and Clay in the wake of the "corrupt bargain" of 1824–25. But their critique of US involvement extended beyond domestic politics. Political instability in the new nations tested US audiences' faith in the universality of republicanism while the cotton industry entrenched slavery and intensified racism in the South. Southerners also feared that Mexicans and Colombians intended to use the Pan-American congress to plot an invasion of Cuba—a scheme that might incite a slave revolt near US shores. For these reasons, southern politicians hardened racial boundaries between Anglo-Americans and Spanish Americans, lambasting their geopolitical neighbors as incapable republicans.[52]

Hidden beneath the belief that Spanish America failed to meet its expectations lay US citizens' fears about Britons' commercial and diplomatic success with the republics. British merchants made appealing trade partners for Spanish Americans. From Mexico to Buenos Aires, Spanish Americans coveted British manufactures and capital. Britons also celebrated Mexico's potential to bolster the global economy. Mexico's silver placed the republic, diplomat Henry George Ward argued, "almost in the first rank of *consuming* nations." British merchants outperformed Americans in the new nations, including Mexico, Chile, and Gran Colombia. Moreover, Mexico had borrowed £6.4 million through interest-bearing bonds in the mid-1820s, allowing the British to influence the nascent nation. British success there troubled Americans. Poinsett complained that British diplomats fostered an anti-American sentiment by convincing Mexicans that "we were the natural Enemies of Mexico." Diplomat Richard Rush interpreted British success with Spanish America as a sign of a potential alliance detrimental to US interests. "It might seem strange, at first," Rush predicted in 1824, "if our next foreign war should be with England . . . having Colombia as her ally." But, as Rush reminded Pennsylvania politician Jonathan Roberts, "stranger things have happened in the history of states."[53]

Mexico received the brunt of Americans' frustration. Certainly, brewing tensions over the Provincia de Texas sharpened the critique of Mexico. Beginning in 1823, waves of Anglo-American settlers flocked to Mexican Texas, seeking to escape economic hardship in the United States and enticed by Mexico's generous land grants to new settlers. The growing presence of Anglo-Americans alarmed Mexican policymakers and increased US interest in the Mexican province. American merchants and diplomats, however, were also disappointed over the lackluster trade with their fellow North Americans. After a lengthy revolution (1810–21), Mexico gained independence as an empire, became a republic in 1823, and had a federal constitution by 1824. Embracing their republic's transcontinental destiny, Mexican officials envisioned that their agricultural products and metals would find markets worldwide and economic liberalism would vanquish bankruptcy. However, Mexico's silver industry did not recover from years of fighting until the mid-nineteenth century. US traders received coins minted in Mexico that lacked uniformity in weight and quality compared to Spain's common monetary standard that had previously appealed to Canton merchants. As such, US merchants in the 1820s turned increasingly to trading in opium, reducing the need for silver. Moreover, to the disappointment of US merchants, Mexicans continued to favor British and European traders. In 1825, the United States received 57 percent of Mexico's commodity exports. By 1830, however, that percentage had dipped to 26 percent as Mexico exported 39 percent of its commodities to Great Britain and 23 percent to France. At the same time, US exports to Mexico dropped from $882,996 in 1824–25 to $481,190 in 1828–29. US consul William Taylor stressed these fluctuations resulted from the reality that US merchants had previously depended on reexports of European manufactures to trade with Spanish Americans. "Our intercourse is declining very rapidly with this Country," Williams complained in August 1826, "as most of the goods . . . are now imported direct from Europe." Writing to Poinsett in 1827, French American Peter Stephen Du Ponceau complained that "Baron Humboldt . . . has given exaggerated views of the Country [of Mexico]." But Humboldt, he added, was "not the only one."[54]

The inter-American discourse that underscored Spanish America's commercial potential had also shaped the justifications for the United States to seize Mexico's far north (present-day Texas, California, New Mexico, Utah, Nevada, Arizona, and parts of Colorado). Spanish Americans' visions of commercial greatness always possessed the potential to spark imperial ambitions. After all, US readers encountered countless passages about Mexico's capacity to alter Pacific commerce. By reading Humboldt's essay, they learned about the defenseless and fertile Alta California. As early as 1818, John Bartow Prevost had alerted Adams to California's potential and of the Russians' desire for the Spanish colony. "The speculations of Humboldt, and his glowing description of the soil and climate of this province," Prevost warned, "have probably given a new direction of ambition of Russia, and determined its Emperor to the acquisition of empire in America." Similar to Humboldt, Prevost remarked that "the port of St. Francis [San Francisco Bay] is one of the most convenient, extensive, and safe in the world, wholly without defence, and in the neighborhood of a feeble, diffused, and disaffected population."

"Under all these circumstances, may we not infer views to the early possession of this harbor," Prevost wondered, "and ultimately to the sovereignty of entire California?"[55]

California's economic dependence on the United States reinforced these beliefs. Mexico's far north became increasingly dependent on US trade in the 1820s. After 1821, Mexican officials opened Alta California's ports to foreign ships, appealing to Anglo-Americans and Europeans. Observing the US ships docked at Santa Barbara a year later, Friar José Señán prayed to God to not "permit these foreigners to take too much of a liking to this Province and then, under free trade, cause the prophecies of certain politicians regarding the Californias to come true!" Meanwhile, US settlers sought new opportunities or a chance to evade debt by heading to Texas to acquire land, while the Santa Fe Trail (opened in 1821) enticed Missourians to trade with Mexico. Receiving vague instructions from Mexico City, Mexican officials welcomed foreign merchants to acquire manufactured goods. Such policies troubled Tadeo Ortiz, who already feared that the "new colony of Columbia" would enable Americans to surround "the Mexican empire from the Atlantic to the Pacific."[56]

These economic changes convinced William Davis Robinson that Mexico's far north appeared up for grabs as early as 1820. The adventurer wrote that "the population of the United States is rapidly rolling towards the Mexican settlements." As St. Louis blossomed into a fur-trading hub, Robinson marveled at the "peculiar manner in which nature" connected St. Louis to Monterey. He encouraged his readers to "anticipate the future importance of this country, when a government made by and for the people shall there be established." Robinson hinted that this "government made by and for the people" could be the United States.[57]

To stake their claims to this contested region, US expansionists twisted the international discourse about Spanish America to argue that Mexicans had failed to realize their territories' economic and commercial promise. Influenced by legends of precious metals and bountiful natural resources, Americans believed that regions such as Mexico's far north held immense potential. By the mid-1820s, however, US expansionists employed racist and anti-Catholic arguments that depicted Mexicans as incapable of capitalizing on the resources of California and Texas. When the Atlantic and Pacific Ship Canal Company bill was introduced in the British House of Commons in 1825, the *Scioto Gazette* maintained that a "canal thro' the Isthmus of Costa

Rica" would resolve Mexico's economic woes. "When this object shall be accomplished," the paper continued, "the prosperity of Mexico will be as rapid as her oppression has been great and continued." The newspaper's tone suggested an intensifying skepticism toward Mexico as well as a desire for its resource-rich land. Some writers were more overt. In 1829, "A Patriot" proposed the Rio Grande as an international boundary, believing that the fertile land north of the river proved "every way desirable to the people of the United States." By contrast, the land south of the river was "unproductive" and therefore "entirely calculated for a lazy, pastoral, mining people like the Mexicans." Such rhetoric implied that only Anglo-Americans could capitalize on the rich natural resources of western North America.[58]

Such misguided beliefs served as justifications to demand Mexico's far north. Although the Adams administration demanded provinces as far south as Sonora and Baja California, the Treaty of Limits (1828) retained the boundaries of the Transcontinental Treaty. Nonetheless, US expansionists had become convinced that they could better realize the commercial potential of Mexico's Pacific territories. In the late 1820s, expansionist George Flower maintained that the United States needed to acquire California to prevent it from falling into British hands. A decade earlier, prorevolutionary Americans began imagining how Spanish American independence would sustain settlements on the Pacific coast. But when such projections failed to materialize, US expansionists began arguing that Mexico represented the means by which their republic would achieve its transcontinental form. "The Peninsula of California affords the best, and most numerous harbours on the pacific," Flower commented. "The possession of this peninsula would form a destined southwestern boundary to the US." He stressed that Mexico would be unable to maintain California and reasoned that "the increase of faction, imbecility, and embarrassment in the Mexican Government"—sparked by rebellions in response to the victory of Manuel Gómez Pedraza in the presidential election of 1828 and the country's bankruptcy—provided an "auspicious period for the peaceable acquisition by purchase."[59]

Rather than a peaceable acquisition, the United States annexed California through war. Historians have underscored how antebellum expansionists craved Oregon and California for their coastal territory. While they recognized California's fertile lands, presidents from Andrew Jackson to James K.

Polk desired the Columbia River basin, San Francisco, and San Diego to gain a greater foothold in the Pacific world. In the 1830s and 1840s, expansionists fixated on California's and Oregon's significance to the Pacific world. Rather than canals, settlers benefitted from improved inland routes, the development of steam power, and later railroads. Attempting to convince the United States to annex California, settler John J. Warner maintained that the distance between the East and West Coasts would be mollified not by a canal but instead by the construction of the transcontinental railroad. In 1835, Jackson attempted to purchase San Francisco from Mexico. Where Old Hickory failed, Young Hickory succeeded. As they negotiated a boundary with Great Britain in Oregon Country, Polk and his fellow expansionists pursued a war against Mexico (1846–48), which secured a boundary at the Rio Grande—and unintentionally propelled the United States toward civil war.[60]

These advocates of manifest destiny argued that US expansion to the Pacific coast was inevitable. This rhetoric would have surprised even the most optimistic expansionists in the first three decades of the nineteenth century. US policymakers struggled to imagine how a settler colony on the Pacific coast would develop rapidly and remain attached to the American union. US settlers hoped that Astoria would secure the fur trade of the Pacific Northwest and serve as a waypoint en route to East Asia. But distance and competition with Chinookan-speaking peoples and European settlers undermined these aspirations. Given the distance between the Columbia River basin and the eastern United States, many Americans articulated several expansionist imaginings such as a separate republic on the Pacific coast or an American republic halted at the Rocky Mountains.

To overcome these fears, US expansionists embraced Spanish Americans' vision of independence. In the early nineteenth century, Spanish American creoles envisioned transforming the commercial world with their transcontinental nations, precious metals, ports on the Pacific Ocean, and interoceanic canals. This vision had been exposed to international audiences, who crafted a transnational discourse about the potential of independent Spanish America. Spanish American expatriates and US expansionists argued that free-trading, independent Spanish American republics would foster the development of the Pacific Northwest. Chilean and Peruvian markets would encourage economic growth and settlement along the Columbian River basin, providing Astorians with specie and precious metals to trade with China and India. Transcontinental nations such as Gran Colombia and

Mexico would sponsor canal projects that would shrink the distance between the United States and the Pacific coast. These visions of Spanish American independence helped Americans imagine how a settler colony on the Pacific coast would thrive and remain attached to the United States.

When independent Spanish America did not live up to these lofty expectations upon immediate independence, however, US policymakers and expansionists reinterpreted the vision to justify annexing California and Mexico's far north. US expansionists erased the political universalism and modernity taking root in Spanish America and instead portrayed those nations as incapable of republican government and capitalism. What had been an anticolonial, mutually reinforcing fantasy of Pacific expansion had become the aggressive, imperialistic language associated with manifest destiny. In the infamous 1845 piece in the *United States Magazine and Democratic Review,* John O'Sullivan argued that California's potential could be best realized by the "Anglo-Saxon" race. Mexico proved too "imbecile and distracted" to "exert any real government authority over such a country"—stunting "the province of all natural growth." He exclaimed: "There is no growth in Spanish America!" The *Democratic Review* added that Mexican policies denied the development and fulfillment of California's "capabilities" and "purposes of creation." With the "Anglo-Saxon foot . . . already on the borders," California would realize its "immense utility to the commerce of the world with the whole eastern Asia." In the decades before antebellum expansionists clamored for war against Mexico, however, Americans imagined spreading their nation from sea to shining sea with the help of their southern sister republics.[61]

# CONCLUSION

Joel Roberts Poinsett witnessed many great events unfold during his travels across the Old and New Worlds. As a young man, he journeyed throughout Napoleonic Europe and watched as republican forces besieged the strongholds of the *ancien régime*. He dined with Russian nobles, trekked the Caucuses, and even conversed with a Persian khan. President James Madison instructed Poinsett in 1810 to observe the revolutions in Chile and Buenos Aires; later, the South Carolinian became the United States' first minister to Mexico in 1825. Despite these exhilarating experiences, Poinsett remained captivated by the rapid expansion of his home country, the United States of America. The itinerant diplomat wrote to a British friend in the autumn of 1832, boasting about the expansion of "frontier settlers" across North America. "I wish you could come and see Man develloping all his energies in this vast and fertile country," Poinsett exclaimed, "contending and overcoming every obstacle opposed to his progress by nature and rapidly extending his domain from the Atlantic to the Pacific."[1]

Poinsett's celebratory remarks in 1832 reveal much of how US expansionists increasingly imagined their republic's aggrandizement in the antebellum era (1830s–50s). Roughly a decade later, antebellum Americans interpreted this seemingly unstoppable movement as their nation's manifest destiny to spread democratic institutions from the Atlantic to the Pacific Oceans. By fixating on Anglo-Americans' rapid westward movement, Poinsett glossed over decades of fits and frustrations.

*Before Manifest Destiny* has stressed that reading manifest destiny back into earlier decades obscures the wide range of assumptions and geopolitical contests that informed how US policymakers undertook their republic's expansion. This conventional narrative erases the multitude of expansionist imaginings of North America and its dependencies, its unrealized geopolitical schemes and rival visions. It strips the story of different directions and possibilities that do not reflect the modern continental boundaries of the United States. It assumes that US policymakers from Benjamin Franklin to James K. Polk successfully imagined and achieved the creation of a westward-bound, transcontinental republic. It shrouds Indigenous hegemony and resistance. It masks fears about neighboring free Black nations and European powers. It rejects the notion that Anglo-Americans would consolidate their national boundaries alongside their Spanish American allies. It portrays frustrated plans to acquire spaces such as Bermuda, Upper Canada, and Cuba as mere blips. It takes the annexation of the Tennessee Valley, Michigan, and the Pacific Northwest for granted. The narrative of manifest destiny left little room for uncertainty and contingency.

This book has uncovered thwarted destinies imagined before antebellum expansionists touted their republic's fate to spread from Maine to California. Between the 1770s and 1820s, US policymakers pursued un-manifest and unfulfilled plans for Bermuda, the Tennessee Valley, Upper Canada, Cuba, and the Pacific Northwest. The in-the-moment interest in these elusive spaces disrupts the notion that leaders of the early republic realized a consistent vision for the United States' expansion. Diplomats, politicians, territorial officials, merchants, and citizens all articulated dynamic imaginings for the union's future boundaries. Some Americans envisioned extensive boundaries, while others sought to impose limits to the Mississippi River or the Rocky Mountains. Whereas a New England soothsayer predicted in 1817 that the United States would annex Canada, Jamaica, and Kamchatka (present-day eastern Russia) by the twenty-first century, a newspaper editor assumed in 1819 that "N. America appears to have been designed by the Great Creator, for several Independent Governments." Far from imagining an embryonic manifest destiny, early US policymakers repeatedly envisioned, reworked, and abandoned destinies that never came to be.[2]

Fear motivated early republic policymakers to embrace this trial-and-error approach to expansion. During these first fifty years, US policymakers identified threats to their republic's survival in all directions. The new nation's military, naval, and financial weaknesses prevented policymakers from directing the Western Hemisphere's geopolitics. To make matters worse, the revolutionary turmoil of the late eighteenth- and early nineteenth-century Atlantic world accentuated the young republic's inability to shape the destiny of contested spaces. Revolutionary Americans dreaded proximity to the British Empire, worrying that British colonies would impede their free-trading aspirations in the Atlantic world and their new nation's stability in the West. Seemingly optimistic expansionists including Thomas Jefferson anticipated breakaway settler republics spawning beyond the Appalachian and Rocky Mountains. Racial anxieties also fueled expansionism. The loyalty of these westward-bound settlers depended on the removal of Native peoples and the spread of slavery in the South. To this end, these policymakers dreaded the consequences of encirclement by free Black populations and powerful Indigenous confederacies. Recovering the contests for elusive spaces such as Bermuda, Upper Canada, and Cuba reveals how US policymakers were far less confident about their nation's expansion. Moreover, US leaders' fears about the fate of the Tennessee Valley, the Michigan Territory, and the Pacific Northwest give little impression that westward expansion to the Pacific coast was inevitable.[3]

Competing visions for the Western Hemisphere exacerbated these fears. Constrained by geopolitical realities, US leaders were forced to engage with complementary and competing alternatives. On the shores of Bermuda, colonists envisioned their archipelago becoming a grand emporium for the Atlantic world amid the US War for Independence. Nestled along the Holston River, western settlers declared independence from North Carolina and championed the spread of republicanism across North America. Around the Great Lakes, Native nations forged loose military confederacies to carve up a pan-Indigenous state and limit the United States to the south and east of the Ohio River. To the south, people of African descent and Cuban planters interpreted the Haitian Revolution as an opportunity to reshape societal structures and economies. Elsewhere in the hemisphere, Spanish American creoles envisaged transforming the Atlantic and Pacific worlds with ocean-connecting canals, precious metals, and free trade. Throughout North America, European officials attempted to expand their empires and gain access to new markets. Bermudians, Franklinites, Native confederates, Black and white Cubans, Spanish Americans, and Europeans reinforced or thwarted the ambitions of US leaders.[4]

When Poinsett penned his letter to his British friend in 1832, several foundational elements associated with manifest destiny had calcified. Between the 1770s and 1820s, US leaders had increasingly touted their nation's supposedly unique role in spreading democracy across the continent, ridding North America of European colonization. By the end of the 1820s, Anglo-Americans had begun making economic and racist justifications for seizing northern Mexico. Masking deep racial anxieties, early republic leaders had pursued the removal of Indigenous peoples along international boundaries and sought to protect the institution of slavery by expanding their slaveholding union. The struggles to absorb Canada and Cuba rendered these territories secondary to the increasingly contested spaces of Texas, Oregon, and California.[5]

Manifest destiny came into clearer focus, however, only after many other destinies were denied. Elements of manifest destiny can certainly be found in the era of the early republic. But reading the antebellum ideology back into earlier decades masks the many thwarted destinies that came before. Early leaders of the republic contemplated a multitude of possibilities for the boundaries of the Americas that were no longer viable by the antebellum era. Nevertheless, these unfulfilled imaginings challenge the belief that a linear evolution in expansionist thought occurred between the American Revolution and the US-Mexico War. At the outset of independence, US policymakers considered Bermuda, Nova Scotia, and the Bahamas critical to their vision of an Atlantic-based, free-trading republic. After the War for Independence, the founders feared that hostile, breakaway states in the trans-Appalachian West would limit the republic to the Atlantic coast. Early nineteenth-century leaders sought to annex Upper Canada to avoid neighboring a powerful pan-Indigenous state in the Great Lakes. Despite their desire to rid the hemisphere of European powers, US policymakers sought to maintain Spanish rule in Cuba to prevent a second Haitian Revolution near Florida's shores. Before the United States invaded northern Mexico, US expansionists struggled to imagine sustaining a settlement on the Pacific coast without the cooperation and support of their Spanish American neighbors. The breakdown of these alternative destinies helped establish the expansionist beliefs and objectives of the antebellum era.[6]

The story of the early American republic's expansion proved contested, dynamic, and un-manifest. Poinsett's interpretation, however, would ultimately prevail for generations. Though not the first to celebrate the rapid movement of settlers, Poinsett wrote at a moment when Euro-Americans began reaching the Southwest and the Pacific coast in greater numbers. In the 1830s and 1840s, Euro-Americans flocked to Texas, California, and Oregon. Distinct economic, technological, and ideological changes were also beginning to transform the republic, influencing how Euro-Americans imagined expansion. Internal improvements shrank distances: roads, canals, and new transportation technology including steamships and later railroads reduced travel time and expedited trade. On the East Coast, industrialization and urbanization shook the economic and social fabric of American society, convincing many Anglo-Americans to seek opportunities in Indigenous and Mexican lands in the West. To justify their encroachment and the spread of slave labor in these lands, expansionists latched onto anti-Catholic tropes and misguided theories about the supposed racial superiority of Protestant "Anglo-Saxons." Masking deep fears about race, industrialization, and disunion, antebellum expansionists flattened the story of expansion by touting their republic's manifest destiny to dominate the continent.[7]

Advocates of manifest destiny would build on this narrative in the following decades. Antebellum expansionists argued that westward expansion was a continuous, inexorable movement that commenced with the founding of Jamestown and Plymouth and carried into their present day. "From the time that the Pilgrim Fathers landed on these shores to the present moment," the *New York Morning News* reported in 1845, "the older settlements have been constantly throwing off a hardy, restless and lawless pioneer population." At the will of Providence, these adventurers conquered "the wilderness" and prepared "the way for more orderly settlers who tread rapidly upon their footsteps." The piece concluded that this "natural" process would "continue until the waves of the Pacific have hemmed in and restrained the onward movement."[8]

President James K. Polk crafted the epilogue for this triumphant march across the continent. The mouthpieces and adventurers of manifest destiny provided Polk with ample ideological and demographic justifications to absorb the Far West. The United States annexed the ten-year-old Republic of Texas in late 1845 and admitted the former republic to the union as a state by February 1846, exacerbating relations with Mexico. Whereas he threatened conflict with Great Britain to secure the 49th parallel as the boundary in the Oregon Country, Polk pursued war outright with Mexico to seize the Southwest. The US-Mexico War concluded in 1848 with the signing of the Treaty of Guadalupe Hidalgo, which established the Rio Grande as an international boundary and ceded Alta California and New Mexico to the US republic for $15 million. By the end of his term, Polk had added over a million square miles to the republic, realizing his country's supposed manifest destiny.[9]

Antebellum Americans ensured that this flattened-out history of US expansion would persist for generations. Certainly, the Treaty of Guadalupe Hidalgo did not sate the appetites of every expansionist, who still craved Cuba, Mexico, Canada, Central America, and even the entire Western Hemisphere. However, Americans began solidifying a narrative that presented Anglo-American leaders and settlers in pursuit of an uncompromising vision of stretching their national domain from sea to sea. These Americans retroactively projected manifest destiny back into the colonial and early national eras, reinterpreting territorial acquisitions and settler invasions as part of a clearsighted plan to extend their dominion to the Pacific coast. In his unfinished history of territorial expansion, Democrat politician Charles Jared Ingersoll pointed to events, including the Louisiana Purchase, as evidence that "providence seem[ed] to have favored the destiny of young America." To craft this story, these expansionists worked backward from California to Virginia to explain how Providence guided their ancestors to expand from Jamestown to San Francisco.[10]

Subsequent generations of historians followed Ingersoll's lead, viewing westward expansion as a "continual process" akin to Frederick Jackson Turner's "frontier thesis" or as a well-executed plan conceived by policymakers. This narrative selectively focused on the grand predictions of optimistic Americans such as Benjamin Franklin, Thomas Jefferson, and John Quincy Adams to demonstrate a continuous desire to dominate North America. As US elites predicted America's transcontinental destiny, westward-bound settlers broke down the geopolitical murkiness and Indigenous autonomy of borderland regions, paving the way for American territorial government and later statehood. Thus, when John O'Sullivan and James K. Polk boasted about their republic's manifest destiny, these antebellum expansionists realized the aspirations of Franklin, Jefferson, and Adams.[11]

Yet as expansionists wrote about inevitability, the antebellum republic continued to encounter obstacles on its path to the Pacific coast. In many ways, Poinsett misconstrued both the past and the present. Certainly, the diplomat from South Carolina observed what appeared to be a seemingly unstoppable westward movement to the Pacific coast. However, these populations expanded into the Far West in part because they had previously met their limits in the maritime Atlantic East, the Caribbean South, and the Canadian North. Poinsett's belief that the United States overcame every obstacle hid the near loss of the Tennessee Valley and the Michigan Territory and downplayed the contested geopolitical situation of the Oregon Country. Though he reinterpreted the past, Poinsett also misunderstood his own times. Before and after Poinsett wrote his letter, Americans—Indigenous, Black, and white—articulated competing visions about the territorial makeup of North America and beyond. Indeed, just a few months prior, Sauk chief Black Hawk, a former ally of Tecumseh, waged war against the United States to reclaim land in Illinois taken by the Treaty of St. Louis (1804).[12]

Advocates of manifest destiny also struggled to conceal contemporary alternatives for the Americas. In the 1830s and 1840s, Anglo-American settlers formed breakaway republics in spaces such as Oregon, California, and Utah—republics that undermined John O'Sullivan's claim that the United States possessed a "manifest destiny to overspread the continent." Settler republics in Oregon and California, a Patriot rebellion in Upper Canada, and Indigenous resistance throughout the continent all reminded US expansionists that the future of North America remained murky. Polk's diplomacy with Great Britain and war with Mexico secured the Far West but did not stop antebellum Americans from proposing new expansionist imaginings. Indeed, in the late 1840s and 1850s, expansionists and proslavery filibusters articulated many unrealized territorial configurations that included Canada, Mexico, Cuba, Santo Domingo, Central America, and even South America. Rapid antebellum expansion intensified disunity over slavery's fate in the United States and unleashed a flurry of short-lived geopolitical schemes in the Civil War era, including the Confederate States of America. Amid today's calls for disunion in the United States, the contingent contest for North America remains unresolved.[13]

The modern boundaries of the United States and the many expansionist imaginings that came before would have surprised Benjamin Franklin. Though he once celebrated the rapid movement of Anglo-American settlers across North America, Franklin dreamed of a confederacy that had a far greater presence in the Atlantic world than on the continent. The many imaginings that followed Franklin's vision reveal the wide-ranging possibilities that existed for early Americans—possibilities that are hidden when narratives privilege inevitable continentalism. The common theme of US expansionism that persisted between the eras of Franklin and Polk was readaptation. Unable to overcome logistical, financial, and military constraints, US expansionists reworked and conceded their ambitions in response to competing visions expressed by the diverse inhabitants of the Americas. As Franklin knew all too well, the story of US expansion was one of unrealized destinies.

# NOTES

## INTRODUCTION

1. Benjamin Franklin, "Proposed Articles of Confederation," On or Before July 21, 1775, Founders Online; Gould, *Among the Powers of the Earth*, 1–2.
2. "Franklin's Sketch of Articles of Peace," [between December 10 and 13, 1782], Founders Online.
3. Isenberg and Richards, "Alternative Wests," 17. On expansionist fears, see Greenberg, *Manifest Manhood*; Hietala, *Manifest Design*.
4. Stourzh, *Franklin and American Foreign Policy*, 59. Several recent studies have quoted and supported Gerald Stourzh's assessment. See Immerman, *Empire for Liberty*, 15; Weeks, *New Cambridge History of American Foreign Relations*, 1:6–11. On Franklin's 1782 demands as a sign of manifest destiny, see Nugent, *Habits of Empire*, xvii. Other examples include Perkins, *Cambridge History of American Foreign Relations, Vol. 1*; Stephanson, *Manifest Destiny*, 15–21; Woods, *John Quincy Adams*, 379–80; Woodworth, *Manifest Destinies*, xi–xii.
5. On the contingency of North America, see Richards, *Breakaway Americas*, 6–14; St. John, "Unpredictable America of William Gwin," 56–84.
6. Isenberg and Richards, "Alternative Wests," 17. For works that have complicated our understanding of manifest destiny, see Burge, *Failed Vision of Empire*; Richards, *Breakaway Americas*, 6–14; St. John, "Unpredictable America of William Gwin," 76; Taylor, *American Republics*, xxiv. Historians have challenged the inevitability of US expansion by implementing Atlantic, borderlands, and continental frameworks. On recent Indigenous histories, see DeLay, *War of a Thousand Deserts*; Witgen, *Seeing Red*, 33–34. For the Atlantic framework, see Furstenberg, "Significance of the Trans-Appalachian Frontier," 659–60;

Gould, *Among the Powers of the Earth*. For an example of a continental study, see Hyde, *Empires, Nations, and Families*. For recent studies that have complicated the narrative of US expansion by situating it in broader global contexts, see Conroy-Krutz, *Christian Imperialism*; Immerwahr, *How to Hide an Empire*; Mills, *World Colonization Made*; Rouleau, *With Sails Whitening Every Sea*. For a recent overview of US empire, see Blaakman and Conroy-Krutz, introduction to *The Early Imperial Republic*, 3–23. On different understandings of geography and evolving mental maps, see St. John, "Contingent Continent," 18–49.

7. For more on fear and race driving US expansion, see Taylor, *American Republics*, xxiv. On securing republicanism, see Cogliano, *Emperor of Liberty*, 1–10; McCoy, *Elusive Republic*, 121–22; Onuf, *Jefferson's Empire*, 53–79. For more on the geopolitical motives, see Lewis, *American Union*; Stagg, *Borderlines in Borderlands*. On the importance of union, see Weeks, *New Cambridge History of American Foreign Relations, Vol. 1*.

8. For more on geopolitical and on-the-ground realities, see Cogliano, *Emperor of Liberty*, 1–10; Kastor, *Nation's Crucible*; Onuf, *Jefferson's Empire*, 55–56. On the role of Indigenous nations in thwarting US expansion and shaping geopolitics, see DeLay, *War of a Thousand Deserts*; Hämäläinen, *Comanche Empire*; Witgen, *Seeing Red*, 33–34. On expansion and fears of proximity to Black populations, see Rothman, *Slave Country*, x–xi.

9. For more on the instability of the revolutionary Atlantic world, see Griffin, *Age of Atlantic Revolution*, 7; Mongey, *Rogue Revolutionaries*, 1–8; Perl-Rosenthal, *Age of Revolutions*, 7–8; Taylor, *American Republics*, 110.

10. On the ideological beliefs of manifest destiny, see Horsman, *Race and Manifest Destiny*; Merk and Merk, *Manifest Destiny and Mission*, vii–ix, 24–60; Richards, *Breakaway Americas*, 8–9.

11. See Gould, *Among the Powers of the Earth*, 2–8; Yokota, *Unbecoming British*.

12. On US interest in Bermuda, see Jarvis, *In the Eye of All Trade*, ch. 6. On fear of proximity to Great Britain in the antebellum era, see Haynes, *Unfinished Revolution*, 204–27.

13. Barksdale, *Lost State of Franklin*; Roney, "Strange Afterlife of the Declaration of Independence."

14. For more on the contest for the Americas in the 1810s and 1820s, see Gould, *Among the Powers of the Earth*, 179–209; Taylor, *American Republics*, 135–39.

15. Histories that treat Michigan as a "native ground" include Nichols, *Peoples of the Inland Sea*; Witgen, *Infinity of Nations*; Witgen, *Seeing Red*. For more on Indigenous-settler relations, see White, *The Middle Ground*. On US interest in Canada, see Lennox, *North of America*.

16. Chambers, *No God but Gain*; Ferrer, *Freedom's Mirror*, 4–17; Ferrer, *Cuba*, 82–95; Karp, *This Vast Southern Empire*.

17. For more on US interest in the Spanish American Wars for Independence, see Fitz, *Our Sister Republics*.
18. For more on the notion of manifest destiny masking all the uncertainty of US expansion, see Isenberg and Richards, "Alternative Wests"; Richards, *Breakaway Americas*; St. John, "Unpredictable America of William Gwin."

# 1. BERMUDA

1. George Washington, "Address to the Inhabitants of Bermuda," September 6, 1775, Founders Online; Jarvis, *In the Eye of All Trade*, 384–92.
2. Gilje, "Commerce and Conquest," 735–37; Stagg, *Borderlines in Borderlands*, 14–15. On "facing east," see Richter, *Facing East from Indian Country*.
3. See Jarvis, *In the Eye of All Trade*, ch. 6; Kerr, *Bermuda and the American Revolution*.
4. For more on Anglophobia and expansionism, see Haynes, *Unfinished Revolution*, ch. 9.
5. Benjamin Franklin, "Proposed Articles of Confederation," On or Before July 21, 1775, Founders Online; John Adams, "I. A Plan of Treaties," June 18, 1776, Founders Online; Stagg, *Borderlines in Borderlands*, 14–15. On the British legacy of American expansionism, see Gould, *Among the Powers of the Earth*, 1–4; Onuf, *Jefferson's Empire*, 6–11, ch. 1; Weeks, *New Cambridge History of American Foreign Relations*, 1:xx. On the breakup of colonial connections in the Atlantic world, see Griffin, *Age of Atlantic Revolution*, 82–86.
6. Montesquieu, *Spirit of Laws*, 311; Armitage, *Ideological Origins of the British Empire*, 100, 173, 195; Breen, *Marketplace of the Revolution*; Gilje, "Conquest and Commerce," 737.
7. John Adams to Edmund Jenings, June 11, 1780, Founders Online; Paine, *Common Sense*, 86; Gould, *Among the Powers of the Earth*, 1–8, 93; Sadosky, *Revolutionary Negotiations*, 98–118; Griffin, *Age of Atlantic Revolution*, 16–17. On American efforts to garner Europeans' respect, see Yokota, *Unbecoming British*, 16–18.
8. John Adams to Patrick Henry, December 8, 1778, Founders Online; Stagg, *Borderlines in Borderlands*, 14–15; Robert Morris to Silas Deane, January 11, 1777, in Smith et al., eds., *Letters of Delegates to Congress, 1774–1789* (hereafter cited as *Letters of Delegates*), 6:84. For more on Nova Scotia during the American War for Independence, see Rawlyk, *Nova Scotia's Massachusetts*, 224, 248.
9. James Lovell to Samuel Holten, December 19, 1780, *Letters of Delegates*, 16:468; Jarvis, *In the Eye of All Trade*, 3–5. For more on Bermuda's connection to Virginia, see Glover and Smith, *Shipwreck that Saved Jamestown*, 212–44.

10. Nathaniel Tucker, *The Bermudian*, 1; George James Bruere, "Answer to the Queries relating to His Majesty's Island of Bermuda," Henry Strachey Papers (1768–1802), Surveys of Colonial Governors, vol. 2, William L. Clements Library (hereafter cited as WLC), University of Michigan, Ann Arbor; Jarvis, *In the Eye of All Trade*, 131–33, 162, 324–25, 350–52; Kerr, *Bermuda and the American Revolution*, 1–7, 11–13.
11. Jarvis, *In the Eye of All Trade*, 387–89. On the practical concerns during the Revolutionary War, see Glover, *Eliza Lucas Pinckney*, 192–207.
12. Jarvis, *In the Eye of All Trade*, 352; Kerr, *Bermuda and the American Revolution*, 13–16, 38–44.
13. St. George Tucker to Thomas Jefferson, June 8, 1775, Founders Online.
14. Henry Tucker to St. George Tucker, March 31, 1774, Tucker-Coleman Papers, box 2, folder 10, Special Collections Research Center, Swem Library, College of William and Mary, Williamsburg, Virginia (hereafter cited as TCP); Henry Tucker to St. George Tucker, March 26, 1775, TCP, box 3, folder 1; St. George Tucker to Richard Rush, October 27, 1813, in Coleman, "Randolph Tucker Letters," 47–52; Jarvis, *In the Eye of All Trade*, 387–89. For more on the British Caribbean and the sugar colonies' role in the Revolutionary War, see O'Shaughnessy, *An Empire Divided*.
15. George Washington to Nicholas Cooke, August 14, 1775, Founders Online; Nicholas Cooke to George Washington, September 2, 1775, Founders Online; Jarvis, *In the Eye of All Trade*, 387–89.
16. St. George Tucker to Richard Rush, October 27, 1813, in Coleman, "Randolph Tucker Letters," 47–52.
17. "Monday, October 2, 1775" and "Wednesday, November 22, 1775," in Ford, *Journals of the Continental Congress* (hereafter *Journals*), 3:268, 362–63.
18. Henry Tucker to St. George Tucker, March 26, 1775, TCP, box 3, folder 1; "The Humble Address of the Council and Assembly of Bermuda to the King's Most Excellent Majesty," June 29, 1776, Bermuda Islands House of Assembly, *Ancient Journals of the House of Assembly*, 1685–88; Jarvis, *In the Eye of All Trade*, 386–409; Kerr, *Bermuda and the American Revolution*, 38–62.
19. Henry Tucker to Benjamin Franklin, August 12, 1775, Founders Online; "Friday, October 10, 1777," Bermuda Islands House of Assembly, *Ancient Journals*, 2:1733; Kerr, *Bermuda and the American Revolution*, 38–42.
20. Silas Deane, "Memoir on the Commerce of America, and Its Importance to Europe," August 15, 1776, in Deane, *The Deane Papers*, 1:192, 195; Robert Morris to Silas Deane, March 30, 1776, in Clark, *Naval Documents of the American Revolution*, 4:578; Kerr, *Bermuda and the American Revolution*, 59–60.

21. Silas Deane to Robert Morris, April 26, 1776, in Clark, *Naval Documents of the American Revolution*, 4:1274–79; Henry Laurens to Elisha Sawyer, January 19, 1776, in Laurens, *Papers of Henry Laurens*, 11:47–49.
22. Silas Deane to Robert Morris, April 26, 1776, in Clark, *Naval Documents of the American Revolution*, 4:1274–79; Bruere, "Answer to the Queries relating to His Majesty's Island of Bermuda," in Henry Strachey Papers (1768–1802), Surveys of Colonial Governors, vol. 2, WLC. For more on the Hamiltonian vision, see Cayton, *Frontier Republic*, 21–22.
23. Benjamin Harrison and Richard Henry Lee to the Commissioners in Paris, February 19, 1777, in Wharton, *Revolutionary Diplomatic Correspondence*, 2:274–75; Silas Deane to Robert Morris, April 26, 1776, in Clark, *Naval Documents of the American Revolution*, 4:1274–79; For more on Britain's naval blockade, see Buel, *In Irons*; Matson, "Revolution, the Constitution, and the New Nation," 1:363–401.
24. Silas Deane to Robert Morris, April 26, 1776, in Clark, *Naval Documents of the American Revolution*, 4:1278.
25. John Adams, "I. A Plan of Treaties," June 18, 1776, Founders Online; Benjamin Franklin, "Sketch of Propositions for a Peace [After September 26, 1776 and Before October 25, 1776]," Founders Online; Gilje, "Conquest and Commerce," 742–47; Gould, *Among the Powers of the World*, 2–8; Sadosky, *Revolutionary Negotiations*, 98–99.
26. The American Commissioners to the Committee for Foreign Affairs, February 28, 1778, Founders Online; Silas Deane to the Committee of Secret Correspondence of the Continental Congress, October 1, 1776, in Clark, *Naval Documents of the American Revolution*, 6:623.
27. Edward Hay to Vice Admiral James Young, September 25, 1775, in Clark, *Naval Documents of the American Revolution*, 2:208–9; "From the St. James Chronicle, *To the Right Hon. John Earl of Sandwich, and the Lords Commissioners for executing the Office of the Lord High Admiral of Great Britain*" (from "Britannus"), *Pennsylvania Packet*, March 2, 1779; Thomas Lyttelton to Lord George Germain, January 27, 1776, in Clark, *Naval Documents of the American Revolution*, 3:536–39.
28. Thomas Lyttelton to Lord George Germain, January 27, 1776, in Clark, *Naval Documents of the American Revolution*, 3:536–39; Vice Admiral Samuel Graves to Philip Stephens, October 9, 1775, in ibid., 2:371–73; George James Bruere to Lord Dartmouth, October 16, 1775, in ibid., 2:486; "July 11, 1776," Bermuda Islands House of Assembly, *Ancient Journals*, 2:1697; "A Letter from St. Kitts, Dated April 20," *London Chronicle*, June 4–6, 1776, in Clark, *Naval Documents of the American Revolution*, 4:1183; For "in defence of trade," see Thomas Jefferson,

"Outline of Argument Concerning Insubordination of Esek Hopkins," August 12, 1776, Founders Online; Jarvis, *In the Eye of All Trade*, 391–412; Nedervelt, "Caught between Realities," 747–69.

29. Gov. George James Bruere to Lord George Germain, April 19, 1777, in Clark, *Naval Documents of the American Revolution*, 8:383; Jarvis, *In the Eye of All Trade*, 416; Kerr, *Bermuda and the American Revolution*, 66.
30. American Commissioners in France to Vergennes, March 18, 1777, in Clark, *Naval Documents of the American Revolution*, 8:689–90; Franco-American Treaty of Alliance, February 6, 1778, Founders Online.
31. Samuel Chase to Thomas Johnson, May 3, 1778, *Letters of Delegates*, 9:572; Lafayette to the Comte de Vergennes, July 3, 1779, in Idzerda, *Lafayette in the Age of the American Revolution*, 2:288; Lafayette to Vergennes, February 2, 1780, in ibid., 2:352; Dull, *French Navy and American Independency*, 106–7; Kerr, *Bermuda and the American Revolution*; Sadosky, *Revolutionary Negotiations*, 100–101.
32. "The Honest Politician," *Pennsylvania Gazette*, August 18 and September 22, 1779.
33. Committee of Congress Observations on a Proposed West Indian Expedition, Philadelphia, September 8, 1778, *Letters of Delegates*, 10:602–4.
34. Committee of Congress Observations on a Proposed West Indian Expedition, Philadelphia, September 8, 1778, *Letters of Delegates*, 10:602–4. For a work that argued that revolutionary leaders anticipated a North America freed of European powers, see Stagg, *Borderlines in Borderlands*, 5–6.
35. Jarvis, *In the Eye of All Trade*, 419–21.
36. James and William Perot to Thomas Prizgar, April 30, 1779, Tudor Company Records, 1752–1897, James and William Perot papers related to capture of Schooner Fanny, 1782–83, box 2, folder 15, Baker Library Special Collections, Harvard Business School; Jarvis, *In the Eye of All Trade*, 425–27; Kerr, *Bermuda and the American Revolution*; Wilkinson, *Bermuda in the Old Empire*, 398–400; Jasanoff, *Liberty's Exiles*, 218–20.
37. Marine Committee to the Eastern Navy Board, January 9, 1779, *Letters of Delegates*, 11:441; Marine Committee to the Eastern Navy Board, November 16, 1778, ibid., 11:221–23; Richard Henry Lee to John Page, March 29, 1779, ibid. 12:262; Jarvis, *In the Eye of All Trade*, 425–27; Buel, *In Irons*, 189.
38. Thomas Jefferson to John Jay, June 19, 1779, Founders Online; Wilkinson, *Bermuda in the Old Empire*, 398–400; Maj. Alexander Dick to Thomas Jefferson, June 18, 1782, in Palmer, *Calendar of Virginia State Papers*, 3:196.
39. George Washington to John Jay, April 23, 1779, Founders Online.
40. John Green to Benjamin Franklin, June 25, 1779, Founders Online; *Pennsylvania Gazette*, May 12, 1779; Thomas Jefferson to St. George Tucker, June 22, 1779, Founders Online.

41. Capt. B. Joell to Timothy Pickering, July 17, 1780, Timothy Pickering Papers, Massachusetts Historical Society (hereafter MHS), Boston; Jarvis, *In the Eye of All Trade*, 409–10, 436.
42. For Samuel Holden Parsons's proposal, see note 14 in Council of War, September 6, 1780, Founders Online; Buel, *In Irons*, 189; Matson, "Revolution, the Constitution, and the New Nation," 363–67. For more on Nova Scotia's importance for American commercial security, see Marshall, *Remaking the British Atlantic*, 30–31. On garnering international respect, see Gould, *Among the Powers of the Earth*.
43. Lord North quoted in Taylor, *American Revolutions*, 296.
44. James Mitchell Varnum to George Washington, October 2, 1781, Founders Online. See also Buel, *In Irons*, 189; Matson, "Revolution, the Constitution, and the New Nation," 363–67.
45. St. George Tucker to George Washington, October 23, 1781, Founders Online.
46. St. George Tucker to George Washington, October 25, 1781; St. George Tucker to George Washington, October 26, 1781, both at Founders Online.
47. "Washington's Summary of British and American Forces," May 1, 1782, Founders Online; Ferling, *Ascent of George Washington*, 56–58.
48. Charles Thompson, *Notes of Debates*, August 5, 6, 1782, in Burnett, *Letters of Members of the Continental Congress*, 6:422–24; James Madison to Edmund Pendleton, August 6, 1782, Founders Online; Robert R. Livingston to George Washington, August 6, 1782, ibid.; George Washington to Robert R. Livingston, August 14, 1782, ibid. For more on the anti-French sentiment in Congress, see Morris, *The Peacemakers*, 15–21.
49. "Harpax," *Freeman's Journal or The North-American Intelligencer*, September 4, 1782.
50. "Harpax," *Freeman's Journal or The North-American Intelligencer*, September 4, 1782.
51. Franklin's Sketch of Articles of Peace, December 10–13, 1782, Founders Online; Morris, *The Peacemakers*, 416.
52. James Mitchell Varnum to George Washington, October 2, 1781, Founders Online; Jarvis, *In the Eye of All Trade*, 393; Taylor *American Revolutions*, 283.
53. Robert Traill to Earl of Shelburne, February 10, 1783, quoted in Wilkinson, *Bermuda in the Old Empire*, 432; William Browne to Lord North, April 30, October 15, 1783, quoted in Jarvis, *In the Eye of All Trade*, 435–37, 450; Kerr, *Bermuda and the American Revolution*, 125–31.
54. George Bascome to St. George Tucker, March 28, 1778, quoted in Kerr, *Bermuda and the American Revolution*, 130–31; Jarvis, *In the Eye of All Trade*, 435–37.
55. On Anglophobia and US expansionism, see Haynes, *Unfinished Revolution*, ch. 9.

56. John Adams to Robert R. Livingston, June 23, 1783, Founders Online; O'Shaughnessy, *Men Who Lost America*, 245; Willcox, *Portrait of a General*, 485n.
57. Samuel Adams to Caleb Davis, December 5, 1778, *Letters of Delegates*, 11:288; Samuel Huntington to John Adams, October 16, 1779, ibid., 14:82.
58. Henry Laurens to John Rutledge, June 3, 1778, *Letters of Delegates*, 10:19-21; Henry Laurens to John Houstoun, August 27, 1778, ibid., 10:510. For more on the Floridas during the war, see DuVal, *Independence Lost*; Wright, *Florida in the American Revolution*, 66.
59. Thomas Jefferson to George Rogers Clark, December 25, 1780, Founders Online. For an in-depth examination of Jefferson's empire of liberty, see Onuf, *Jefferson's Empire*, 14-15, 53-56.
60. Benjamin Franklin to the Conde d'Aranda, April 7, 1777, Founders Online; Stagg, *Borderlines in Borderlands*, 15-30; Wright, *Florida in the American Revolution*, 64-65.
61. "Tuesday, October 17, 1780," in Ford, *Journals*, 18:945-46; Patrick Henry to Bernardo de Gálvez, in Kinnaird, *Annual Report of the American Historical Association, 1945. Vol. 2: Spain in the Mississippi Valley, 1765-1794* (hereafter *Spain in the Mississippi Valley*), 248-49. On the trans-Appalachian West in an Atlantic context, see Furstenberg, "Significance of the Trans-Appalachian Frontier," 659-60.
62. On fear of British proximity, see Lennox, *North of America*, 17-19, ch. 1.
63. Thomas Paine to Thomas Jefferson, September 23, 1803, Founders Online; Latimer, *1812*, 316-17; Wilkinson, *Bermuda from Sail to Steam*, 2:684-737.

## 2. THE STATE OF FRANKLIN

1. Adam Stephen to James Madison, November 25, 1787, Founders Online. For more on the state of Franklin, see Barksdale, *Lost State of Franklin*; Williams, *History of the Lost State of Franklin*; Kastor, "Equitable Rights and Privileges," 193-226; Roney, "Strange Afterlife of the Declaration of Independence," 246-72.
2. On the founders' vision for the West, see Onuf, "Liberty, Development, and Union," 179-213; Witgen, *Seeing Red*, ch.1.
3. On breakaway republics and intrigue, see Richards, *Breakaway Americas*, 7-14. Richards examines a series of breakaway Americas (Texas, Oregon, California, etc.) that did not necessarily seek union with the United States. The Franklinites sought union but contemplated other futures outside of the early republic; see also Narrett, *Adventurism and Empire*. On early republic settlers as agents of manifest destiny, see Owsley and Smith, *Filibusters and Expansionists*, ch. 2.

4. On settler influence on US policy, see Ablavsky, *Federal Ground*, 15; Griffin, *American Leviathan*, 10; Hinderaker, *Elusive Empires*, 187–267.
5. Gould, *Among the Powers of the Earth*, 8–9, 113–22; McCoy, *Elusive Republic*, ch. 3.
6. George Washington to Benjamin Harrison, October 10, 1784, Founders Online; Banning, *Sacred Fire of Liberty*, 58–68.
7. Abigail Adams to Cotton Tufts, February 21, 1786, Founders Online; Sheffield, *Commerce of the American States*, 235–39; Taylor, *American Revolutions*, 347.
8. Sheffield, *Commerce of the American States*, 235–39, 254.
9. Richard Henry Lee to James Madison, November 20, 1784, Founders Online; "To the People of America," *The Virginia Gazette, or, The American Advertiser*, January 3, 1784; McCoy, *Elusive Republic*, 90–100. For more on postwar Americans' cultural insecurities, see Yokota, *Unbecoming British*.
10. "To the People of the United States," *Carlisle Gazette*, July 5, 1786, quoted in Onuf, *Origins of the Federal Republic*, 160.
11. Thomas Jefferson to George Washington, March 15, 1784, Founders Online; Gordon-Reed and Onuf, *"Most Blessed of the Patriarchs,"* 317–18; Tucker and Hendrickson, *Empire of Liberty*, 30–32. For more on Virginians' views on the West in the 1780s, see Glover, *Fate of Revolution*, 49–53.
12. John Adams, October 25, 1775, Founders Online; Barksdale, *Lost State of Franklin*, 20–35; Calloway, *American Revolution in Indian Country*, 208–12.
13. Richard Henry Lee to James Madison, May 30, 1785, Founders Online.
14. Barksdale, *Lost State of Franklin*, 36–40; Onuf, *Origins of the Federal Republic*, 38–39, 167.
15. David Campbell to Arthur Campbell, December 27, 1784, Arthur Campbell Papers, 1752–1811, box 1, folder 3, Filson Historical Society, Louisville, KY (hereafter cited as FHS); Ablavsky, *Federal Ground*, 40–45; Barksdale, *Lost State of Franklin*, 54–58; For more on western elites' land speculating schemes, see Blaakman, "Marketplace of American Federalism," 598–99.
16. Barksdale, *Lost State of Franklin*, 54–58.
17. Roney, "Strange Afterlife of the Declaration of Independence," 246–48.
18. John Sevier to Governor Alexander Martin, March 22, 1785, in Sevier et al., *Sevier Family History with the Collected Letters of Gen. John Sevier* (hereafter *Collected Letters of Gen. Sevier*), 60; David Campbell to Arthur Campbell, December 27, 1784, Campbell Papers, 1752–1811, box 1, folder 3, FHS; Barksdale, *Lost State of Franklin*, 53–61. On war with Indigenous nations and western unity in early America, see Silver, *Our Savage Neighbors*; Parkinson, *Common Cause*.
19. John Sevier to Governor Alexander Martin, March 22, 1785, *Collected Letters of Gen. Sevier*, 60; Barksdale, *Lost State of Franklin*, 53–61; Choppin Roney, "The Strange Afterlife of the Declaration of Independence," 252–54.

20. *Hartford Courant*, May 23, 1785; "A Manifesto, To the Inhabitants of the Counties of Washington, Sullivan, and Green," *Freeman's Journal or The North-American Intelligencer*, November 16, 1785; Barksdale, *Lost State of Franklin*, 62–64; Onuf, *Origins of the Federal Republic*, 159.
21. *The Freeman's Journal or The North-American Intelligencer*, November 30, 1785; John Sevier to Richard Caswell, May 14, 1785, *Collected Letters of Gen. Sevier*, 61–62; Barksdale, *Lost State of Franklin*, 60–70. On masculinity in the trans-Appalachian West, see Sachs, *Home Rule*.
22. Richard Henry Lee to James Madison, May 30, 1785, Founders Online; James Madison to James Monroe, May 29, 1785, Founders Online; Friend, *Kentucke's Frontiers*, 134–36.
23. Patrick Henry to Thomas Jefferson, September 10, 1785, Founders Online; Onuf, *Origins of the Federal Republic*, 17; Kastor, "Equitable Rights and Privileges," 193–226. For more on interstate land speculating in the postwar era, see Blaakman, "Marketplace of American Federalism," 583–608.
24. Thomas Jefferson to George Washington, July 10, 1785, Founders Online; Thomas Jefferson to Richard Henry Lee, July 12, 1785, Founders Online; Kastor, "Equitable Rights and Privileges," 193–226.
25. Richard Henry Lee to James Madison, May 30, 1785, Founders Online; Arthur Campbell to Isaac Shelby, February 27, 1783, Isaac Shelby Papers, 1760–1839, box 1, folder 1, FHS.
26. Arthur Campbell to Patrick Henry, June 7, 1785, Palmer, *Calendar of Virginia State Papers*, 4:32; James Madison to Thomas Jefferson, January 9, 1785, Founders Online; Onuf, *Origins of the Federal Republic*, 155; Kastor, "Equitable Rights and Privileges," 193–226. For Kentucky's influence on James Madison, see Banning, *Sacred Fire of Liberty*, 58–68; McCoy, "James Madison and Visions of American Nationality," 226–58.
27. "Memorial. To the Honourable the Congress of the United States of America, January 17, 1785," in Palmer, *Calendar of Virginia State Papers*, 4:4–5. The Franklinites who signed the memorial were Gilbert Christian, John Anderson, David Looney, and John Adair. See Williams, *History of the Lost State of Franklin*, 45–55.
28. "Memorial. To the Honourable the Congress of the United States of America, January 17, 1785," in Palmer, *Calendar of Virginia State Papers*, 4:4–5; Kastor, "Equitable Rights and Privileges," 193–226; Williams, *History of the Lost State of Franklin*, 45–55.
29. *Freeman's Journal*, January 12, 1785; Onuf, *Origins of the Federal Republic*, 154–55.
30. Arthur Campbell to Patrick Henry, July 26, 1785, in Palmer, *Calendar of Virginia State Papers*, 4:44.

31. Arthur Campbell to James Madison, October 28, 1785, Founders Online; Kastor, "Equitable Rights and Privileges," 217–18.
32. James Madison to Lafayette, March 20, 1785, Founders Online; Arthur Campbell to James Madison, October 28, 1785, Founders Online; Kastor, "Equitable Rights and Privileges," 217–18; Banning, *Sacred Fire of Liberty*, 58–68.
33. John Sevier to Patrick Henry, July 19, 1785, in Palmer, *Calendar of Virginia State Papers*, 4:43; Kastor, "Equitable Rights and Privileges," 193–226.
34. Barksdale, *Lost State of Franklin*, 60–70.
35. "To the Honorable Continental Congress, March 12, 1785," quoted in Williams, *History of the Lost State of Franklin*, 82–84; Barksdale, *Lost State of Franklin*, 60–70.
36. Patrick Henry to Thomas Jefferson, September 10, 1785, Founders Online; Barksdale, *Lost State of Franklin*, 65–67; Roney, "Strange Afterlife of the Declaration of Independence," 262–63; Williams, *History of the Lost State of Franklin*, 82–89.
37. Jefferson, *Notes on the State of Virginia*, 164–65; Calloway, *American Revolution in Indian Country*, 208–12; Barksdale, *Lost State of Franklin*, 105–6. For more on the significance of land to settlers' concept of liberty, see Hinderaker, *Elusive Empires*, 187–267.
38. Treaty of Dumplin Creek, June 10, 1785, *Collected Letters of Gen. Sevier*, 63; Joseph Martin to Richard Caswell, September 19, 1785, Penelope Johnson Allen Cherokee Collection, 1775–1878, Tennessee State Library and Archives, Tennessee Virtual Archive; Calloway, *American Revolution in Indian Country*, 208–12; Barksdale, *Lost State of Franklin*, 105–6.
39. Treaty of Dumplin Creek, June 10, 1785, *Collected Letters of Gen. Sevier*, 63; Faulkner, *Massacre at Cavett's Station*, 21–22.
40. "Indian Talk Enclosed Also with the Above, and the String of Beads Referred to, Found Enclosed," September 19, 1785, in Palmer, *Calendar of Virginia State Papers*, 4:56; Calloway, *American Revolution in Indian Country*, 208–12; Witgen, *Seeing Red*, 18–20.
41. Barksdale, *Lost State of Franklin*, 105–6; Calloway, *American Revolution in Indian Country*, 208–12.
42. "Domestic Intelligence," *Freeman's Journal or The North-American Intelligencer*, October 5, 1785; David Campbell to Arthur Campbell, August 14, 1787, Campbell Papers, box 1, folder 4, FHS; "Extract of a letter from a gentleman in Washington, to his friend in this city," *The Independent Gazetteer*, August 6, 1785. See also Arthur Campbell to Patrick Henry, June 7, 1785, in Palmer, *Calendar of Virginia State Papers*, 4:32. On the overlap of Native communities and white settlements in the early stages of colonization, see Aron, *How the West Was Lost*,

14–30; for more on Thomas Jefferson's views about Native assimilation, see Witgen, *Seeing Red,* 38–63.

43. *The Freeman's Journal or The North-American Intelligencer,* January 4, 1786. For more on the Franklinites' Constitution, see Arthur Campbell to James Madison, October 28, 1785, Founders Online; Barksdale, *Lost State of Franklin,* 67–71.
44. *Freeman's Journal or The North-American Intelligencer,* September 28, 1785; Barksdale, *Lost State of Franklin,* 64–65, 72–74.
45. Tristram Dalton to John Adams, October 18, 1785, Founders Online; Thomas Jefferson to Archibald Stuart, January 25, 1786, Founders Online.
46. On Chief Kaiyah-tahee's hopes, see Calloway, *American Revolution in Indian Country,* ch. 7. On Spanish intrigue, see DuVal, *Independence Lost,* 313–20.
47. William Cocke to Benjamin Franklin, June 15, 1786, in Franklin, *Works of Benjamin Franklin,* 11:257–58.
48. Benjamin Franklin to William Cocke, August 12, 1786, in Franklin, *Works of Benjamin Franklin,* 11:273–74.
49. David Campbell to Arthur Campbell, August 14, 1787, Campbell Papers, box 1, folder 4, FHS; Barksdale, *Lost State of Franklin,* 72–84.
50. Judge David Campbell to Governor Richard Caswell, November 30, 1786, quoted in Williams, *History of the Lost State of Franklin,* 115–17; *Pennsylvania Gazette,* August 30, 1786; Old Tassel, Speech, quoted in Calloway, *American Revolution in Indian Country,* 208–12; Barksdale, *Lost State of Franklin,* 100–117; Faulkner, *Massacre at Cavett's Station,* 22–23.
51. Otto to Vergennes, August 13, 1786, quoted in Bancroft, *History of the Formation of the Constitution,* 2:378; Banning, *Sacred Fire of Liberty,* 58–68; Glover, *Fate of the Revolution,* 50–52; McCoy, "James Madison and Visions of American Nationality," 240–41. For more on treaty-worthiness, see Gould, *Among the Powers of the Earth.*
52. Otto to Vergennes, September 10, 1786, in Bancroft, *History of the Formation of the Constitution,* 2:389–93; Banning, *Sacred Fire of Liberty,* 58–68; Glover, *Fate of the Revolution,* 50–52; McCoy, "James Madison and Visions of American Nationality," 240–41; Griffin, *American Leviathan,* 187–97.
53. William Graham to Arthur Campbell, September 24, 1786, Campbell Papers, box 1, folder 4, FHS; Furstenberg, "Significance of the Trans-Appalachian Frontier," 659–60; Banning, *Sacred Fire of Liberty,* 58–68; Glover, *Fate of the Revolution,* 50–52; McCoy, "James Madison and Visions of American Nationality," 240–41; Griffin, *American Leviathan,* 187–97.
54. Otto to Vergennes, August 23, 1786, in Bancroft, *History of the Formation of the Constitution,* 2:385; Thomas Jefferson to James Madison, January 30, 1787, Founders Online.

55. Otto to Vergennes, March 5, 1787, in Bancroft, *History of the Formation of the Constitution*, 2:415.
56. "A Copy of two letters from a gentleman at the Falls of Ohio, to his friend in New England, December 4, 1786," in Kaminski, *Commentaries on the Constitution*, 1:152–54; Williams, *Lost State of Franklin*, 123–25.
57. "Copy of two letters," in Kiminski, *Commentaries on the Constitution*, 1:152–54; Williams, *Lost State of Franklin*, 123–25; Witgen, *Seeing Red*, 22–23, 40.
58. "Copy of two letters," in Kiminski, *Commentaries on the Constitution*, 1:154; Williams, *Lost State of Franklin*, 123–25.
59. James Madison to George Washington, March 18, 1787, Founders Online; see also Edmund Randolph to James Madison, March 7, 1787, Founders Online; Williams, *Lost State of Franklin*, 123–25.
60. "Records of Sumner Court, April Term 1787," in Ramsey, *Annals of Tennessee to the End of the Eighteenth Century*, 502–3; *Maryland Journal*, November 6, 1787, in *Collected Letters of Gen. Sevier*, 85–86.
61. David Campbell to Arthur Campbell, August 14, 1787, Campbell Papers, box 1, folder 4, FHS; *Maryland Journal*, July 27, 1787, quoted in Williams, *Lost State of Franklin*, 183; Sevier to Benjamin Franklin, November 2, 1787, *Collected Letters of Gen. Sevier*, 85–86; Barksdale, *Lost State of Franklin*, 130–31. On westerners' support for a strong national government, see Onuf, *Origins of the Federal Republic*, 155–58; Griffin, *American Leviathan*, 14–15.
62. Constitution of the United States, Article IV, Section 3; Barksdale, *Lost State of Franklin*, 130–31; Roney, "Strange Afterlife of the Declaration of Independence," 263.
63. *The Federalist No. 6* "[14 November 1787]," Founders Online.
64. Williams, *Lost State of Franklin*, 183–88.
65. "James Wilson, December 4, 1787," in Merrill, *Documentary History of the Ratification of the Constitution*, 2:477; Williams, *Lost State of Franklin*, 185. For more on the forward-thinking nature of the Federalists, see Onuf, *Origins of the Federal Republic*, chs. 7–9; Glover, *Fate of the Revolution*, 53.
66. "Genuine Information XI," *Maryland Gazette*, February 5, 1788; "Thursday August 30, 1787," in Madison, *Notes of Debates in the Federal Convention of 1787*, 554–62.
67. *The Federalist No. 10* [22 November 1787], Founders Online.
68. Arthur Campbell to James Madison, October 28, 1785, Founders Online; Onuf, *Origins of the Federal Republic*, 155–58; Kastor, "Equitable Rights and Privileges," 217–18.
69. *Poughkeepsie Journal*, April 22, 1788; Barksdale, *Lost State of Franklin*, 132–36.
70. *Columbian Herald, or, The Independent Courier of North-America*, August 14, 1788; Barksdale, *Lost State of Franklin*, 137–38.

71. "Records of Sumner Court, April Term 1787," in Ramsey, *Annals of Tennessee to the End of the Eighteenth Century,* 502–3; Adam Stephen to James Madison, November 25, 1787, Founders Online; Arthur Campbell to Gov. Randolph, December 5, 1787, in Palmer, *Calendar of Virginia State Papers,* 4:363–64; David Campbell to Arthur Campbell, August 14, 1787, Campbell Papers, box 1, folder 4, FHS.
72. Richard Winn to Henry Knox, August 5, 1788, in Lowrie, *American State Papers: Indian Affairs,* 1:28; Faulkner, *Massacre at Cavett's Station,* 21–24.
73. Miró's Offer to Western Americans, April 20, 1789, in Kannaird, *Spain in the Mississippi Valley, 1765–1794,* 270–71; don Diego de Gardoqui to Conde de Floridablanca, April 22, 1788, in Kaminski, *Documentary History of the Ratification of the Constitution Digital Edition,* http://rotunda.upress.virginia.edu/founders/RNCN-03-17-02-0045; DuVal, *Independence Lost,* 313–20; Narrett, *Adventurism and Empire,* 115–86.
74. John Sevier to don Diego de Gardoqui, September 12, 1788, *Collected Letters of Gen. Sevier,* 95–96.
75. John Sevier to don Diego de Gardoqui, September 12, 1788, *Collected Letters of Gen. Sevier,* 96–97. On speculation in the Muscle Shoals, see Whitaker, "Muscle Shoals Speculation, 1783–1789," 377–86.
76. Barksdale, *Lost State of Franklin,* 142–44.
77. John Brown Cutting to Thomas Jefferson, July 11, 1788, Founders Online; James Madison to George Washington, September 26, 1788, Founders Online; Barksdale, *Lost State of Franklin,* 143; Williams, *History of the Lost State of Franklin,* ch. 31.
78. Barksdale, *Lost State of Franklin,* 167–69; Narrett, *Adventurism and Empire,* 115–86.
79. "Location of the Capital, September 4, 1789," Founders Online; McCoy, "James Madison and Visions of American Nationality," 226–58.
80. On the contested nature of the West, see Narrett, *Adventurism and Empire;* Richards, *Breakaway Americas.*
81. David Campbell to Richard Caswell, November 30, 1786, quoted in Williams, *History of the Lost State of Franklin,* 115–17. For more on Anglo-Americans spreading republicanism with or without the United States, see Richards, *Breakaway Americas,* 6–14, 17–49. On Crockett, see Wallis, *David Crockett,* 10–11.

# 3. THE MICHIGAN AND UPPER CANADA BORDERLANDS

1. Isaac Brock to Lord Liverpool, August 29, 1812, in Harrison, *Messages and Letters of William Henry Harrison* (hereafter *Letters of WHH*), 2:102–3.

2. Witgen, *Seeing Red*, 38–88. On Michigan as a native ground, see Nichols, *Peoples of the Inland Sea*.
3. For Indigenous autonomy in the Great Lakes, see Witgen, *An Infinity of Nations*; White, *The Middle Ground*.
4. On British plans for Upper Canada, see Taylor, *Civil War of 1812*, 45–51. On US expansionism into Canada, see Horsman, "On to Canada," 1–24.
5. This book uses "Indian" when referring to an official government title or when quoting a primary source. Otherwise, the book uses "Indigenous" or "Native" when speaking broadly about multiple Native nations. On learning to live with a British Canada, see Taylor, *Civil War of 1812*, 12. On Indigenous influence on geopolitics and US expansionist thinking, see DeLay, *War of a Thousand Deserts*, xviii–xix. On the importance of the Midwest to the story of removal, see Seeley, *Race, Removal, and the Right to Remain*, 17–23; Witgen, *Seeing Red*.
6. On native grounds, see Duval, *Native Ground*. On Michigan as a native ground see Nichols, *Peoples of the Inland Sea*. See also Dowd, *Spirited Resistance*, 27–36; White, *The Middle Ground*, xiv, 314.
7. Calloway, *Indian World of George Washington*, 332–42; Hinderaker, *Elusive Empires*.
8. "Extracts of Correspondence on Indian Affairs, October 1792," Founders Online; Nichols, *Red Gentlemen and White Savages*, 164–65; Calloway, *Indian World of George Washington*, 435–37; Witgen, *Seeing Red*, 65–66.
9. Nichols, *Red Gentlemen and White Savages*, 165.
10. "General Wayne's Orderly Book," *Michigan Pioneer and Historical Collections* (hereafter MPHC), 34:546–48; Speech of Nanaume, November 1807, MPHC, 40:249; Hatter, *Citizens of Convenience*, 76–77; Nichols, *Red Gentlemen and White Savages*, 165.
11. Yanik, *Fall and Recapture of Detroit*, 12–17; Taylor, *Civil War of 1812*, 153–55; Cangany, *Frontier Seaport*, 106–8.
12. Darby, *Tour from the City of New-York to Detroit*, 188. For more on Detroit's incorporation into the Atlantic world, see Cangany, *Frontier Seaport*, chs. 1–3. For more on Mackinac's commercial connections, see Hyde, *Empires, Nations, and Families*, 9–11.
13. Frederick Bates to Sarah Bates, May 5, 1799, in Marshall, *The Life and Papers of Frederick Bates*, 1:45–48.
14. The Inhabitants of the Michigan Territory to James Madison, December 10, 1811, Founders Online; Miles, *Dawn of Detroit*, 190; Taylor, *Civil War of 1812*, 153–54.
15. Winthrop Sargent to Timothy Pickering, September 30, 1796, in Carter, *Territorial Papers of the United States* (hereafter TPUS), 2:580; Winthrop Sargent to Timothy Pickering, August 14, 1797, TPUS, 2:622–24. For more on British

merchants' scheme to purchase Michigan, see Nichols, *Peoples of the Inland Sea*, 132; Bald, *Detroit's First American Decade*, 108–15.

16. Jay Treaty, November 19, 1794, in Miller, *Treaties and Other International Acts*, 2:246–47; Hull, *Memoirs of the Campaign of the North Western Army*, 15–16; Estes, *Jay Treaty Debate*, 29; Hatter, *Citizens of Convenience*, 8–9; Taylor, *Civil War of 1812*, 153–55.

17. Jeremiah Dubois to Jeremiah Dubois [father and son], March 4, 1819, Jeremiah G. Dubois Letters, WLC; Jeremiah Dubois to Jeremiah Dubois, June 21, 1819, Jeremiah G. Dubois Letters, WLC; Inhabitants of the Michigan Territory to James Madison, December 10, 1811, Founders Online; Taylor, *Civil War of 1812*. For more on settlers' hatred toward Indigenous people, see Silver, *Our Savage Neighbors*.

18. Solomon Sibley to the US Congress, December 6, 1804, quoted in Cangany, *Frontier Seaport*, 139; Yanik, *Fall and Recapture of Detroit*, 12–17; Miles, *Dawn of Detroit*, 190–99.

19. Miles, *Dawn of Detroit*, 190–99; Lee, "Indian Boundary Line," 40–41; Yanik, *Fall and Recapture of Detroit*, 12–17.

20. Perkins, *Prologue to War*, 140–41; Gilje, *Free Trade and Sailors' Rights*, 99–101, 156–58.

21. Thomas Forsyth to William Clark, December 23, 1812, in Libby, "Forsyth to Clark," 194; Sugden, *Tecumseh*, 117, 156–58; Nichols, *Peoples of the Inland Sea*, 142–44; White, *The Middle Ground*, 497–512; Dowd, *Spirited Resistance*, 115–20; DuVal, "How Native Nations Survived," 63–82; Lee, "Indian Boundary Line," 39–42.

22. Augustus Woodward to William Hull, August 12, 1807, MPHC, 40:173–77; Miles, *Dawn of Detroit*, 190–201; Sugden, *Tecumseh*, 156–58. US officials often worried about the movements of Indigenous peoples. See Seeley, *Race, Removal, and the Right to Remain*, 164–67.

23. Augustus Woodward to William Hull, August 12, 1807, MPHC, 40:173–77. For more on the US-Canada border, see Hatter, *Citizens of Convenience*.

24. Augustus Woodward to Frederick Bates, August 12, 1807, in Marshall, *Life and Papers of Frederick Bates*, 1:172–74; Jasper Grant to William Hull, September 8, 1807, MPHC, 31:601–4; William Hull to Jasper Grant, September 3, 1807, MPHC, 31:598–600; Miles, *Dawn of Detroit*, 195–201; Yanik, *Fall and Recapture of Detroit*, 16–18.

25. Augustus Woodward to William Hull, August 12, 1807, MPHC, 40:173–77. On US interest in Canada, see Lennox, *North of America*, 17–18.

26. Augustus Woodward to William Hull, August 12, 1807, MPHC, 40:173–77; William Hull to Henry Dearborn, August 13, 1807, MPHC, 40:181.

27. John Graves Simcoe to Sir Joseph Banks, January 8, 1791, in Cruikshank, *Correspondence of Lieut. Governor Simcoe,* 1:18; Alexander McKee to John Graves Simcoe, August 22, 1793, ibid., 2:35. On British plans for Upper Canada, see Craig, *Upper Canada,* 21–43; Taylor, *Civil War of 1812,* 15–36, 46–51.
28. Thomas Jefferson to Henry Dearborn, August 28, 1807, Founders Online; Speech of Nanaume, November 1807, MPHC, 40:249; Wallace, *Jefferson and the Indians,* 239, 304–18.
29. Thomas Jefferson to Henry Dearborn, August 28, 1807, Founders Online; Witgen, *Seeing Red,* 78–81.
30. Miles, *Dawn of Detroit,* 203–5; Yanik, *Fall and Recapture of Detroit,* 17; Sugden, *Tecumseh,* 158–60.
31. Sugden, *Tecumseh,* 158–60; Witgen, *Seeing Red,* 21–22, 140.
32. The Chiefs and Warriors of the Ottawa, Chippewa, Potawatomi, and Wyandot Nations to James Madison, November 13, 1811, Founders Online; John R. Williams to William Boyd and Henry Suydam, April 28, 1812, John R. Williams Papers, Burton Historical Collection (hereafter BHC), Detroit Public Library; Sugden, *Tecumseh,* 158–60; Witgen, *Seeing Red,* 21–22, 140.
33. Nichols, *Peoples of the Inland Sea,* 141–46; Sugden, *Tecumseh,* 160, 183–89.
34. Speech of Indian Chiefs to William Hull, MPHC, 40:306; Owens, *Mr. Jefferson's Hammer,* 199–207; Sugden, *Tecumseh,* 183–89; Dowd, *Spirited Resistance,* 138–41.
35. Tecumseh's Speech to Governor Harrison, August 20, 1810, *Letters of WHH,* 1:465; Ostler, *Surviving Genocide,* 146–52; Seeley, *Race, Removal, and the Right to Remain,* 164–65.
36. Owens, *Mr. Jefferson's Hammer,* 216–20; Yanik, *Fall and Recapture of Detroit,* 20–21; Sugden, *Tecumseh,* 236; Perkins, *Prologue to War,* 282–83.
37. The Inhabitants of the Michigan Territory to James Madison, December 10, 1811, Founders Online; Yanik, *Fall and Recapture of Detroit,* 22.
38. The Chiefs and Sachems of the Wyandot Nation to James Madison, February 5, 1812, Founders Online.
39. Thomas Forsyth to William Clark, May 27, 1812, Thomas Forsyth Papers, Missouri History Museum Archives (hereafter MSM), St. Louis; Ostler, *Surviving Genocide,* 157–60.
40. "Indian Hostilities," *National Intelligencer,* March 26, 1812.
41. William Hull to William Eustis, March 6, 1812, MPHC, 40:362–68; John R. Williams to William Boyd and Henry Suydam, April 28, 1812, John R. Williams Papers, BHC; Stagg, *Mr. Madison's War,* 191–200.
42. James Witherell to Amy Witherell, June 9, 1812, BFH Witherell Papers, box 1, BHC; William Hull to William Eustis, March 6, 1812, MPHC, 40:362–68; Taylor, *Civil War of 1812,* 125–26.

43. John R. Williams to William Boyd and Henry Suydam, April 28, 1812, John R. Williams Papers, box 3, BHC.
44. John R. Williams to William Boyd and Henry Suydam, July 21, 1812, John R. Williams Papers, box 3, BHC; Taylor, *Civil War of 1812*, 158–61; Hickey, *War of 1812*, 81–82; Yanik, *Fall and Recapture of Detroit*, 23–24, 36–37, 40–52.
45. Hull, *Memoirs of the Campaign of the North Western Army*, 45–50; Lennox, *North of America*, 17–18; Ostler, *Surviving Genocide*, 177; Taylor, *Civil War of 1812*, 158–61.
46. Hull, *Defence of Brigadier General W. Hull*, 50; William Hull to William Eustis, July 21, 1812, in Cruikshank, *Documents Relating to the Invasion of Canada*, 78; Sugden, *Tecumseh*, 284–85; Stagg, *Mr. Madison's War*, 200.
47. Colonel Elliott to Colonel Claus, July 15, 1812, in Cruikshank, *Documents Relating to the Invasion of Canada*, 62–63; Sugden, *Tecumseh*, 284–85; Stagg, *Mr. Madison's War*, 200.
48. John R. Williams to William Boyd and Henry Suydam, July 21, 1812, John R. Williams Papers, box 3, BHC; Hickey, *War of 1812*, 81–82; Stagg, *Mr. Madison's War*, 197–200.
49. On the surrender of Mackinac, see Porter Hanks to William Hull, August 4, 1812, in Cruikshank *Documents Relating to the Invasion of Canada*, 67–69; Hickey, *War of 1812*, 81–82; Taylor, *Civil War of 1812*, 160–63.
50. William Hull to Henry Dearborn, August 13, 1807, MPHC, 40:184–85; Thomas Forsyth to William Clark, December 23, 1812, in Libby, "Forsyth to Clark," 190–92.
51. William Hull to Henry Dearborn, August 13, 1807, MPHC, 40:184–85; Forbes, *Report of the Trial of General Hull*, 140; Lewis Cass to John S. Gano, August 12, 1812, in Hamlin, *Quarterly Publication of the Historical and Philosophical Society of Ohio*, 15:85; Hickey, *War of 1812*, 81–82; Sugden, *Tecumseh*, 287.
52. Isaac Brock to William Hull, August 15, 1812, in Cruikshank, *Documents Relating to the Invasion of Canada*, 144; "General Tecumseh," *Daily National Intelligencer*, January 28, 1813.
53. Isaac Shelby to William Eustis, September 5, 1812, *Letters of WHH*, 2:111; Stagg, *Mr. Madison's War*, 205–11.
54. Isaac Shelby to William Eustis, September 5, 1812, *Letters of WHH*, 2:111; Stagg, *Mr. Madison's War*, 205–11.
55. Isaac Shelby to William Eustis, September 5, 1812, *Letters of WHH*, 2:111; Thomas Forsyth to William Clark, July 20, 1813, Forsyth Papers, MSM; Harrison, "They had won their battle, too," in Brunsman, *Border Crossings*, 127; Owens, *Red Dreams, White Nightmares*, 206; Sugden, *Tecumseh*, 187–89, 310–14.
56. Solomon Sibley to Edward Hempstead, November 16, 1812, Solomon Sibley Papers, Box 36, BHC; Thomas Forsyth to William Clark, February 20, 1813,

Forsyth Papers, MSM; Isaac Shelby to William Eustis, September 5, 1812, *Letters of WHH*, 2:111. For works that dismiss the possibility of Tecumseh's dream, see Sugden, *Tecumseh*, 187–89; Dowd, *Spirited Resistance*, 181–83.

57. "Brock's Proclamation Following the Surrender of Detroit," August 16, 1812, in Cruikshank, *Documents Relating to the Invasion of Canada*, 155; Antal, *A Wampum Denied*, x–xiii; Antal, "Michigan Ceded," 7–18; Craig, *Upper Canada*, 73–76.

58. John Strachan to Thomas Jefferson, January 30, 1815, Founders Online; Hickey, *War of 1812*, 85–86; Taylor, *Civil War of 1812*, 203–12; Yanik, *Fall and Recapture of Detroit*, 149.

59. James Madison to Henry Dearborn, October 7, 1812, Founders Online; Craig, *Upper Canada*, 75–79; Hickey, *War of 1812*, 127–28.

60. Hickey, *The War of 1812*, 127–28.

61. Lewis Cass to John Armstrong, December 17, 1813, MPHC, 40:551; Stagg, *Mr. Madison's War*, 321–31, 387–400.

62. John Armstrong to James Madison, May 1, 1814, Founders Online; Duncan McArthur to George Croghan, June 6, 1814, Duncan McArthur Letterbooks, volume 1, BHC; Antal, *A Wampum Denied*, 391; Stagg, *Mr. Madison's War*, 321–31, 387–400.

63. Augustus B. Woodward to James Monroe, March 5, 1815, TPUS, 10:513–14; Duncan McArthur to James Monroe, February 6, 1815, TPUS, 10:503–5.

64. John Quincy Adams to James Monroe, September 5, 1814, in Manning, *Diplomatic Correspondence of the United States: Canadian Relations*, 1:647; Antal, *A Wampum Denied*, 390–91.

65. For works on Indigenous removal and resistance in and around Michigan, see Bowes, *Land too Good for Indians*; Seeley, *Race, Removal, and the Right to Remain*, 17–23; Witgen, *Seeing Red*. For recent works on the removal of the southeastern Native peoples, see Ostler, *Surviving Genocide*; Saunt, *Unworthy Republic*; Snyder, *Great Crossings*, 5–17.

66. Lewis Cass to John Armstrong, December 4, 1813, MPHC, 40:544; James Monroe to Albert Gallatin, John Quincy Adams, and James A. Bayard, April 15, 1813, in Manning, *Diplomatic Correspondence of the United States: Canadian Relations*, 1:212–13.

67. Lewis Cass to William H. Crawford, July 30, 1816, TPUS, 10:661–63; Nichols, *Peoples of the Inland Sea*, 157–58; Taylor, *Civil War of 1812*, 430–37; Witgen, *Seeing Red*, 76–81.

68. Norton, *Journal of Major John Norton*, 315; Lewis Cass to William H. Crawford, July 30, 1816, TPUS, 10:661–63; Antal, *A Wampum Denied*, 71–72; Treaty with the Wyandot, 1818, in Keppler, *Indian Affairs*, 2:164; Nichols, *Peoples of the Inland Sea*, 157–58; Radojewski, "Rush-Bagot Agreement," 280–99; Taylor, *Civil War of 1812*, 430–37; Witgen, *Seeing Red*, 76–81.

69. Nichols, *Peoples of the Inland Sea*, 154-55.
70. *Detroit Gazette*, November 28, 1817; "President's Message," *Detroit Gazette*, January 2, 1818; Ostler, *Surviving Genocide*, 197-200; Witgen, *Seeing Red*, 121-25, 348.
71. *Detroit Gazette*, November 28, 1817; James Witherell to B. F. H. Witherell, February 17, 1816, B. F. H. Witherell Papers, BHC.
72. Ostler, *Surviving Genocide*, 197-206.
73. Taylor, *Civil War of 1812*, 12.
74. Bowes, *Land Too Good for Indians*, 45-48; Richards, *Breakaway Americas*, 50-52; Weeks, *New Cambridge History of American Foreign Relations*, 1:151-52.
75. "President's Message," *Ohio Observer*, December 23, 1830; Snyder, *Great Crossings*, 46-47; Owens, *Red Dreams, White Nightmares*, 13-14.

# 4. CUBA

1. For more on the Guamacaro Revolt of 1825, see Barcia, *Great African Slave Revolt*.
2. For more on early US interest in Cuba, see Chambers, *No God but Gain*; Ferrer, *Cuba*; Langley, *Struggle for the American Mediterranean*, 28-60.
3. For more on the role played by people of African descent in shaping geopolitics, see White, *Encountering Revolution*; Schneider, *Occupation of Havana*. For the visions of people of African descent, see Dubois, *Avengers of the New World*, 104-8; Ferrer, "Speaking of Haiti," 223-47.
4. Thomas Jefferson to James Madison, April 27, 1809, Founders Online. On neighborhood, see Lewis, *American Union and the Problem of Neighborhood*. For more on preserving Spanish rule, see Chambers, *No God but Gain*. Racial anxieties had animated Anglo-American expansion since the colonial era. See, for example, Silver, *Our Savage Neighbors*. For more on the expansion and protection of slavery in the antebellum era, see Karp, *This Vast Southern Empire*, chs. 2 and 3; Hietala, *Manifest Design*, ch. 2.
5. White, *Encountering Revolution*, 1-3; Klooster, *Revolutions of the Atlantic World*, 186.
6. Thomas Jefferson to Robert R. Livingston, April 18, 1802, Founders Online; Scott, *Common Wind*, xvii, 204-5; Tucker and Hendrickson, *Empire of Liberty*, 126-30; Girard, "Liberté, Égalité, Esclavage," 55-77.
7. "Haitian Declaration of Independence, January 1, 1804," in Blaufarb, *Revolutionary Atlantic*, 392; Gaffield, *Haitian Connections*, 2-15, 65.
8. "Aponte's Rebellion, Cuba, 1812," in Geggus, *Haitian Revolution*, 190; Ferrer, *Cuba*, 74; Ferrer, "Speaking of Haiti," 234-35; Scott, *Common Wind*, xvii, 204-5.

9. Thomas Jefferson to James Madison, February 12, 1799, Founders Online; White, *Encountering Revolution*, 124–25.
10. "November 20, 1791," Obras de D. Francisco de Arango y Parreño, in Geggus, *Haitian Revolution*, 192–93; Luis de Las Casas to Príncipe, December 16, 1795, in Geggus, *Haitian Revolution*, 186–87; Scott, *Common Wind*, 15–17, 120–21, 163; Ferrer, *Freedom's Mirror*, 17, 233; Ferrer, *Cuba*, 67–69.
11. "January 17, 1793," Obras de D. Francisco de Arango y Parreño, in Geggus, *Haitian Revolution*, 192–93; Ferrer, *Freedom's Mirror*, 10; Chambers, *No God but Gain*, 23.
12. "January 17, 1793," Obras de D. Francisco de Arango y Parreño, in Geggus, *Haitian Revolution*, 192–93; Ferrer, *Freedom's Mirror*, 10; Scott, *Common Wind*, 5; Chambers, *No God but Gain*, 23.
13. Tench Coxe to Thomas Jefferson, March 20, 1802, Founders Online (emphasis in original); White, *Encountering Revolution*, 160–64; Rothman, *Slave Country*, 22–30; Tucker and Hendrickson, *Empire of Liberty*, 126. On John Adams's diplomacy with Toussaint Louverture, see Johnson, *Diplomacy in Black and White*.
14. On informal empire over Cuba, see Chambers, *No God but Gain*, 21–42; Schneider, *Occupation of Havana*, 314–15.
15. Tench Coxe to Thomas Jefferson, March 20, 1802, Founders Online; Schneider, *Occupation of Havana*, 314–15; Chambers, *No God but Gain*, 21–42.
16. Davis, *The Gulf*, 100–101; Kastor, *Nation's Crucible*, 64–65.
17. Thomas Jefferson to William C. C. Claiborne, October 29, 1808, Founders Online; Shaler, "Essay III," in Stagg, "Political Essays of William Shaler"; Lewis, *American Union and the Problem of Neighborhood*, 34–36.
18. William C. C. Claiborne to Thomas Jefferson, December 24, 1810, Founders Online; Lewis, *American Union and the Problem of Neighborhood*, 34–36.
19. *Aurora*, April 14, 1809, quoted in White, *Encountering Revolution*, 171–72; William C. C. Claiborne to Robert Smith, May 14, 1809, in Rowland, *Official Letter Books of W. C. C. Claiborne*, 4:352.
20. James Sterrett to Nathaniel Evans, June 24, 1809, quoted in Rothman, *Slave Country*, 91; White, *Encountering Revolution*, 169–202.
21. *Annals of Congress*, House of Representatives, 11th Congress, 1st Session, 461–62.
22. Maurice Rogers to James Madison, January 26, 1809, Founders Online; Shaler, "Essay III," in Stagg, "Political Essays of William Shaler"; Stagg, *Borderlines in Borderlands*, 95–133.
23. "From the *Tennessee Herald* of Sept. 5," *National Intelligencer*, October 6, 1812; Horne, *Negro Comrades of the Crown*, 35–36; Horne, *Race to Revolution*, ch. 1.
24. Cusick, *Other War of 1812*, x, 295–300; Landers, "Black Community and Culture," 117–34.

25. Hunter, *Speech of the Hon. William Hunter, Feb. 2d, 1813*, 27–29; Lt. Col. Smith to Gov. Mitchell, June 20, 1812, in Davis, "US Troops in Spanish East Florida," 101; Horne, *Negro Comrades of the Crown*, 35–36; Cusick, *Other War of 1812*, 183; Rothman, *Slave Country*, 139–40.
26. John Quincy Adams to Hyde de Neuville, July 28, 1821, in Adams, *Writings of John Quincy Adams*, 7:153–54; Millett, *Maroons of Prospect Bluff*; Owsley, and Smith, *Filibusters and Expansionists*, 103–17.
27. Thomas S. Jesup to James Monroe, August 21, 1816, Thomas S. Jesup Collection, WLC; Lewis, *American Union and the Problem of Neighborhood*, 91–93; Chambers, *No God but Gain*, 92.
28. Thomas S. Jesup to James Monroe, September 8, 1816, Thomas J. Jesup Collection, WLC.
29. Pérez, *Cuba in the American Imagination*, 25–26.
30. Chambers, *No God but Gain*, 79–83; Ferrer, *Freedom's Mirror*, 4–5.
31. "Philanthropos" to James Madison, October 6, 1816, Founders Online; Chambers, *No God but Gain*, 79–83; Ferrer, *Freedom's Mirror*, 4–5.
32. Chambers, *No God but Gain*, 79–83, 93.
33. Poinsett, *Notes on Mexico*, 289; Chambers, *No God but Gain*, 88; Ferrer, *Cuba*, 70–71; Mulcahy, *Hubs of Empire*, 120–22.
34. Poinsett, *Notes on Mexico*, 288–89, 293–95.
35. T. Ford to Joel Roberts Poinsett, May 20, 1823, Joel Roberts Poinsett Papers, vol. 2, folder 8, Historical Society of Pennsylvania (hereafter HSP), Philadelphia; William Johnson to Joel Roberts Poinsett, ibid., vol. 2, folder 6; Chambers, *No God but Gain*, 90–105.
36. John Warner to John Quincy Adams, March 28, 1824, *Despatches from United States Consuls in Havana, Cuba, 1783–1906*, Reel 3, National Archives, Washington, DC (hereafter *Despatches from Havana*); Thomas Wilcock to John Quincy Adams, May 27, 1818, quoted in Chambers, *No God but Gain*, 105.
37. Richard Rush to Jonathan Roberts, October 23, 1823, Jonathan Roberts Papers (Collection 558), box 3, folder 16, HSP; Lewis, *American Union and the Problem of Neighborhood*, 173–79.
38. José María Heredia to Francisco Hernández Morejón, November 6, 1823, in Luciani, *Heredia in New York*, 4, 33–34; James Monroe to James Madison, September 26, 1822, Founders Online; John Quincy Adams, Diary Entry, September 30, 1822, in LaFeber, *Adams and American Continental Empire*, 128; Ferrer, *Cuba*, 86.
39. John Quincy Adams, Diary Entry, September 27, 1822, in LaFeber, *Adams and American Continental Empire*, 126–27; "Communicated for the Centinel," *Fayetteville Weekly Observer*, April 10, 1823; Chambers, *No God but Gain*, 105–9; Lewis, *American Union and the Problem of Neighborhood*, 172–73.

40. John Quincy Adams, Diary Entry, September 27, 1822, in LaFeber, *Adams and American Continental Empire*, 128; Langley, *Struggle for the American Mediterranean*, 39–46.
41. Canning's Memorandum to the Cabinet on Spanish American Policy, November 15, 1822, in Blaufarb, *Revolutionary Atlantic*, 492–94; Chambers, *No God but Gain*, 105–9; Langley, *Struggle for the American Mediterranean*, 39–46; Schneider, *Occupation of Havana*, chs. 1 and 2.
42. John Mountain to John Quincy Adams, July 18, 1823, *Despatches from Havana*, Reel 3; José María Heredia to Francisco Hernández Morejón, November 6, 1823, in Luciani, *Heredia in New York*, 33, 240n4; Ferrer, *Cuba*, 82–90.
43. John C. Calhoun to Andrew Jackson, March 30, 1823, in Jackson, *Papers of Andrew Jackson*, 5:266–67; Lewis, *American Union and the Problem of Neighborhood*, 173–79.
44. Chambers, *No God but Gain*, 118–22.
45. John Quincy Adams to Hugh Nelson, April 28, 1823, in Adams, *Writings of John Quincy Adams*, 7:369–76; John C. Calhoun to Andrew Jackson, March 30, 1823, in Jackson, *Papers of Andrew Jackson*, 5:266–67. See also Schneider, *Occupation of Havana*, 316; Pérez, *Cuba in the American Imagination*, 25–26; Langley, "Slavery, Reform, and American Policy," 72–73.
46. John Quincy Adams to Hugh Nelson, April 28, 1823, in Adams, *Writings of John Quincy Adams*, 7:369–76.
47. Thomas Jefferson to James Monroe, June 23, 1823, Founders Online; James Monroe to Thomas Jefferson, June 30, 1823, Founders Online; W. H. Sumner to John Adams, May 3, 1823, Founders Online.
48. Jonathan Roberts to Nathan Roberts, February 14, 1825, Jonathan Roberts Papers, box 3, folder 20, HSP.
49. S. A. Rainey to N. Talcott, June 19, 1825, Eben William Sage Papers, box 2, folder 25, MHS; Barcia, *Great African Slave Revolt*, 3; Chambers, *No God but Gain*, 143–54.
50. "Revolt in Cuba," *Maryland Gazette*, July 7, 1825; "Further Particulars of the Insurrection at Matanzas. In a letter to the Editors of the *New York Daily Advertiser*," *American Daily Advertiser*, July 6, 1825; S. A. Rainey to Eben William Sage, August 14, 1825, Sage Papers, box 2, folder 1825, MHS; Ephron William Webster to Eben William Sage, November 13, 1825, ibid.; "Havana," *Providence Patriot, Columbian Phenix*, September 24, 1825.
51. Henry Clay to Henry Middleton, May 10, 1825, in Manning, *Diplomatic Correspondence Concerning the Independence of the Latin-American Nations*, 1:247–48; Joel Roberts Poinsett to Henry Clay, March 18, 1826, in ibid., 3:1655; Patrick Mackie to George Canning, November 20, 1823, in Webster, *Britain and the Independence of Latin America*, 1:440.

52. Simón Bolívar to Francisco de Paula Santander, July 10, 1825, in Bolívar, *Selected Writings*, 2:518; Bolívar to Santander, December 23, 1822, in ibid., 1:307; Bolívar to Santander, May 20, 1825, in ibid. 2:498–99.
53. Seaton, *Register of Debates in Congress*, House of Representatives, 19th Congress, 1st Session, 2449–51; Lynch, *Simón Bolívar*, 288–89; Torget, *Seeds of Empire*, 78–80.
54. Lewis, *American Union and the Problem of Neighborhood*, 198–208; Fitz, *Our Sister Republics*, 218–20.
55. *Niles' Weekly Register*, June 1826, 233; Lewis, *American Union and the Problem of Neighborhood*, 198–208; Fitz, *Our Sister Republics*, 217–20.
56. *Niles' Weekly Register*, June 1826, 170; Fitz, *Our Sister Republics*, 217–20.
57. Alexander H. Everett to John Quincy Adams, November 30, 1825, in Hale, *Cuba: The Everett Letters on Cuba*, 6–10; Alexander H. Everett to Henry Clay, January 7, 1827, in Manning, *Diplomatic Correspondence Concerning the Independence of the Latin-American Nations*, 3:2139–40.
58. *Weekly Raleigh Register*, October 7, 1825; Joel R. Poinsett to Henry Clay, May 12, 1827, in Manning, *Diplomatic Correspondence Concerning the Independence of the Latin-American Nations*, 3:1660.
59. *Niles' Weekly Register*, June 1826, 171–72.
60. Patrick Mackie to George Canning, November 20, 1823, in Webster, *Britain and the Independence of Latin America*, 1:440; George Canning to Edward J. Dawkins, March 18, 1826, in ibid., 1:408.
61. Joel R. Poinsett to Martin Van Buren, October 14, 1829, in Manning, *Diplomatic Correspondence Concerning the Independence of the Latin-American Nations*, 3:1705; Van Young, *A Life Together*, 404–6.
62. "Senate of the United States, Wednesday, March 1," *American Watchman and Delaware Advertiser*, March 10, 1826; *Register of Debates in Congress*, House of Representatives, 19th Congress, 1st Session, 2449–51; William Tudor to Joel Roberts Poinsett, February 3, 1827, Joel Roberts Poinsett Papers, vol. 4, folder 3, HSP.
63. "Patriot, and the *Nashville Republican*, Western Boundary," *Indiana State Journal*, September 24, 1829. US expansionists expressed many reasons for their interest in Texas. For more on the role of the cotton industry in shaping US interest in Texas, see Torget, *Seeds of Empire*. For more on Comanche imperialism, see DeLay, *War of a Thousand Deserts*. For more on the expansion and protection of slavery, see Karp, *This Vast Southern Empire*, chs. 2 and 3; Hietala, *Manifest Design*, ch. 2; Campbell, *Empire for Slavery*; Taylor, *American Republics*, 315–29.
64. Burge, *Failed Vision of Empire*, 67–86; Weeks, *New Cambridge History of American Foreign Relations*, 1:213–15; Karp, *This Vast Southern Empire*, 57–69; Horsman, *Race and Manifest Destiny*, 279–83.

65. On the role of sectional politics contributing to the thwarted effort to annex Cuba, see Perkins, *Cambridge History of American Foreign Relations*, 1:198.
66. On anxious aggrandizement, see Hietala, *Manifest Design*, ch. 2.
67. Karp, *This Vast Southern Empire*, 57–69.
68. Thomas Jefferson to William C. C. Claiborne, October 29, 1808, Founders Online.

## 5. THE PACIFIC NORTHWEST

1. Guadalupe Victoria, "Proclamation," November 23, 1825, *American Monitor*, 416.
2. On the collapse of Spanish America and US westward expansion, see Owsley and Smith, *Filibusters and Expansionists*, 1–6; Weber, *Spanish Frontier in North*, 296–301. On US struggles to establish a territorial presence on the Pacific coast, see Kastor, *William Clark's World*, 8–9, 210–11; Ronda, *Astoria and Empire*, 327–36.
3. For more on cooperative imperialism between the American republics, see Fitz, "Monroe Doctrine and the Indigenous Americas," 802–7. On Pan-American unity, see Fitz, *Our Sister Republics*. On Spanish America and the economic development of the US, see Herrera, "Rise and Fall of a Speculative Bubble," 132–34; Truett, *Fugitive Landscapes*, 9; Whitaker, *United States and the Independence of Latin America*. On the collapse of the Spanish Empire and its consequences for US expansion, see Lewis, *American Union and the Problem of Neighborhood*; Narrett, "Liberation and Conquest," 23–50.
4. For more on mutually reinforcing developments in Latin America and the US West, see McGuinness, *Path of Empire*, 12. On republicanism and free trade, see Reeder, *Smugglers, Pirates, and Patriots*, 5–6. On antebellum expansion to the Pacific coast, see Graebner, *Empire on the Pacific*, 217–20; Pletcher, *Diplomacy of Annexation*, 3, 60–100.
5. For more on Anglo-Americans' interest in the Pacific world, see Mapp, *Elusive West*, 3–5; Yokota, *Unbecoming British*, 115–19, 159–61.
6. John Jacob Astor to Thomas Jefferson, October 18, 1813, Founders Online; Ross, *First Settlers on the Oregon or Columbia River*, 100; Robbins, *Oregon*, 33–40; Tyler, *Leveraging an Empire*, 5–19; Weeks, *John Quincy Adams and American Global Empire*, 31.
7. Franchère, *Narrative of a Voyage to the Northwest Coast of America*, 270; Daehnke, *Chinook Resilience*, 44–45; Robbins, *Oregon*, 27–28. On *Illahee* and the "so many little sovereignties" that defined the Columbia River basin, see Whaley, *Oregon and the Collapse of Illahee*, chs. 1–2.

8. "July 20, 1813," in Jones, *Annals of Astoria*, 203; Robbins, *Oregon*, 27–28.
9. Tyler, *Leveraging an Empire*, 7–19; Weeks, *John Quincy Adams and American Global Empire*, 31.
10. Ross, *First Settlers on the Oregon or Columbia River*, 101; Thomas Jefferson to John Jacob Astor, May 24, 1812, Founders Online.
11. Caldas, *Semanario del Nuevo Reyno de Granada*, 11–13; Del Castillo, *Crafting a Republic for the World*, 27–29, 85; Lynch, *Spanish American Revolutions*, 32–34; Tutino, *Making a New World*, 8–10, 36; Jin Xu, *Empire of Silver*, 204.
12. Molina, *Compendio de la historia civil del Reyno de Chile*, 331; Lynch, *Spanish American Revolutions*, 13–15, 32–34; Walker, *Exquisite Slaves*, 22–24. For New Spain's networks with China, see Slack, "Orientalizing New Spain," 97–127.
13. Caldas, *Semanario del Nuevo Reyno de Granada*, 13–14; Appel, "Francisco José de Caldas," 80–81; McFarlane, *Colombia Before Independence*, 311–21.
14. "Bolívar's Jamaica Letter, September 6, 1815," in Blaufarb, *Revolutionary Atlantic*, 452. On colonial legacies see Castillo, *Crafting a Republic for the World*, 1–2. See also Lasso, *Erased*, 11–22; Lynch, *Simón Bolívar*, 159–66.
15. The collapse of the Spanish Empire commanded the attention of Americans and Europeans. See Blaufarb, "The Western Question," 764–86.
16. Samuel Gilman to William Tudor, May 23, 1824, Letters Received by William Tudor, 1824–1828, folder 1, MHS; Jared Sparks to Joel Roberts Poinsett, August 9, 1825, Joel Roberts Poinsett Papers, vol. 3, folder 4, HSP; Fitz, *Our Sister Republics*, 47–53, 159–60; Gould, "Entangled Histories, Entangled Worlds," 764–86; Mapp, *Elusive West*, 114–19.
17. Torres, *Exposition of the Commerce of Spanish America*, 9; Fitz, *Our Sister Republics*, 47–53, 159–60; John Adams to James Lloyd, March 30, 1815, Founders Online; Lazo, *Letters from Filadelfia*, 98–102; Lynch, *Spanish American Revolutions*, 24–26; Weinberg, *Manifest Destiny*, 43.
18. Humboldt, *Political Essay on the Kingdom of New Spain*, 2:79–80; Van Young, *Stormy Passage*, 273.
19. "Idea of Mexican Wealth, From the Travels of Humboldt," *Providence Patriot, Columbian Phenix*, November 10, 1819; Lynch, *Spanish American Revolutions*, 14; Reeder, *Smugglers, Pirates, and Patriots*, 4–5.
20. Torres, *Exposition of the Commerce of Spanish America*, 11; Kanki, *Letters on the United provinces of South America*, 241; Mapp, *Elusive West*, 114–19.
21. Torres, *Exposition of the Commerce of Spanish America*, 41; Pitkin, *A statistical view of the commerce of the United States of America*, 166; John Adams to James Lloyd, March 30, 1815, Founders Online; Norwood, *Trading Freedom*, 33. The statistical numbers about ghost exports and Spanish silver come from Javier

Cuenca-Esteban's "British 'Ghost' Exports, American Middlemen, and the Trade to Spanish America, 1790–1819," 64, 71–72, 80–81; Yokota, *Unbecoming British*, 115–19, 159–61.

22. "A Merchant of Philadelphia" [James Yard], *Spanish America and the United States*, 21, 56. For more on US trade with the Spanish Caribbean, see Chambers, *No God but Gain*, 20–30; Cuenca-Esteban, "Trends and Cycles in US Trade with Spain and the Spanish Empire, 1790–1819," 521–43; Irigoin, "End of a Silver Era," 215–20.

23. Henry Clay, "Emancipation of the South American States," March 24, 1818, in Clay, *Speeches of Henry Clay*, 1:169; Fitz, *Our Sister Republics*, 175–76.

24. Richard Rush to Caesar A. Rodney and John Graham, July 18, 1817, in Manning, *Diplomatic Correspondence Concerning the Independence of the Latin-American Nations*, 1:44; Richard Rush to J. B. Prevost, July 18, 1817, Rodney Family Papers, Rodney Collection, box 5, folder 12, Delaware Historical Society, Wilmington; Theodorick Bland to James Monroe, November 15, 1817, quoted in Stewart, "South American Commission," 48; Lewis, *American Union and the Problem of Neighborhood*, 105–6.

25. Theodorick Bland to John Quincy Adams, November 2, 1818, in Manning, *Diplomatic Correspondence Concerning the Independence of the Latin-American Nations*, 2:997–1005; Goebel, "British-American Rivalry in the Chilean Trade," 190–202; Lynch, *Spanish American Revolutions*, 24–26.

26. J. B. Prevost to John Quincy Adams, March 8, 1818, *Despatches from Special Agents of the Department of State, 1794–1906* (hereafter *Despatches from Special Agents*) M37, roll 4, National Archives, Washington, DC.

27. Theodorick Bland to John Quincy Adams, November 2, 1818, in Manning, *Diplomatic Correspondence Concerning the Independence of the Latin-American Nations*, 2:997–1005; *Philadelphia Gazette*, April 3, 1819; "Trade to China," *Raleigh Register*, May 22, 1818; "Congressional," *National Intelligencer*, December 31, 1822; Weeks, *John Quincy Adams and American Global Empire*, 55–58.

28. John Quincy Adams to Richard C. Anderson, May 27, 1823, in Adams, *Writings of John Quincy Adams*, 7:467–68; Bemis, *John Quincy Adams and the Foundations of American Foreign Policy*, 366; Fitz, *Our Sister Republics*, 176–81; Weinberg, *Manifest Destiny*, 59–67; Weeks, *John Quincy Adams and American Global Empire*, 168–69.

29. "The Mouth of the Columbia," *St. Louis Enquirer*, August 18, 1819; Norwood, *Trading Freedom*, 105–6.

30. "Extract of a Report of an Intelligent Citizen, Travelling in South-America, to a Distinguished Statesman of the United States," *Daily National Journal*, October 23, 1824.

31. "Diary Entry, March 9, 1824," in LaFeber, *John Quincy Adams and American Continental Empire*, 38; Ronda, *Astoria and Empire*, 314–15; St. John, "Contingent Continent," 18–49.
32. John Lowe to Marquess of Londonderry (Robert Stewart, Lord Castlereagh), July 20, 1822, in Stewart, *Correspondence, Despatches, and Other Papers*, 480–81.
33. Humboldt, *Political Essay on the Kingdom of New Spain*, 1:45; "Mexico," *National Advocate, for the Country*, December 5, 1820; Herrera, "Rise and Fall of a Speculative Bubble," 132–34.
34. James Biddle to John Quincy Adams, October 2, 1817, Nicholas Biddle Papers, vol. 5, p. 15, HSP; James Biddle to Thomas Cadwalader, January 28, 1818, Cadwalader Family Papers, series 3, box 99, folder 16, HSP; Robinson, *Memoirs of the Mexican Revolution*, 364; McGuinness, *Path of Empire*, 29.
35. Ortiz de Ayala, *Resumen de la estadística del imperio mexicano*, 59; Herrera, "Rise and Fall of a Speculative Bubble," 136–42; Timmons, *Tadeo Ortiz*, 12–22. On Mexico's topography, see Guardino, *The Dead March*, 305.
36. Simón Bolívar, "Address Delivered at the Inauguration of the Second National Congress of Venezuela in Angostura," February 15, 1819, in Bolívar, *Selected Writings*, 1:197; Simón Bolívar to José de San Martín, August 24, 1821, in ibid., 1:277; Pedro Gual to Simón Bolívar, June 25, 1822, in ibid., 1:333; McFarlane, *Colombia Before Independence*, 311–21; Lynch, *Bolívar*, 167–75; Parker, *Panama Fever*, 15.
37. "Mexico," *National Advocate, for the Country*, December 5, 1820; Kanki, *Letters on the United provinces of South America*, 241; "Reflections upon the state of America, with reference to Europe, and other parts of the world, by a Native of Cusco," *State Journal*, May 10, 1826; Fitz, *Our Sister Republics*, 50–51.
38. *Annals of Congress*, House of Representatives, 17th Congress, 2nd Session, 693–94; Ronda, *Astoria and Empire*, 330–31; Schroeder, "Rep. John Floyd," 333–46.
39. "English Canal Company," *Scioto Gazette*, May 12, 1825; "Exploration of the Northwest Coast, January 16, 1826," House of Representatives, 19th Congress, 1st session, 21.
40. Ortiz, *Resumen de la estadística del imperio mexicano*, 57–58; Weeks, *New Cambridge History of American Foreign Relations*, 1:114–20. For more on the Holy Alliance, see Sexton, *Monroe Doctrine*, 30–31, and ch. 3.
41. Hugh White to Thomas Jefferson, January 18, 1823; Founders Online; Whitaker, *United States and the Independence of Latin America*, 185–86, 345; Lewis, *American Union and the Problem of Neighborhood*, 165–87; Fitz, *Our Sister Republics*, 189.
42. John Quincy Adams to Richard Rush, July 22, 1823; Monroe, *Writings of James Monroe*, 6:356–57; Sexton, *Monroe Doctrine*, 30–31.

43. Lynch, *Simón Bolívar*, 212–14.
44. Lewis A. Tarascon, "Circular re. road from Missouri to Columbia Rivers," July 3, 1824, Founders Online; Whaley, *Oregon and the Collapse of Illahee*, 74–83.
45. James M. Bradford to Josiah Stoddard Johnston, December 21, 1824, Josiah Stoddard Johnston Papers, box 2, folder 11, HSP.
46. George Canning to the Earl of Liverpool, July 7, 1826, in Stapleton, *Some Official Correspondence of George Canning*, 2:73–74; Robbins, *Oregon*, 40–42; Ronda, *Astoria and Empire*, 331–33; St. John, "Contingent Continent," 18–49; Whaley, *Oregon and the Collapse of Illahee*, 74–83.
47. Lewis Williams, "To the citizens of the thirteenth Congressional district of North Carolina," March 1, 1825, in Cunningham, *Circular Letters of Congressmen*, 3:1295; R. L. Colt to Joel Roberts Poinsett, October 7, 1829, Gilpin Family Papers, Poinsett section, HSP. On the contested nature of Oregon, see Richards, *Breakaway Americas*, 183–87; St. John, "Contingent Continent," 18–49.
48. William Tudor to Thomas Handasyd Perkins, December 5, 1824, William Tudor personal archive, box 2, folder 26, Harvard University Archives, Cambridge, MA (hereafter HUA); Tudor to Perkins, July 11, 1824, William Tudor personal archive, box 2, folder 24, HUA; Perkins to Tudor, September 12, 1824, William Tudor personal archive, box 2, folder 25, HUA; Daniel Wadsworth Coit to Daniel Lathrop Coit, April 3, 1826, Daniel Wadsworth Coit correspondence, 1823–28, Connecticut Historical Society, Hartford; Tudor to Perkins, June 17, 1827, William Tudor personal archive, box 2, folder 29, HUA.
49. Goebel, "British-American Rivalry in the Chilean Trade," 190–202.
50. Isaac Foster Coffin Journals, ca. 1820–25, Appleton Family Papers, box 36, folder 2, vol. 87, MHS; Michael Hogan to Joel Roberts Poinsett, August 1, 1827, Joel Roberts Poinsett Papers, vol. 4, box 14, HSP; Goebel, "British-American Rivalry in the Chilean Trade," 190–202.
51. Antonio José Cañaz to John Quincy Adams, February 8, 1825, in Manning, *Diplomatic Correspondence Concerning the Independence of the Latin-American Nations*, 2:881; John Williams to Henry Clay, November 24, 1826, Department of State, *Despatches from US Ministers to Central America, 1824–1906*, Microfilm Reel 2; Herrera, "Rise and Fall of a Speculative Bubble," 141–50.
52. Fitz, *Our Sister Republics*, 217–20.
53. Ward, *Mexico in 1827*, 1:25; Joel Roberts Poinsett to Martin Van Buren, August 2, 1829, Gilpin Papers, Poinsett section, HSP; Richard Rush to Jonathan Roberts, July 1824, Jonathan Roberts Papers, box 3, folder 19, HSP; Guyatt, "Adams Doctrine," 841–42; Haynes, *Unfinished Revolution*, 211–14; Whitaker, *United States and the Independence of Latin America*, 73, 98.
54. William Taylor to James Madison, August 10, 1826, Founders Online; Peter S. Du Ponceau to Joel Roberts Poinsett, August 15, 1827, Joel Roberts Poinsett

Papers, vol. 4, folder 13, HSP; Irigoin, "End of a Silver Era," 217–25; Norwood, *Trading Freedom*, 61–65; Tutino, *Mexico City, 1808*, 252. On Mexico's exports, see Kuntz-Ficker and Tena-Junguito, "Mexico's Foreign Trade in a Turbulent Era," 62. On US exports to Mexico (based on real export prices of 1840/41–1844/45), see Salvucci, "The Origins and Progress of US-Mexican Trade, 1825–1884," 704. On Anglo-American migrations to Texas in the 1820s, see Richards, *Breakaway Americas*, 17–19; Weeks, *New Cambridge History of American Foreign Relations*, 1:163–65.

55. J. B. Provost to John Quincy Adams, November 11, 1818, in Lowrie, *American State Papers: Miscellaneous*, 2:1007–13.
56. Fr. José Señán to Fr. Juan Cortés, November 17, 1822, in Señán, *Letters of José Señán*, 168; Ortiz, *Resumen de la estadística del imperio mexicano*, 57; Weber, *The Mexican Frontier*, 11–14, 122–46, 196–202; Guardino, *The Dead March*, 305–15; Reséndez, *Changing National Identities at the Frontier*, 5–6, 268.
57. Robinson, *Memoirs of the Mexican Revolution*, 365–67, 370–71.
58. "English Canal Company," *Scioto Gazette*, May 12, 1825; "Western Boundary," *Indiana State Journal*, September 24, 1829; Fitz, *Our Sister Republics*, 194–239; Guardino, *The Dead March*, 17–25.
59. George Flowers, Pamphlet, ca. 1829, Gilpin Papers, Poinsett Section, HSP; Van Young, *Stormy Passage*, 204–5.
60. Graebner, *Empire on the Pacific*, 217–20; Pletcher, *Diplomacy of Annexation*, 94–95. For more on the US-Mexico War, see Greenberg, *A Wicked War*.
61. "Annexation," *United States Magazine and Democratic Review* 17, no. 1 (1845): 5–10.

# CONCLUSION

1. Joel Roberts Poinsett to Frances Tyrell, October 10, 1832, Gilpin Family Papers, Poinsett section, HSP; Regele, *Flowers, Guns, and Money*, 1–2, 23–25, 51–53.
2. "From the New England Galaxy: Anno Domini 2000 Anticipated!" *Detroit Gazette*, June 5, 1817; *Franklin Gazette*, March 1, 1819.
3. On fear driving expansionism, see Taylor, *American Republics*, 6–8. On the instability of the Atlantic revolutionary age, see Griffin, *Age of Atlantic Revolution*, 148–49, 183–84, 216.
4. On geopolitical schemes in the early republic era, see Narrett, *Adventurism and Empire*, 3–8.
5. On connections between early republic and antebellum expansionist ideology, see Perkins, *Cambridge History of American Foreign Relations, Vol. 1*. On signs

of an embryonic manifest destiny taking shape, see Shire, *Threshold of Manifest Destiny.*

6. For more on the alternatives for the Americas, see St. John, "Contingent Continent," 18-49.
7. For the general beliefs associated with manifest destiny, see Howe, *What Hath God Wrought,* ch. 18; Richards, *Breakaway Americas,* 13-14, 187. On fears about manhood and industrialization and their relationship to manifest destiny, see Greenberg, *Manifest Manhood.* On the emergence of new racist ideas that supported manifest destiny, see Horsman, *Race and Manifest Destiny,* 5-6. On racial anxieties and manifest destiny, see Hietala, *Manifest Design.*
8. "The Popular Movement," *New York Morning News,* May 24, 1845, quoted in Merk and Merk, *Manifest Destiny and Mission,* 22-23.
9. Richards, *Breakaway Americas,* 254-55; Weeks, *New Cambridge History of American Foreign Relations,* 1:178-202.
10. Charles Jared Ingersoll Papers (Collection 1812), box 5, "Louisiana," 201, HSP.
11. Turner, "Significance of the Frontier in American History," 197-227. On the United States and the breakdown of borderlands, see Adelman and Aron, "From Borderlands to Borders," 814-41. On a consistent vision of a continental empire, see Perkins, *Cambridge History of American Foreign Relations, Vol. 1;* Weeks, *Building the Continental Empire;* Woodworth, *Manifest Destinies,* xi-xii.
12. For more on the many articulations of expansionism in the nineteenth century, see St. John, "Contingent Continent," 18-49. On the contested nature of the antebellum North American continent, see Taylor, *American Republics.*
13. "Annexation," *United States Magazine and Democratic Review* 17, no. 1 (1845): 5-6. On breakaway republics, see Richards, *Breakaway Americans,* 6-7, 12-14, 266-67. On alternative territorial schemes in the Civil War and postwar eras, see Burge, *Failed Vision of Empire,* chs. 5-7; St. John, "Unpredictable America of William Gwin," 56-84. On the divisiveness of manifest destiny, see Greenberg, "Mercenary Ambivalence," 265-78.

# BIBLIOGRAPHY

## ABBREVIATIONS

| | |
|---|---|
| BHC | Burton Historical Collection, Detroit Public Library |
| CHS | Connecticut Historical Society, Hartford |
| FHS | Filson Historical Society, Louisville |
| HSP | Historical Society of Pennsylvania, Philadelphia |
| HUA | Harvard University Archives, Cambridge, MA |
| MHS | Massachusetts Historical Society, Boston |
| MPHC | Michigan Pioneer and Historical Collections |
| MSM | Missouri History Museum Archives, St. Louis |
| TPUS | Territorial Papers of the United States |
| WLC | William L. Clements Library, University of Michigan |

## MANUSCRIPT COLLECTIONS

Penelope Johnson Allen Cherokee Collection, 1775–1878, Tennessee State Library and Archives, Tennessee Virtual Archive

American Science and Medicine Collection, WLC

Nicholas Biddle Papers, HSP
Cadwalader Family Papers, HSP
Arthur Campbell Papers, 1752–1811, FHS
Daniel Wadsworth Coit Correspondence, 1823–28, CHS
Jeremiah G. Dubois Letters, WLC
Thomas Forsyth Papers, MSM
Gilpin Family Papers, Poinsett section, HSP
Henry Hamilton Papers, 1768–1933, Houghton Library, Harvard University
Charles Jared Ingersoll Papers (Collection 1812), HSP
Thomas S. Jesup Collection, WLC
Josiah Stoddard Johnston Papers, HSP
Duncan McArthur Letterbooks, BHC
James and William Perot papers related to capture of Schooner Fanny, 1782–83, Baker Library Special Collections, Harvard Business School
Timothy Pickering Papers, MHS
Joel Roberts Poinsett Papers, HSP
Jonathan Roberts Papers (Collection 558), HSP
Rodney Family Papers, Rodney Collection, Delaware Historical Society, Wilmington
Eben William Sage Papers, MHS
Isaac Shelby Papers, 1760–1839, FHS
Henry Strachey Papers (1768–1802), Surveys of Colonial Governors, WLC
Tucker-Coleman Papers, Special Collections Research Center, Swem Library, College of William and Mary, Williamsburg, VA
William Tudor Personal Archive, Harvard University Archives, Cambridge
Letters Received by William Tudor, 1824–1828, MHS
John R. Williams Papers, BHS
B. F. H. Witherell Papers, BHS

## STATE DOCUMENTS AND PAPERS

Bermuda Islands House of Assembly. *Ancient Journals of the House of Assembly of Bermuda*. 2 vols. Hamilton, Bermuda: G. V. Lee, 1890.
Burnett, Edmund Cody. *Letters of Members of the Continental Congress*. 7 vols. Washington, DC: Carnegie Institution of Washington, 1921–36.
Carter, Clarence Edwin, et al., eds. *Territorial Papers of the United States*. 28 vols. Washington, DC: Government Printing Office, 1934–75.
Clark, William Bell, et al., eds. *Naval Documents of the American Revolution*. 12 vols. Washington, DC: Naval History Division, Dept. of the Navy, 1966–2005.

Ford, Worthington C., et al., eds. *Journals of the Continental Congress, 1774–1789*. 34 vols. Washington, DC: Government Printing Office, 1904–37.
Keppler, Charles J. *Indian Affairs: Laws and Treaties*. 7 vols. Washington, DC: Government Printing Office, 1904–71.
Lowrie, Walter, et al., eds. *American State Papers: Indian Affairs*. 2 vols. Washington, DC: Gales and Seaton, 1832–34.
Lowrie, Walter, et al., eds. *American State Papers: Miscellaneous*. Washington, DC: Gales and Seaton, 1832–34.
Miller, David Hunter, ed. *Treaties and Other International Acts of the United States of America*. 8 vols. Washington, DC: Government Printing Office, 1931–48.
Palmer, William P. *Calendar of Virginia State Papers and Other Manuscripts*. 11 vols. Richmond, VA: James E. Goode, Printer, 1875–93.
Seaton, William Winston, and Joseph Gales, eds. *Register of Debates in Congress*. Washington, DC: Gales and Seaton, 1825–37.
Smith, Paul H., et al., eds. *Letters of Delegates to Congress, 1774–1789*. 26 vols. Washington, DC: Library of Congress, 1976–2000.
US Department of State. *Despatches from Special Agents of the Department of State, 1794–1906*. National Archives, Washington, DC.
US Department of State. *Despatches from United States Consuls in Havana, Cuba, 1783–1906*. National Archives, Washington, DC.
US Department of State. *Despatches from US Ministers to Central America, 1824–1906*. National Archives, Washington, DC.
Webster, C. K., *Britain and the Independence of Latin America, 1812–1830: Select Documents from the Foreign Office Archives*. 2 vols. New York: Octagon Books, 1970.
Wharton, Francis, ed. *The Revolutionary Diplomatic Correspondence of the United States*. 6 vols. Washington, DC: Government Printing Office, 1886–89.

## DIGITAL ARCHIVES

Founders Online
    Adams Papers
    Papers of Benjamin Franklin
    Papers of Alexander Hamilton
    Jay Papers
    Papers of Thomas Jefferson
    Papers of James Madison
    Papers of George Washington

Kaminski, John P., et al., eds. *The Documentary History of the Ratification of the Constitution Digital Edition*. Charlottesville: University of Virginia Press, 2009. http://rotunda.upress.virginia.edu/founders/RNCN-03-17-02-0045.

## NEWSPAPERS AND MAGAZINES

*American Daily Advertiser* (Philadelphia)
*Aurora and General Advertiser* (Philadelphia)
*The American Monitor* (London, UK)
*Bangor Register* (ME)
*Columbian Herald, or, The Independent Courier of North-America* (Charleston, SC)
*Detroit Gazette* (MI)
*Franklin Gazette* (Philadelphia)
*Freeman's Journal or The North-American Intelligencer* (Philadelphia)
*Hartford Courant* (CT)
*Indiana State Journal* (Indianapolis)
*Louisville Public Advertisement* (KY)
*Maryland Gazette* (Baltimore)
*Mississippian* (Vicksburg, MS)
*National Advocate, for the Country* (New York City)
*National Intelligencer* (Washington, DC)
*New York Morning News*
*Niles' Weekly Register* (Baltimore)
*Ohio Observer* (Hudson)
*Pennsylvania Gazette* (Philadelphia)
*Pennsylvania Packet* (Philadelphia)
*Philadelphia Gazette*
*Poughkeepsie Journal* (NY)
*Providence Patriot, Columbian Phenix* (Providence, RI)
*Scioto Gazette* (Chillicothe, OH)
*St. Louis Enquirer* (MO)
*State Journal* (Jackson, MS)
*United States Magazine and Democratic Review* (New York City)
*Virginia Gazette* (Williamsburg)
*Virginia Gazette, or, The American Advertiser* (Williamsburg)
*The Washington City Weekly Gazette* (Washington, DC)
*Weekly Raleigh Register* (NC)

# PUBLISHED PRIMARY SOURCES

Adams, John Quincy. *John Quincy Adams and American Continental Empire: Letters, Papers, and Speeches.* Edited by Walter LaFeber. Chicago: Quadrangle Books, 1965.

Adams, John Quincy. *Writings of John Quincy Adams.* 7 vols. Edited by Worthington Chauncey Ford. New York: Macmillan, 1913-17.

"A Merchant of Philadelphia" [James Yard]. *Spanish America and the United States; Or, Views of the Actual Commerce of the United States with the Spanish Colonies.* Philadelphia: M. Carey & Son, 1818.

Blaufarb, Rafe, ed. *The Revolutionary Atlantic: Republican Visions, 1760-1830, A Documentary History.* New York: Oxford University Press, 2018.

Bolívar, Simón. *Selected Writings of Bolívar.* 2 vols. Compiled by Vicente Lecuna, translated by Lewis Bertrand, edited by Harold A. Bierck Jr. New York: Colonial Press, 1951.

Caldas, Francisco José de. *Semanario del Nuevo Reyno de Granada.* Bogotá, 1808.

Channing, William E. *Thoughts on the Evils of a Spirit of Conquest, and on Slavery: A Letter on the Annexation of Texas to the United States.* London: John Green, 1837.

Clay, Henry. *The Papers of Henry Clay.* 10 vols. Edited by James F. Hopkins and Mary W. M. Hargreaves. Lexington: University Press of Kentucky, 1959-91.

———. *The Speeches of Henry Clay.* 2 vols. Edited by Calvin Colton. New York: A. S. Barnes & Co., 1857.

Coleman, George P., ed. "Randolph Tucker Letters." *William and Mary Quarterly* 42, no. 3 (Jan. 1934): 47-52.

Cruikshank, E. A., ed. *The Correspondence of Lieut. Governor John Graves Simcoe, with Allied Documents Relating to His Administration of the Government of Upper Canada.* 5 vols. Toronto: Ontario Historical Society, 1923-31.

———. *The Documentary History of the Campaign upon the Niagara Frontier in the Year 1813.* Welland: Lundy's Lane Historical Society, 1902.

———. *Documents Relating to the Invasion of Canada and the Surrender of Detroit.* Ottawa: Government Printing Bureau, 1912.

Cummingham, Noble E., Jr. *Circular Letters of Congressmen to Their Constituents 1789-1829.* 3 vols. Chapel Hill: University of North Carolina Press, 1978.

Darby, William. *A Tour from the City of New-York to Detroit, in the Michigan Territory, Made between the 2d of May and the 22d of September, 1818.* New York: Kirk & Mercein, 1819.

Davis, T. Frederick, ed. "United States Troops in Spanish East Florida, 1812-1813." *Florida Historical Quarterly* 9, no. 4 (April 1931): 3-21.

Deane, Silas. *The Deane Papers: Collections of the New-York Historical Society*. New York: New-York Historical Society, 1887–1891.

Forbes, Lt. Col. James G. *Report of the Trial of Brig. General William Hull; Commanding the North-Western Army of the United States by a Court Martial Held at Albany on Monday, 3d January, 1814, and Succeeding Days*. New York: Eastburn, Kirk, and Co., 1814.

Franchère, Gabriel. *Narrative of a Voyage to the Northwest Coast of America in the Years 1811, 1812, 1813, and 1814; or the First American Settlement on the Pacific*. New York: Redfield, 1854.

Franklin, Benjamin. *The Works of Benjamin Franklin, Including the Private as Well as the Official and Scientific Correspondence, Together with the Unmutilated and Correct Version of the Autobiography*. 12 vols. Edited by John Bigelow. New York: G. P. Putnam's Sons, 1904.

Geggus, David, ed. *The Haitian Revolution: A Documentary History*. Indianapolis: Hackett Publishing, 2014.

Hale, Edward E. *Cuba: The Everett Letters on Cuba*. Boston: Geo. H. Ellis, Printer, 1897.

Hamlin, L. Belle, ed. *Quarterly Publication of the Historical and Philosophical Society of Ohio*. 18 vols. Cincinnati: Abingdon Press, 1906–24.

Harrison, William Henry. *Messages and Letters of William Henry Harrison*. 2 vols. Edited by Logan Esarey. Indianapolis: Indiana Historical Commission, 1922.

Holroyd, John, Lord Sheffield. *Observations on the Commerce of the American States*. London: J. Debrett, 1784.

Hull, William. *Memoirs of the Campaign of the North Western Army of the United States, A.D. 1812. In a Series of Letters Addressed to the Citizens of the United States*. Boston: True & Greene, 1824.

Humboldt, Alexander von. *Political Essay on the Kingdom of New Spain*. Translated by John Black. 4 vols. London: Longman, Hurst, Rees, Orme, and Brown, 1822.

Hunter, William. *Speech of the Hon. William Hunter, in secret session of the Senate of the United States, Feb. 2d, 1813: On the proposition for seizing and occupying the province of East-Florida by the troops of the U. States*. Newport: Rousmaniere & Barber, 1813.

Idzerda, Stanley J., et al., eds. *Lafayette in the Age of the American Revolution: Selected Letters and Papers, 1776–1790*. 5 vols. Ithaca, NY: Cornell University Press, 1977–83.

Jackson, Andrew. *The Papers of Andrew Jackson*. 10 vols. Edited by Sam B. Smith et al. Knoxville: University of Tennessee Press, 1980–.

Jones, Robert F. *Annals of Astoria: The Headquarters Log of the Pacific Fur Company on the Columbia River, 1811–1813*. New York: Fordham University Press, 1999.

Kanki, Vicente Pazos. *Letters on the United provinces of South America, addressed to the Hon. Henry Clay, speaker of the House of representatives in the U. States*. New York: J. Seymour, 1819.

Kaminski, John P., et al., eds. *Commentaries on the Constitution: Public and Private*. Madison: State Historical Society of Wisconsin, 1981–95.

Kinnaird, Lawrence, ed. *Annual Report of the American Historical Association for the Year 1945. Volume 2: Spain in the Mississippi Valley, 1765–1794*. Washington, DC: Government Printing Office, 1949.

Laurens, Henry. *The Papers of Henry Laurens*. 17 vols. Edited by David R. Chesnutt et al. Columbia: University of South Carolina Press, 1968–2003.

Libby, Dorothy, ed. "Thomas Forsyth to William Clark, December 23, 1812." *Ethnohistory* 8, no. 2 (Spring 1961): 179–95.

Luciani, Frederick, ed. *José María Heredia in New York, 1823–1825: An Exiled Cuban Poet in the Age of Revolution, Selected Letters and Verse*. Albany: SUNY Press, 2020.

Madison, James. *Notes of Debates in the Federal Convention of 1787 Reported by James Madison*. Columbus: Ohio University Press, 1985.

Manning, William R., ed. *Diplomatic Correspondence of the United States: Canadian Relations, 1784–1860*. 4 vols. Washington DC: Carnegie Endowment for International Peace, 1940–45.

Manning, William R., ed. *Diplomatic Correspondence of the United States Concerning the Independence of the Latin-American Nations*. 3 vols. New York: Oxford University Press, 1925–26.

Marshall, Thomas Maitland, ed. *The Life and Papers of Frederick Bates*. 2 vols. New York: Arno Press, 1975.

*Michigan Pioneer and Historical Collections*. 40 volumes. Lansing: Wynkoop Hallenbeck Crawford, 1874–1929.

Molina, Juan Ignacio. *Compendio de la historia civil del Reyno de Chile, Escrito en Italiano por el Abate Don Juan Ignacio Molina. Parte segunda, Traducida al Español, y aumentada con varias notas por don Nicolas de la Cruz y Bahamonde*. Madrid: La Imprenta de Sancha, 1795.

Monroe, James. *The Writings of James Monroe, Including a Collection of His Public and Private Papers and Correspondence Now for the First Time Printed*. 7 vols. Edited by Stanislaus Murray Hamilton. New York: G. P. Putnam's Sons, 1898–1903.

Montesquieu, Charles, Baron de. *The Spirit of Laws*. [1748]. Translated by Thomas Nugent. New York: Colonial Press, 1899.

Norton, John. *The Journal of Major John Norton, 1816*. Edited by Carl F. Klinck and James J. Talman. Toronto: Champlain Society, 1970.

Onís, Luis de. *Memoir upon the Negotiations Between Spain and the United States of America, Which Led to the Treaty of 1819*. Translated by Tobias Watkins. Washington, DC: E. DeKrafft, Printer, 1821.

Ortiz de Ayala, Simón Tadeo. *Resumen de la estadística del imperio mexicano*. Mexico City: Universidad Nacional Autónoma de México, 1991.

Paine, Thomas. *Common Sense*. [1776]. Reprint edited by Isaac Kramnick. New York: Penguin Books, 1986.

———. *The American Crisis*. [1776–83]. Reprint edited by Andrew S. Trees. New York: Barnes and Noble, 2010.

Pitkin, Timothy. *A Statistical View of the Commerce of the United States of America: Its Connection with Agriculture and Manufactures: and an Account of the Public Debt, Revenues, and Expenditures of the United States. With a Brief Review of the Trade, Agriculture, and Manufactures of the Colonies, Previous to Their Independence*. New York: James Eastburn & Co., 1817.

Poinsett, Joel Roberts. *Notes on Mexico Made in the Autumn of 1822: Accompanied by an Historical Sketch of the Revolution, and Translations of Official Reports on the Present State of that Country*. London: John Miller, 1825.

Robinson, William Davis. *Memoirs of the Mexican Revolution: Including a narrative of the expedition of General Xavier Mina. With some observations on the practicability of opening a commerce between the Pacific and Atlantic oceans*. . . . Philadelphia: Lydia R. Bailey, 1820.

Ross, Alexander. *Adventures of the First Settlers on the Oregon or Columbia River: Being a Narrative of the Expedition Fitted Out by John Jacob Astor, to Establish the "Pacific Fur Company"; With an Account of Some Tribes on the Coast of the Pacific*. London: Smith, Elder, and Co., 1849.

Rowland, Dunbar, ed. *Official Letter Books of W. C. C. Claiborne, 1801–1816*. 6 vols. Jackson, MS: State Department of Archives and History, 1917.

Schoolcraft, Henry Rowe. *Narrative journal of travels through the northwestern regions of the United States; extending from Detroit through the great chain of American lakes, to the sources of the Mississippi river. Performed as a member of the expedition under Governor Cass. In the year 1820*. Albany, NY: E. & E. Hosford, 1821.

Señán, José. *The Letters of José Señán, O.F.M. Mission San Buenaventura, 1796–1823*. Translated by Paul D. Nathan. Edited by Lesley Byrd Simpson. Los Angeles: John Howell Books, 1962.

Sevier, Cora Bales, and Nancy S. Madden, eds. *Sevier Family History with the Collected Letters of Gen. John Sevier, First Governor of Tennessee*. Washington, DC: Privately published, 1961.

Stagg, J. C. A., ed. "The Political Essays of William Shaler." *William and Mary Quarterly* 59 (April 2002): 449–80.

Stapleton, Edward J., ed. *Some Official Correspondence of George Canning*. 2 vols. London: Longmans, Green, and Co., 1887.

Stewart, Robert, Lord Castlereagh. *Correspondence, Despatches, and Other Papers of Viscount Castlereagh, Second Marquess of Londonderry*. Vol. 2. Edited by Charles William Vane. London: John Murray, 1853.

Torres, Manuel. *An Exposition of the Commerce of Spanish America*. Philadelphia: G. Palmer, 1816.
Tucker, Nathaniel. *The Bermudian: A Poem*. Hull: Joseph Simmons, 1808.
Ward, Henry George. *Mexico in 1827*. 2 vols. London: Henry Colburn, 1828.

## SECONDARY SOURCES

Ablavsky, Gregory. *Federal Ground: Governing Property and Violence in the First US Territories*. New York: Oxford University Press, 2021.
Adelman Jeremy, and Stephen Aron. "From Borderlands to Borders: Empires, Nation-States, and the Peoples in between in North American History." *American Historical Review* 104 (June 1999): 814–41.
Antal, Sandy. "Michigan Ceded: Why and Wherefore?" *Michigan Historical Review* 38, no 1. (Spring 2012): 1–26.
———. *A Wampum Denied: Procter's War of 1812*. Ottawa: Carleton University Press, 1997.
Appel, John Wilton. "Francisco José de Caldas: A Scientist at Work in Nueva Granada." *Transactions of the American Philosophical Society* 84, no. 5 (1994), 1–154.
Armitage, David. *The Ideological Origins of the British Empire*. New York: Cambridge University Press, 2000.
Aron, Stephen. *How the West Was Lost: The Transformation of Kentucky from Daniel Boone to Henry Clay*. Baltimore: Johns Hopkins University Press, 1996.
Bald, F. Clever. *Detroit's First American Decade: 1796–1805*. Ann Arbor: University of Michigan Press, 1948.
Bancroft, George. *History of the Formation of the Constitution of the United States*. 2 vols. New York: D. Appleton and Co., 1889.
Banning, Lance. *The Sacred Fire of Liberty: James Madison and the Founding of the Federal Republic*. Ithaca, NY: Cornell University Press, 1995.
Barcia, Manuel. *The Great African Slave Revolt of 1825: Cuba and the Fight for Freedom in Matanzas*. Baton Rouge: Louisiana State University Press, 2012.
Barksdale, Kevin T. *The Lost State of Franklin: America's First Secession*. Lexington: University Press of Kentucky, 2009.
Bemis, Samuel Flagg. *John Quincy Adams and the Foundations of American Foreign Policy*. New York: Alfred A. Knopf, 1949.
Blaakman, Michael A. "The Marketplace of American Federalism: Land Speculation Across State Lines in the Early Republic." *Journal of American History* 107, no. 3 (Dec. 2020): 583–608.

Blaakman, Michael A., and Emily Conroy-Krutz. Introduction to *The Early Imperial Republic: From the American Revolution to the US-Mexico War*, edited by Michael A. Blaakman, Emily Conroy-Krutz, and Noelani Arista, 3–23. Philadelphia: University of Pennsylvania Press, 2023.

Blaufarb, Rafe. "The Western Question: The Geopolitics of Latin American Independence." *American Historical Review* 12, no. 3 (2007): 764–86.

Bowes, John P. *Land too Good for Indians: Northern Indian Removal.* Norman: Oklahoma University Press, 2016.

Breen, T. H. *The Marketplace of the Revolution: How Consumer Politics Shaped American Independence.* New York: Oxford University Press, 2004.

Brunsman, Denver Alexander, Joel Stone, and Douglas D. Fisher, eds. *Border Crossings: The Detroit River Region in the War of 1812.* Detroit: Detroit Historical Society, 2012.

Buel, Richard, Jr. *In Irons: Britain's Naval Supremacy and the American Revolutionary Economy.* New Haven, CT: Yale University Press, 1998.

Burge, Daniel J. *A Failed Vision of Empire: The Collapse of Manifest Destiny, 1845–1872.* Lincoln: University of Nebraska Press, 2022.

Calloway, Colin G. *The American Revolution in Indian Country: Crisis and Diversity in Native American Communities.* New York: Cambridge University Press, 1995.

———. *The Indian World of George Washington: The First President, the First Americans, and the Birth of the Nation.* New York: Oxford University Press, 2018.

Campbell, Randolph B. *An Empire for Slavery: The Peculiar Institution in Texas, 1821–1865.* Baton Rouge: Louisiana State University Press, 1989.

Cangany, Catherine. *Frontier Seaport: Detroit's Transformation into an Atlantic Entrepôt.* Chicago: University of Chicago Press, 2014.

Cayton, Andrew R. L. *The Frontier Republic: Ideology and Politics in the Ohio Country, 1780–1825.* Kent, OH: Kent State University Press, 1986.

Chambers, Stephen M. *No God but Gain: The Untold Story of Cuban Slavery, the Monroe Doctrine, and the Making of the United States.* New York: Verso, 2015.

Cogliano, Francis D. *Emperor of Liberty: Thomas Jefferson's Foreign Policy.* New Haven, CT: Yale University Press, 2014.

Conroy-Krutz, Emily. *Christian Imperialism: Converting the World in the Early American Republic.* Ithaca, NY: Cornell University Press, 2015.

Craig, Gerald M. *Upper Canada: The Formative Years 1784–1841.* New York: Oxford University Press, 1963.

Cuenca-Esteban, Javier. "British 'Ghost' Exports, American Middlemen, and the Trade to Spanish America, 1790–1819." *William and Mary Quarterly* 71, no. 1 (Jan. 2014): 63–98.

———. "Trends and Cycles in US Trade with Spain and the Spanish Empire, 1790–1819." *Journal of Economic History* 41, no. 2 (June 1984): 521–43.

Cusick, James G. *The Other War of 1812: The Patriot War and the American Invasion of Spanish East Florida*. Athens: University of Georgia Press, 2003.

Daehnke, Jon D. *Chinook Resilience: Heritage and Cultural Revitalization on the Lower Columbia River*. Seattle: University of Washington Press, 2017.

Davis, Jack E. *The Gulf: The Making of an American Sea*. New York: Liveright, 2017.

DeConde, Alexander. *This Affair of Louisiana*. New York: Scribner, 1976.

DeLay, Brian. *War of a Thousand Deserts: Indian Raids and the US-Mexican War*. New Haven, CT: Yale University Press, 2008.

Del Castillo, Lina. *Crafting a Republic for the World: Scientific, Geographic, and Historiographic Inventions of Colombia*. Lincoln: University of Nebraska Press, 2018.

Dowd, Gregory Evans. *A Spirited Resistance: The North American Indian Struggle for Unity, 1745–1815*. Baltimore: Johns Hopkins University Press, 1992.

Dull, Jonathan R. *The French Navy and American Independency: A Study of Arms and Diplomacy, 1774–1787*. Princeton, NJ: Princeton University Press, 1975.

DuVal, Kathleen. "How Native Nations Survived the Imperial Republic." In *The Early Imperial Republic: From the American Revolution to the US-Mexico War*, edited by Michael A. Blaakman, Emily Conroy-Krutz, and Noelani Arista, 63–82. Philadelphia: University of Pennsylvania Press, 2023.

———. *Independence Lost: Lives on the Edge of the American Revolution*. New York: Random House, 2015.

———. *The Native Ground: Indians and Colonists in the Heart of the Continent*. Philadelphia: University of Pennsylvania Press, 2006.

Edmunds, R. David. *The Potawatomis: Keepers of the Fire*. Norman: University of Oklahoma Press, 1978.

Esteban, Javier Cuenca. "Trends and Cycles in US Trade with Spain and the Spanish Empire, 1790–1819." *Journal of Economic History* 44, no. 2 (June 1984): 521–43.

Estes, Todd. *The Jay Treaty Debate: Public Opinion, and the Evolution of Early American Political Culture*. Amherst: University of Massachusetts Press, 2006.

Faulkner, Charles H. *Massacre at Cavett's Station: Frontier Tennessee During the Cherokee Wars*. Knoxville: University of Tennessee Press, 2013.

Ferling, John E. *The Ascent of George Washington: The Hidden Political Genius of an American Icon*. New York: Bloomsbury Publishing, 2009.

Ferrer, Ada. *Cuba: An American History*. New York: Scribner, 2021.

———. *Freedom's Mirror: Cuba and Haiti in the Age of Revolution*. New York: Cambridge University Press, 2014.

———. "Speaking of Haiti: Slavery, Revolution, and Freedom in Cuban Slave Testimony." In *The World of the Haitian Revolution*, edited by David Patrick Geggus et al., 223–47. Bloomington: Indiana University Press, 2009.

Fitz, Caitlin. "The Monroe Doctrine and the Indigenous Americas." *Diplomatic History* 47, no. 5 (Nov. 2023): 802–22.

———. *Our Sister Republics: The United States in an Age of American Revolutions*. New York: Liveright, 2016.

Friend, Craig Thompson. *Kentucke's Frontiers*. Indianapolis: Indiana University Press, 2010.

Furstenberg, François. "The Significance of the Trans-Appalachian Frontier in Atlantic History." *American Historical Review* 113, no. 3 (June 2008): 647–77.

Gilje, Paul A. "Commerce and Conquest in Early American Foreign Relations, 1750–1850." *Journal of the Early Republic* 37, no. 4 (Winter 2017): 538–54.

———. *Free Trade and Sailors' Rights in the War of 1812*. New York: Cambridge University Press, 2013.

Girard, Philippe R. "'Liberté, Égalité, Esclavage': French Revolutionary Ideals and the Failure of the Leclerc Expedition to Saint-Domingue." *French Colonial History* 6 (2005): 55–77.

Glover, Lorri. *Eliza Lucas Pinckney: An Independent Woman in the Age of Revolution*. New Haven, CT: Yale University Press, 2020.

———. *The Fate of the Revolution: Virginians Debate the Constitution*. Baltimore: Johns Hopkins University Press, 2016.

Glover, Lorri, and Daniel Blake Smith. *The Shipwreck that Saved Jamestown: The* Sea Venture *Castaways and the Fate of America*. New York: Henry Holt, 2008.

Goebel, Dorthy Burne. "British-American Rivalry in the Chilean Trade." *Journal of Economic History* 2, no 2. (Nov. 1942): 190–202.

Gordon-Reed, Annette, and Peter S. Onuf. *"Most Blessed of the Patriarchs": Thomas Jefferson and the Empire of the Imagination*. New York: Liveright, 2016.

Gould, Eliga H. *Among the Powers of the Earth: The American Revolution and the Making of a New World Empire*. Cambridge, MA: Harvard University Press, 2012.

———. "Entangled Histories, Entangled Worlds: The English-Speaking Atlantic as a Spanish Periphery." *American Historical Review* 112, no. 3 (June 2007): 764–86.

Graebner, Norman A. *Empire on the Pacific: A Study in American Continental Expansion*. New York: Ronald Press Co., 1955.

Greenberg, Amy S. *Manifest Manhood and the Antebellum American Empire*. New York: Cambridge University Press, 2005.

———. "Mercenary Ambivalence: Military Violence in Antebellum America's Wars of Empire." In *The Early Imperial Republic: From the American Revolution to the US-Mexico War*, edited by Michael A. Blaakman, Emily Conroy-Krutz, and Noelani Arista, 265–78. Philadelphia: University of Pennsylvania Press, 2023.

———. *A Wicked War: Polk, Clay, Lincoln, and the 1846 US Invasion of Mexico*. New York: Vintage, 2012.

Griffin, Patrick. *The Age of Atlantic Revolution: The Fall and Rise of a Connected World*. New Haven: Yale University Press, 2023.

———. *American Leviathan: Empire, Nation, and Revolutionary Frontier.* New York: Hill and Wang, 2007.

Guardino, Peter. *The Dead March: A History of the Mexican-American War.* Cambridge: Harvard University Press, 2017.

Guyatt, Nicholas. "The Adams Doctrine and an 'Empire of States.'" *Diplomatic History* 47, no. 5 (Nov. 2023): 823–44.

Hämäläinen, Pekka. *The Comanche Empire.* New Haven, CT: Yale University Press, 2008.

Hatter, Lawrence B. A. *Citizens of Convenience: The Imperial Origins of American Nationhood on the US-Canadian Border.* Charlottesville: University of Virginia Press, 2017.

Haynes, Sam W. *Unfinished Revolution: The Early American Republic in a British World.* Charlottesville: University of Virginia Press, 2010.

Herrera, Jose Maria. "The Rise and Fall of a Speculative Bubble: Geostrategic Concerns, Public Debate, and the Promotion of an American Trans-Oceanic Canal in the 1820s." *American Nineteenth Century History* 19, no. 2 (2018): 131–58.

Hickey, Donald R. *The War of 1812: A Forgotten Conflict.* Urbana: University of Illinois Press, 1989.

Hietala, Thomas R. *Manifest Design: Anxious Aggrandizement in Late Jacksonian America.* Ithaca, NY: Cornell University Press, 1985.

Hinderaker, Eric. *Elusive Empires: Constructing Colonialism in the Ohio Valley, 1673–1800.* New York: Cambridge University Press, 1997.

Horne, Gerald. *Negro Comrades of the Crown: African Americans and the British Empire Fight the U.S. before Emancipation.* New York: NYU Press, 2012.

———. *Race to Revolution: The U.S. and Cuba during Slavery and Jim Crow.* New York: Monthly Review Press, 2014.

Horsman, Reginald. "On to Canada: Manifest Destiny and United States Strategy in the War of 1812." *Michigan Historical Review* 13, no. 2 (Fall 1987): 1–24.

———. *Race and Manifest Destiny: The Origins of American Racial Anglo-Saxonism.* Cambridge, MA: Harvard University Press, 1981.

Howe, Daniel Walker. *What Hath God Wrought: The Transformation of America, 1815–1848.* New York: Oxford University Press, 2007.

Hudson, Linda S. *Mistress of Manifest Destiny: A Biography of Jane McManus Storm Cazneau, 1807–1878.* Austin: Texas State Historical Association, 2001.

Hyde, Anne F. *Empires, Nations, and Families: A History of the North American West, 1800–1860.* Lincoln: University of Nebraska Press, 2011.

Immerman, Richard H. *Empire for Liberty: A History of American Imperialism from Benjamin Franklin to Paul Wolfowitz.* Princeton, NJ: Princeton University Press, 2010.

Immerwahr, Daniel. *How to Hide an Empire: A History of the Greater United States.* New York: Farrar, Straus and Giroux, 2019.

Irigoin, Alejandra. "The End of a Silver Era: The Consequences of the Breakdown of the Spanish Peso Standard in China and the United States, 1780s–1850s." *Journal of World History* 20, no. 2 (June 2009): 207–44.

Isenberg, Andrew C., and Thomas Richards Jr. "Alternative Wests: Rethinking Manifest Destiny." *Pacific Historical Review* 86, no. 1 (Feb. 2017): 4–17.

Jarvis, Michael J. *In the Eye of All Trade: Bermuda, Bermudians, and the Maritime Atlantic World, 1680–1783.* Chapel Hill: University of North Carolina Press, 2010.

Jasanoff, Maya. *Liberty's Exiles: American Loyalists in the Revolutionary World.* New York: Vintage, 2011.

Johnson, Ronald. *Diplomacy in Black and White: John Adams, Toussaint Louverture, and Their Atlantic World Alliance.* Athens: University of Georgia Press, 2014.

Karp, Matthew. *This Vast Southern Empire: Slaveholders at the Helm of American Foreign Policy.* Cambridge, MA: Harvard University Press, 2016.

Kastor, Peter. "'Equitable Rights and Privileges': The Divided Loyalties in Washington County, Virginia, During the Franklin Separatist Crisis." *Virginia Magazine of History and Biography* 105, no. 1 (Spring 1997): 193–226.

———. *The Nation's Crucible: The Louisiana Purchase and the Creation of America.* New Haven, CT: Yale University Press, 2004.

———. *William Clark's World: Describing America in an Age of Unknowns.* New Haven, CT: Yale University Press, 2011.

Kerr, Winfred Brenton. *Bermuda and the American Revolution: 1760–1783.* Hamden, CT: Archon Books, 1969.

Klooster, Wim. *Revolutions of the Atlantic World: A Comparative History.* New York: NYU Press, 2018.

Kuntz-Ficker, Sandra, and Antonio Tena-Junguito. "Mexico's Foreign Trade in a Turbulent Era (1821–1870): A Reconstruction." *Revista de Historia Económica / Journal of Iberian and Latin American Economic History* 36, no. 1 (March 2018): 149–82.

Landers, Jane. "Black Community and Culture in the Southeastern Borderlands." *Journal of the Early Republic* 18, no. 1 (Spring 1998): 117–34.

Langley, Lester D. "Slavery, Reform, and American Policy in Cuba, 1823–1878." *Revista de Historia de América* no. 65/66 (Jan.–Dec. 1968): 71–84.

———. *Struggle for the American Mediterranean: United States–European Rivalry in the Gulf-Caribbean, 1776–1904.* Athens: University of Georgia Press, 1976.

Lasso, Marixa. *Erased: The Untold Story of the Panama Canal.* Cambridge, MA: Harvard University Press, 2019.

Latimer, Jon. *1812: War with America*. Cambridge, MA: Belknap Press of Harvard University Press, 2009.

Lazo, Rodrigo. *Letters from Filadelfia: Early Latino Literature and the Trans-American Elite*. Charlottesville: University of Virginia Press, 2020.

Lee, Robert. "The Indian Boundary Line and the Imperialization of US-Indian Affairs." In *The Early Imperial Republic: From the American Revolution to the US-Mexico War*, edited by Michael A. Blaakman, Emily Conroy-Krutz, and Noelani Arista, 27–44. Philadelphia: University of Pennsylvania Press, 2023.

Lennox, Jeffers. *North of America: Loyalists, Indigenous Nations, and the Borders of the Long American Revolution*. New Haven: Yale University Press, 2022.

Lewis, James E., Jr. *The American Union and the Problem of Neighborhood: The United States and the Collapse of the Spanish Empire, 1783–1829*. Chapel Hill: University of North Carolina Press, 1998.

Lynch, John. *Simón Bolívar: A Life*. New Haven, CT: Yale University Press, 2006.

———. *The Spanish American Revolutions, 1808–1826*. New York: W. W. Norton, 1973.

Mapp, Paul. *The Elusive West and the Contest for Empire, 1713–1763*. Chapel Hill: University of North Carolina Press, 2011.

Marshall, P. J. *Remaking the British Atlantic: The United States and the British Empire after American Independence*. New York: Oxford University Press, 2012.

Matson, Cathy. "The Revolution, the Constitution, and the New Nation." In *The Cambridge Economic History of the United States, Vol. 1: The Colonial Era*, edited by Stanley L. Engerman and Robert E. Gallman. New York: Cambridge University Press, 1996.

McCoy, Drew R. *The Elusive Republic: Political Economy in Jeffersonian America*. Chapel Hill: University of North Carolina Press, 1980.

———. "James Madison and Visions of American Nationality in the Confederation Period." In *Beyond Confederation: Origins of the Constitution and American National Identity*, edited by Richard Beeman et al., 226–58. Chapel Hill: University of North Carolina Press, 1987.

McDonnell, Michael A. *Masters of Empire: Great Lakes Indians and the Making of America*. New York: Hill and Wang, 2015.

McFarlane, Anthony. *Colombia Before Independence: Economy, Society, and Politics Under Bourbon Rule*. Cambridge: Cambridge University Press, 1993.

McGuinness, Aims. *Path of Empire: Panama and the California Gold Rush*. Ithaca, NY: Cornell University Press, 2007.

Merk, Frederick, and Lois Bannister Merk. *Manifest Destiny and Mission in American History*. New York: Knopf, 1963.

Miles, Tiya. *The Dawn of Detroit: A Chronicle of Slavery and Freedom in the City of Straits*. New York: New Press, 2017.

Millett, Nathaniel. *The Maroons of Prospect Bluff and Their Quest for Freedom in the Atlantic World*. Gainesville: University Press of Florida, 2013.

Mills, Brandon. *The World Colonization Made: The Racial Geography of Early American Empire*. Philadelphia: University of Pennsylvania Press, 2020.

Mongey, Vanessa. *Rogue Revolutionaries: The Fight for Legitimacy in the Greater Caribbean*. Philadelphia: University of Pennsylvania Press, 2020.

Morris, Richard B. *The Peacemakers: The Great Powers and American Independence*. New York: Harper & Row, 1965.

Morrison, Dane. *Eastward of Good Hope: Early America in a Dangerous World*. Baltimore: Johns Hopkins University Press, 2021.

———. *True Yankees: The South Seas and the Discovery of American Identity*. Baltimore: Johns Hopkins University Press, 2014.

Mulcahy, Matthew. *Hubs of Empire: The Southeastern Lowcountry and British Caribbean*. Baltimore: Johns Hopkins University Press, 2014.

Narrett, David E. *Adventurism and Empire: The Struggle for Mastery in the Louisiana-Florida Borderlands*. Chapel Hill: University of North Carolina Press, 2015.

Narrett, David E. "Liberation and Conquest: John Hamilton Robinson and US Adventurism Toward Mexico, 1806–1819." *Western Historical Quarterly* 40, no. 1 (Spring 2009): 23–50.

Nedervelt, Ross. "Caught Between Realities: The American Revolution, the Continental Congress, and Political Turmoil in the Bahama Islands." *Journal of Imperial and Commonwealth History* 43, no. 5 (2015): 747–69.

Nichols, David Andrew. *Peoples of the Inland Sea: Native Americans and Newcomers in the Great Lakes Region, 1600–1870*. Athens: Ohio University Press, 2018.

———. *Red Gentlemen and White Savages: Indians, Federalists, and the Search for Order on the American Frontier*. Charlottesville: University of Virginia Press, 2008.

Norwood, Dael A. *Trading Freedom: How Trade with China Defined Early America*. Chicago: Chicago University Press, 2022.

Nugent, Walter. *Habits of Empire: A History of American Expansion*. New York: Alfred A. Knopf, 2008.

O'Shaughnessy, Andrew Jackson. *An Empire Divided: The American Revolution and the British Caribbean*. Philadelphia: University of Pennsylvania Press, 2000.

———. *The Men Who Lost America: British Leadership, the American Revolution, and the Fate of the Empire*. New Haven, CT: Yale University Press, 2013.

Onuf, Peter S. *Jefferson's Empire: The Language of American Nationhood*. Charlottesville: University of Virginia Press, 2000.

———. "Liberty, Development, and Union: Visions of the West in the 1780s." *William and Mary Quarterly* 43, no. 2 (April 1986): 179–213.

———. *The Origins of the Federal Republic: Jurisdictional Controversies in the United States, 1775–1787*. Philadelphia: University of Pennsylvania Press, 1983.

Ostler, Jeffrey. *Surviving Genocide: Native Nations and the United States from the American Revolution to Bleeding Kansas*. New Haven, CT: Yale University Press, 2019.

Owens, Robert M. *Mr. Jefferson's Hammer: William Henry Harrison and the Origins of American Indian Policy*. Norman: University of Oklahoma Press, 2008.

———. *Red Dreams, White Nightmares: Pan-Indian Alliances in the Anglo-American Mind, 1763–1815*. Norman: University of Oklahoma Press, 2015.

Owsley, Frank Lawrence, Jr., and Gene A. Smith. *Filibusters and Expansionists: Jeffersonian Manifest Destiny, 1800–1821*. Tuscaloosa: University of Alabama Press, 1997.

Pagden, Anthony. *Lords of All the World: Ideologies of Empire in Spain, Britain and France, c. 1500–1800*. New Haven, CT: Yale University Press, 1995.

Parker, Charles H. *Global Interactions in the Early Modern Age*. New York: Cambridge University Press, 2010.

Parker, Matthew. *Panama Fever: The Epic Story of One of the Greatest Human Achievements of all Time—the Building of the Panama Canal*. New York: Doubleday, 2007.

Parkinson, Robert G. *The Common Cause: Creating Race and Nation in the American Revolution*. Chapel Hill: University of North Carolina Press, 2016.

Perdue, Theda, and Michael Green. *The Cherokee Nation and the Trail of Tears*. New York: Viking, 2007.

Pérez, Louis A. *Cuba in the American Imagination: Metaphor and the Imperial Ethos*. Chapel Hill: University of North Carolina Press, 2008.

Perkins, Bradford. *The Cambridge History of American Foreign Relations, Vol. I: The Creation of a Republican Empire, 1776–1865*. Cambridge: Cambridge University Press, 1993.

———. *Prologue to War: England and the United States, 1805–1812*. Berkeley: University of California Press, 1961.

Perl-Rosenthal, Nathan. *The Age of Revolutions: And the Generations Who Made It*. New York: Basic Books, 2024.

Pletcher, David M. *The Diplomacy of Annexation: Texas, Oregon, and the Mexican War*. Columbia: University of Missouri Press, 1973.

———. *The Diplomacy of Involvement: American Economic Expansion Across the Pacific, 1784–1900*. Columbia: University of Missouri Press, 2001.

Pompeian, Edward P. *Sustaining Empire: Venezuela's Trade with the United States during the Age of Revolutions, 1797–1828*. Baltimore: Johns Hopkins University Press, 2022.

Radojewski, Christopher Mark. "The Rush-Bagot Agreement: Canada-US Relations in Transition." *American Review of Canadian Studies* 47, no. 3 (Sept. 2017): 280–99.

Ramsey, J. G. M. *The Annals of Tennessee to the End of the Eighteenth Century: Comprising Its Settlement, as the Watauga Association, from 1769 to 1777; A Part of North-Carolina, from 1777–1784; The State of Franklin, from 1784 to 1788; A Part of North-Carolina, from 1788 to 1790; The Territory of the U. States South of the Ohio, from 1790 to 1796; The State of Tennessee, from 1796 to 1800*. Philadelphia: J. B. Lippincott, 1860.

Rawlyk, George A. *Nova Scotia's Massachusetts: A Study of Massachusetts–Nova Scotia Relations, 1630 to 1784*. Montreal: McGill-Queen's University Press, 1973.

Reed, Joshua L. *The Sea Is My Country: The Maritime World of the Mahaks*. New Haven, CT: Yale University Press, 2015.

Reeder, Tyson. *Smugglers, Pirates, and Patriots: Free Trade in the Age of Revolution*. Philadelphia: University of Pennsylvania Press, 2019.

Regele, Lindsay Schakenbach. *Flowers, Guns, and Money: Joel Roberts Poinsett and the Paradoxes of American Patriotism*. Chicago: University of Chicago Press, 2023.

Reséndez, Andrés. *Changing National Identities at the Frontier: Texas and New Mexico, 1800–1850*. New York: Cambridge University Press, 2005.

Richards, Thomas, Jr. *Breakaway Americans: The Unmanifest Future of the Jacksonian United States*. Baltimore: Johns Hopkins University Press, 2020.

Richter, Daniel K. *Facing East from Indian Country: A Native History of Early America*. Cambridge, MA: Harvard University Press, 2001.

Robbins, William G. *Oregon: This Storied Land*. Seattle: University of Washington Press, 2020.

Ronda, James P. *Astoria and Empire*. Lincoln: University of Nebraska Press, 1990.

Roney, Jessica Chopin. "1776, Viewed from the West." *Journal of the Early Republic* 37, no. 4 (Winter 2017): 655–700.

———. "The Strange Afterlife of the Declaration of Independence: The State of Franklin, 1784–c. 1789." In *Ireland and America: Empire, Revolution, and Sovereignty*, edited by Patrick Griffin and Francis D. Cogliano, 246–72. Charlottesville: University of Virginia Press, 2021.

Rothman, Adam. *Slave Country: American Expansion and the Origins of the Deep South*. Cambridge, MA: Harvard University Press, 2005.

Rouleau, Brian. *With Sails Whitening Every Sea: Mariners and the Making of an American Maritime Empire*. Ithaca, NY: Cornell University Press, 2014.

Rozbicki, Michal Jan. *Culture and Liberty in the Age of the American Revolution*. Charlottesville: University of Virginia Press, 2011.

Sachs, Honor. *Home Rule: Households, Manhood, and National Expansion on the Eighteenth-Century Kentucky Frontier*. New Haven, CT: Yale University Press, 2015.

Sadosky, Leonard J. *Revolutionary Negotiations: Indians, Empires, and Diplomats in the Founding of America*. Charlottesville: University of Virginia Press, 2009.

Saler, Bethel. *The Settlers' Empire: Colonialism and State Formation in America's Old Northwest.* Philadelphia: University of Pennsylvania Press, 2014.

Salvucci, Richard J. "The Origins and Progress of US-Mexican Trade, 1825-1884." *Hispanic American Historical Review* 71, no. 4 (Nov. 1991): 697-735.

Saunt, Claudio. *Unworthy Republic: The Dispossession of Native Americans and the Road to Indian Territory.* New York: W. W. Norton, 2020.

———. *West of the Revolution: An Uncommon History of 1776.* New York: W. W. Norton, 2014.

Schneider, Elena. *The Occupation of Havana: War, Trade, and Slavery in the Atlantic World.* Chapel Hill: University of North Carolina Press, 2018.

Schroeder, John H. "Rep. John Floyd, 1817-1829: Harbinger of Oregon Territory." *Oregon Historical Quarterly* 70, no. 4 (Dec. 1969): 333-46.

Scott, Julius S. *The Common Wind: Afro-American Currents in the Age of the Haitian Revolution.* New York: Verso, 2018.

Seeley, Samantha. *Race, Removal, and the Right to Remain: Migration and the Making of the United States.* Chapel Hill: University of North Carolina Press, 2022.

Seijas, Tatiana, and Jake Frederick. *Spanish Dollars and Sister Republics: The Money That Made Mexico and the United States.* Lanham: Rowman & Littlefield, 2017.

Sexton, Jay. *The Monroe Doctrine: Empire and Nation in Nineteenth-Century America.* New York: W. W. Norton, 2011.

Shire, Laurel Clark. *The Threshold of Manifest Destiny: Gender and National Expansion in Florida.* Philadelphia: University of Pennsylvania Press, 2016.

Silver, Peter. *Our Savage Neighbors: How Indian War Transformed Early America.* New York: W. W. Norton, 2008.

Slack, Edward R., Jr. "Orientalizing New Spain: Perspectives on Asian Influence in Colonial Mexico." *México y la Cuenca del Pacífico* 43 (Jan.-April, 2012): 97-127.

Snyder, Christina. *Great Crossings: Indians, Settlers, and Slaves in the Age of Jackson.* New York: Oxford University Press, 2017.

Stagg, J. C. A. *Borderlines in Borderlands: James Madison and the Spanish-American Frontier, 1776-1821.* New Haven, CT: Yale University Press, 2009.

———. *Mr. Madison's War: Politics, Diplomacy, and Warfare in the Early American Republic, 1783-1830.* Princeton, NJ: Princeton University Press, 1983.

Starkey, Armstrong. *European and Native American Warfare, 1675-1815.* Norman: University of Oklahoma Press, 1998.

Stephanson, Anders. *Manifest Destiny: American Expansionism and the Empire of Right.* New York: Hill and Wang, 1995.

Stewart, Watt. "The South American Commission, 1817-1818." *Hispanic American Historical Review* 9, no. 1 (Feb. 1929): 31-59.

St. John, Rachel. "Contingent Continent." *Pacific Historical Review* 86, no. 1 (Feb. 2017): 18–49.

———. *Line in the Sand: A History of the Western US-Mexico Border*. Princeton, NJ: Princeton University Press, 2011.

———. "The Unpredictable America of William Gwin: Expansion, Secession, and the Unstable Borders of Nineteenth-Century North America." *Journal of the Civil War Era* 6, no. 1 (March 2016): 56–84.

Stourzh, Gerald. *Benjamin Franklin and American Foreign Policy*. Chicago: University of Chicago Press, 1969.

Sugden, John. *Tecumseh: A Life*. New York: Henry Holt, 1998.

Taylor, Alan. *American Republics: A Continental History of the United States, 1783–1850*. New York: W. W. Norton, 2021.

———. *American Revolutions: A Continental History, 1750–1804*. New York: W. W. Norton, 2016.

———. *The Civil War of 1812: American Citizens, British Subjects, Irish Rebels, and Indian Allies*. New York: Vintage Books, 2010.

———. *The Internal Enemy: Slavery and War in Virginia, 1772–1832*. New York: W. W. Norton, 2013.

Timmons, Wilbert H. *Tadeo Ortiz: Mexican Colonizer and Reformer*. El Paso: Texas Western Press, 1974.

Torget, Andrew J. *Seeds of Empire: Cotton, Slavery, and the Transformation of the Texas Borderlands, 1800–1850*. Chapel Hill: University of North Carolina Press, 2015.

Tucker, Robert W., and David C. Hendrickson. *Empire of Liberty: The Statecraft of Thomas Jefferson*. New York: Oxford University Press, 1990.

Turner, Frederick Jackson. "The Significance of the Frontier in American History." *Annual Report of the American Historical Association for the Year 1893*. Washington, DC: Government Printing Office, 1894.

Tutino, John. *Making a New World: Founding Capitalism in the Bajío and Spanish North America*. Durham, NC: Duke University Press, 2011.

———. *Mexico City, 1808: Power, Sovereignty, and Silver in an Age of War and Revolution*. Albuquerque: University of New Mexico Press, 2018.

Truett, Samuel. *Fugitive Landscapes: The Forgotten History of the US-Mexico Borderlands*. New Haven, CT: Yale University Press, 2006.

Tyler, Jacki Hedlund. *Leveraging an Empire: Settler Colonialism and the Legalities of Citizenship in the Pacific Northwest*. Lincoln: University of Nebraska Press, 2021.

Van Young, Eric. *A Life Together: Lucas Alamán and Mexico, 1792–1853*. New Haven, CT: Yale University Press, 2021.

———. *Stormy Passage: Mexico from Colony to Republic, 1750–1850*. Lanham, MD: Rowman & Littlefield, 2022.

Walker, Tamara J. *Exquisite Slaves: Race, Clothing, and Status in Colonial Lima*. New York: Cambridge University Press, 2017.

Wallace, Anthony F. C. *Jefferson and the Indians: The Tragic Fate of the First Americans*. Cambridge, MA: Harvard University Press, 1999.

Wallis, Michael. *David Crockett: The Lion of the West*. New York: W. W. Norton, 2011.

Weber, David J. *The Mexican Frontier, 1821–1846: The American Southwest under Mexico*. Albuquerque: University of New Mexico Press, 1982.

———. *The Spanish Frontier in North America*. New Haven, CT: Yale University Press, 1992.

Weeks, William Earl. *Building the Continental Empire: American Expansion from the Revolution to the Civil War*. Chicago: Ivan R. Dee, 1996.

———. *John Quincy Adams and American Global Empire*. Lexington: University Press of Kentucky, 1992.

———. *The New Cambridge History of American Foreign Relations, Volume 1: Dimensions of the Early American Empire, 1754–1865*. Cambridge: Cambridge University Press, 2013.

Weinberg, Albert K. *Manifest Destiny: A Study of Nationalist Expansionism in American History*. Chicago: Quadrangle, 1963.

Whaley, Gray H. *Oregon and the Collapse of Illahee: US Empire and the Transformation of an Indigenous World, 1792–1859*. Chapel Hill: University of North Carolina Press, 2010.

Whitaker, Arthur Preston. "The Muscle Shoals Speculation, 1783–1789." *Mississippi Valley Historical Review* 13, no. 3 (Dec. 1926): 377–86.

———. *The United States and the Independence of Latin America, 1800–1830*. New York: W. W. Norton, 1964.

White, Ashli. *Encountering Revolution: Haiti and the Making of the Early Republic*. Baltimore: Johns Hopkins University Press, 2010.

White, Richard. *The Middle Ground: Indians, Empires, and Republics in the Great Lakes Region, 1650–1815*. New York: Cambridge University Press, 1991.

Wilkinson, Henry C. *Bermuda from Sail to Steam: The History of the Island from 1784 to 1901*. 2 vols. London: Oxford University Press, 1973.

———. *Bermuda in the Old Empire: A History of the Island from the Dissolution of the Somers Island Company Until the End of the American Revolutionary War: 1684–1784*. New York: Oxford University Press, 1950.

Willcox, William B. *Portrait of a General: Sir Henry Clinton in the War of Independence*. New York: Knopf, 1962.

Williams, Samuel Cole. *History of the Lost State of Franklin*. New York: Press of the Pioneers, 1933.

Witgen, Michael. *An Infinity of Nations: How the Native New World Shaped Early North America*. Philadelphia: University of Pennsylvania Press, 2012.

———. *Seeing Red: Indigenous Land, American Expansion, and the Political Economy of Plunder in North America*. Chapel Hill: University of North Carolina Press, 2022.

Wood, Gordon S. *The Radicalism of the American Revolution*. New York: Alfred A. Knopf, 1991.

Woods, Randall. *John Quincy Adams: A Man for the Whole People*. New York: Dutton, 2024.

Woodworth, Steven E. *Manifest Destinies: America's Westward Expansion and the Road to the Civil War*. New York: Knopf, 2010.

Wright, J. Leitch, Jr. *Florida in the American Revolution*. Gainesville: University Press of Florida, 1975.

Jin Xu. *Empire of Silver: A New Monetary History of China*. Translated by Stacy Mosher. New Haven, CT: Yale University Press, 2021.

Yanik, Anthony J. *The Fall and Recapture of Detroit in the War of 1812: In Defense of William Hull*. Detroit: Wayne State University Press, 2011.

Yokota, Kariann Akemi. *Unbecoming British: How Revolutionary America Became a Postcolonial Nation*. New York: Oxford University Press, 2010.

Zagarri, Rosemarie. "The Significance of the 'Global Turn' for the Early American Republic: Globalization in the Age of Nation-Building." *Journal of the Early Republic* 31, no. 1 (Spring 2011): 1–37.

# INDEX

Adams, Abigail, 45
Adams, John, 34, 47, 61, 119, 153, 155; on free trade, 14–15, 37; views on expansion, 5, 13
Adams, John Quincy, 2, 8, 107, 125, 132, 134, 136, 137, 139, 157, 158, 160, 162, 170, 172, 174, 182; and the Monroe Doctrine, 133, 166; and the Transcontinental Treaty, 158; views on Cuba, 125, 127, 130–31, 133, 137, 140
American Revolution, 5, 12, 15, 16, 44, 48, 49, 59, 60, 61, 77, 82, 180
Anishinaabe, 7, 81–82, 86, 89, 93, 109, 110; control of Michigan, 80, 91, 101; resisting removal, 108
Articles of Confederation: admission of new states, 57, 68; and expansion, 1, 90; and Indigenous nations, 58; weaknesses of, 40–41, 61
Astor, John Jacob, 111, 148, 150
Astoria, 8, 146, 148–49, 150, 157, 158–59, 160, 164, 168, 175
Atlantic revolutions, impact on US expansion, 4, 41, 78, 111

Atlantic world: common wind of, 117, 118; US policymakers' commercial visions of, 12, 20, 36–37, 39

Bahamas, 24, 37, 40, 180
Battle of Fallen Timbers, 83–84, 87, 90, 104
Battle of Tippecanoe, 95, 96–97
Bermuda: and the British Empire, 13, 16, 17, 23–24, 26–27, 35–36, 41; location in the Atlantic world, 12, 15; and North America, 15, 16; and privateering, 15, 26–28, 29; US interest in, 3, 4, 5, 6–7, 11–12, 13, 18, 20–23, 24–25, 29–30, 31–34, 35, 40–41, 178, 179, 180
Bermudians: envision independence, 19, 31–32, 36; and the gunpowder plot, 11, 18
Bolívar, Simón: and Cuba, 136–37, 138–39; and interoceanic canals, 152, 162–63; and the Panama congress, 137, 139, 166

British Empire, 1, 14, 22, 23, 24, 36, 37, 45, 64, 82, 97; and Native peoples, 80–81, 82, 83–84, 85–86, 90, 91, 98, 100, 102, 104, 105, 106–7, 112; US anxiety of independence from, 7, 12, 13–14, 22; US fears of, 13, 37–38, 39–40, 41, 179. *See also* Bermuda; Cuba; Upper Canada

Brock, Isaac, 79, 102, 104

Bruere, George James, 16, 18, 20, 21, 23–24, 27, 28, 29

Caldas, Francisco José de, 151, 152

Calhoun, John C., 130–31, 132, 133, 134, 142

Campbell, Arthur, 52–55, 57, 60, 70–71, 72

Campbell, David, 48, 49, 52, 59, 63, 68, 72, 76, 77

Canada, 1, 2, 5, 13, 15, 24, 25, 27, 29, 33, 36, 37, 38, 44, 55, 83, 85, 86, 90, 97, 98, 99, 103, 106, 108, 111, 125, 136, 149, 168, 178, 180, 182, 183. *See also* Lower Canada; Upper Canada

Canning, George, 131–32, 133, 140, 167–68

Cass, Lewis, 81, 100, 101, 106, 108–10, 111, 112–13

Cazneau, Jane McManus Storm, 2

Cherokees, 75, 77, 108. *See also* Chickamauga Cherokees; Overhill Cherokees

Chickamauga Cherokees, 63–64, 71, 72–73, 74; and the Cherokee-American wars, 51

Chile, 151, 157–58, 160, 162, 168–70, 171, 177

Chinookan peoples, 4, 8, 146, 149–50, 160, 165, 166, 167, 168, 175

Claiborne, William C. C., 122–23, 126

Clatsops, 149, 168

Clay, Henry, 107, 136, 137, 139, 141, 156, 165, 170

Comcomly, 149, 160

Confederation Congress, 45, 48, 52; and the Jay-Gardoqui Treaty, 65, 66, 67; and the state of Franklin, 44, 53, 56–57, 58, 60, 61, 62, 68–69, 77

Congress (US), 85, 95, 133, 165; and the Columbia River basin, 163–64; and the creation of territories, 75, 84, 87, 156; debates over the Panama Congress, 137–40, 141, 170–71

Continental Association Agreement of 1774, 16, 17, 18, 19

Continental Congress, 20, 21, 23, 24, 25, 26; and Bermuda, 16, 17, 18, 21, 28, 33, 36

Corps of Discovery, 148, 161–62, 164

Cuba: British interest in, 115, 131–32, 133, 140; Cubans' plans for, 115, 119, 127, 130, 135, 136, 140, 179; and enslaved resistance on, 114, 117–18, 135–36, 179; and Gran Colombia, 115, 134, 136–37, 138–39, 140, 171; and Haiti, 8, 114, 117–19, 120, 122, 135, 141, 143; and Mexico, 134, 136, 137, 138, 139; and the Monroe Doctrine, 132–33, 166; and piracy, 128–29; and slavery, 114, 115, 119, 128, 131, 143, 144; Spanish maintenance of, 115, 132, 143; and US expatriates, 126, 127, 135–36; US policymakers' interest in, 2, 3, 4, 5, 7, 8, 114–15, 120, 121–22, 123–24, 125–26, 130–31, 133–34, 138, 140–41, 142–44, 178, 179, 180, 182, 183; and US trade, 154, 156

Deane, Silas, 27, 33, 40; advocates conquering Bermuda, 20–23, 24
Dearborn, Henry, 90, 91
Dessalines, Jean-Jacques, 117
Detroit, 80, 84, 86, 97, 101, 103, 105, 106, 110; African American community of, 89–90; British occupation of, 82–83, 84, 85, 104; French *habitants* of, 84–85; and Native nations, 87, 88, 89, 95, 98, 111; US surrender of, 101–2, 103, 104
Dragging Canoe, 58, 71, 73

Far West, 5, 181, 183. *See also* Pacific Northwest
Florida, 1, 3, 13, 15, 22, 24, 29, 37, 38, 39, 67, 76, 115, 120, 124–25, 126, 131, 139, 141, 156, 158, 180
France, 14, 20, 23, 27, 32, 33, 39, 40, 65, 82, 84–85, 121–22, 124, 172; and the Franco-American alliance of 1778, 24–26, 30, 31, 35, 41; and the French Revolution, 116, 155; and Haiti, 116–17, 119, 135; and the Holy Alliance, 132, 133
Franklin (state), 7, 61–62, 69–71, 78, 82, 179; challenges US westward expansion, 42–44, 49, 50, 51–56, 59, 61, 65–68, 71–74, 77–78; and the Chickamauga Cherokees, 63, 71, 72, 73; collapse of, 71–74; constitution of, 60; and Benjamin Franklin, 49, 62, 68; intrigue with Spain, 62, 73–74; and North Carolina, 48, 49, 50, 60–61, 62–63, 69, 71, 74, 75–76; and the Overhill Cherokees, 48, 49, 56, 57–60, 63–64, 72–73; rejected by Congress, 56–57, 61; threatens war with Spain, 65–66, 67; and the Treaty of Coyotee, 63, 72; and the Treaty of Dumplin Creek, 58, 59, 60, 63, 72; and the US Constitution, 68–69
Franklin, Benjamin, 19, 28, 178, 182; and Bermuda, 17–18, 22, 34; as a diplomat, 22, 24, 34, 39; and the state of Franklin, 49, 62, 68; and unrealized visions of expansion, 1–2, 5, 13, 34, 37, 183–84

Gran Colombia, 145, 161, 171; and canal projects, 161, 162–63, 166, 175–76; and Cuba, 115, 134, 136–37, 138–39, 140, 171; as a transcontinental nation, 158, 175
Great Britain. *See* British Empire
Guamacaro Revolt, 114, 135–36

Haiti, 4, 8, 25, 116–17, 118, 119, 120, 122, 133, 135, 137, 140, 141, 143
Haitian Revolution, 116–17, 122, 132, 141; impact on Atlantic slavery, 117–20, 135; influence on US policy toward Cuba, 8, 114–15, 119–20, 122–23, 126, 129, 133, 134, 143, 144; and the Louisiana Purchase, 121; as a source of inspiration, 117–18, 179
Hudson's Bay Company (HBC), 148, 166–68
Hull, William, 87, 103; and concerns of a British-Native alliance, 89, 90; and fears of Native nations, 86, 98–99, 100–101; and surrender of Detroit, 101–2; as territorial governor, 87–88, 89; and treaties with Native peoples, 92–93; and Upper Canada, 90–91, 97–100, 102

*Illahee*, 149, 150, 160
Indigenous peoples: and pan-Indigenous unity, 5, 7–8, 79–80, 81–82, 83, 84, 87, 88, 90, 91, 92, 93, 94–95, 96, 102, 103, 104, 105, 107, 111, 112, 113, 179; resistance to US expansion, 2, 7, 38, 51, 67, 73, 75, 80, 81–82, 91, 93, 94, 108, 183; US policy toward, 47, 51, 57–59, 67, 79–80, 81, 82–83, 86, 87, 88, 89–90, 91–92, 93, 96, 98–99, 107–11, 112–13, 147, 166, 179, 180; US removal of, 8, 47, 58, 60, 81, 86, 92, 93, 107, 108–11, 112–13, 147, 179, 180; US settler violence toward, 42, 50–51, 63, 72–73, 76, 82–83, 86, 93, 99, 106, 146. *See also specific nations*

Jay-Gardoqui Treaty (1786), 64, 67, 77; westerners' rejection of, 65, 66
Jefferson, Thomas, 2, 17, 18, 28, 29, 41, 51, 55, 87, 120, 165; and Cuba, 115, 121–22, 123, 134, 143–44; and "empire of liberty," 7, 38–39, 57–58, 79–80; and Haiti, 117, 118, 119, 120, 121, 143; and the Louisiana Purchase, 121, 143; and Native peoples, 59, 79–80, 91–92, 105, 109; and Upper Canada, 91; and westward expansion, 46–47, 52, 61, 65, 80, 93, 148, 150, 179, 182

Kaiyah-tahee (Old Tassel), 58–59, 62, 63–64, 72–73
Kanki, Vincente Pazos, 155, 163
Kentucky, 51, 52, 54, 56, 62, 65, 66, 70, 73, 77, 83

Louisiana Purchase, 2, 120, 121, 123, 143, 182
Louverture, Toussaint, 117, 118; fears of a Cuban Toussaint, 115
Lower Canada, 91, 97
Loyalists (British), 18, 29, 35, 50, 91; and privateering, 7, 18, 22, 27–28, 29, 30, 38, 41

Mackinac, 80, 84, 89, 95, 100–101, 102, 103, 104
Madison, James, 4, 33, 42, 55, 65, 72, 75, 80, 93, 95, 96, 112, 119, 124, 127, 177; and Canada, 97, 98, 105; and Cuba, 122, 123–24; and territorial expansion, 44, 51, 53, 54–55, 67, 69, 70–71, 76
manifest destiny, 3, 5–6, 8–9, 12, 13, 37, 40, 62, 76, 80, 111, 112, 115, 142, 143, 175, 176, 178, 179–80, 181–82, 183; conventional narrative of, 1–2, 5, 43, 146, 177–78, 181, 182
Mexico, 55, 121, 122, 124, 128, 132, 151, 152–54, 156, 158–59, 160, 164, 167, 168, 171, 177; and Cuba, 134, 136, 137, 138, 139; and an interoceanic canal, 161, 162, 163; as a transcontinental nation, 145, 153–54, 162; US aggression toward, 5, 8, 142, 146, 147, 171–74, 175–76, 180, 181–82, 183
Michigan, 3, 8, 80, 84, 85, 87, 88, 89, 90, 93, 95, 96, 97, 99, 101, 102, 103, 104, 105, 111, 112, 178, 179, 183; Anishinaabe peoples' control of, 7, 79–80, 81–82, 84, 86, 100–101, 108, 111; as a buffer state, 5, 80, 91, 104, 106–7; and the Canadian border, 8,

79–80, 81, 86, 87, 97, 98, 106, 108, 110; Wyandots of, 109
Mississippi River, 1, 7, 39, 43, 44, 45, 54, 61, 64, 65, 67, 73, 77, 111, 117, 121, 122, 123, 159, 178
Monroe, James, 8, 106, 108, 110, 112, 119, 126, 130, 131, 132, 133, 134, 156–57, 159, 165
Monroe Doctrine, 132–33, 134, 165–66

Native peoples. *See* Indigenous peoples; *specific nations*
North West Company (NWC), 108, 148, 150, 160
Northwest Ordinances, 43, 53, 69, 77
Nova Scotia, 1, 13, 15, 22, 29, 32, 33, 34, 37–38, 40, 44, 131, 180

Ohio River, 4, 5, 7, 43, 53, 66, 79, 81, 83, 87, 88, 94, 100, 103, 104, 179
Oregon Country, 149, 160, 167, 175, 181, 183. *See also* Pacific Northwest
Ortiz, Tadeo, 162, 164, 173
O'Sullivan, John, 2, 142, 176, 182, 183
Overhill Cherokees: and the state of Franklin, 7, 43, 48, 49, 56, 72–73; and the Treaty of Coyotee, 63–64; and the Treaty of Dumplin Creek, 57–60, 61; and the Treaty of Hopewell, 59, 62, 63

Pacific Northwest: as an Indigenous space, 146; and the Monroe Doctrine, 133, 165–66; and Spanish America, 5, 158, 159, 165, 166, 175;

US struggles to annex, 3, 8, 160, 163, 166, 167, 168, 175, 179
Panama Congress, 137, 139, 140, 166, 170–71; southern politicians' rejection of, 137–40
Peru, 151, 153, 155, 157, 163, 165, 168–69
Poinsett, Joel Roberts, 128, 129, 136, 139, 170, 171, 172, 177, 179–80, 182–83

Royal Navy (British), 25, 29, 40; and Bermuda, 12, 19, 21, 23, 24; and Cuba, 131, 134, 143; prevents US invasion of Bermuda, 4, 7, 11, 35

Sevier, John, 49, 50–51, 55, 56, 57, 58, 60, 61, 62–63, 68–69, 71–75, 76, 78
Spain: and the Bourbon reforms, 151–52; and Chile, 151, 157; and intrigue in the West, 42, 62, 73–74, 75; and the Mississippi River, 45, 54, 61, 64–67; and Native resistance, 67, 125; and New Spain, 64, 151, 154; and the Pacific Northwest, 150, 156, 158; and Peru, 151; and policy toward Cuba, 115, 118–19, 120, 121, 127, 130, 131, 132, 135, 141, 143, 154, 155–56; and US War for Independence, 26, 30, 32, 39
Spanish America: visions of, 4, 7, 8, 130, 145, 146, 150–52, 153, 154–55, 156, 159–60, 161, 163, 164, 168, 172, 175–76, 179; wars for independence of, 115, 128, 130, 137, 145, 146, 152, 160–61

Tecumseh, 78, 88, 93, 94, 100, 102, 107, 112, 183; death of, 105; and

Tecumseh (*continued*)
  pan-Indigenous unity, 7–8, 79, 80, 88, 92, 93, 94, 95, 96, 111; and Upper Canada, 100, 102, 103–4
Tennessee Valley, 3, 4, 7, 41, 42, 47, 48, 49, 51, 53, 56, 57, 60, 61–62, 63, 67, 71, 74, 75–76, 77, 178, 179, 183
Tenskwatawa, 78, 89, 91, 92, 100, 109, 111; and the Battle of Prophetstown, 95, 96; and a pan-Indigenous state, 88, 93–94, 111; spiritual teachings of, 79, 88
Texas, 2, 3, 5, 6, 137, 142, 143–44, 152, 156, 158, 171, 172, 173, 180, 181
Tipton, John, 56, 63, 71, 75
trans-Appalachian West, 55, 67, 82; US policymakers' visions for, 5, 38–39, 41, 42–47, 52, 57, 69–70, 75, 76–77, 179, 180; westerners' visions for, 53–54, 61–62, 66, 76
Transcontinental Treaty (1819), 8, 126, 143, 146, 147, 158, 159, 165, 174
Treaty at the Foot of the Rapids (1817), 110
Treaty of Detroit (1807), 93
Treaty of Fort Dearborn (1809), 94
Treaty of Fort Wayne (1809), 94
Treaty of Ghent (1814), 81, 107, 109, 112, 127, 150
Treaty of Greenville (1795), 79, 83, 88, 96
Treaty of Guadalupe Hidalgo (1848), 181, 182
Tucker, Henry, 17–18, 19, 23; and an independent Bermuda, 19–20

Tucker, St. George, 17, 18, 23, 29, 33, 36; and Bermuda's independence, 31–32, 36

United States. *See* manifest destiny; *specific policymakers and locations*
Upper Canada, 3, 80, 85, 86, 87, 89, 93, 95, 107, 108, 110, 179; creation of, 91, 104; dependence on Native peoples, 80, 91, 104, 107; US invasion of, 98–100, 102, 105, 111–12; US policymakers' desire for, 3, 7–8, 80, 81, 87, 90–91, 92, 97–98, 106, 111–12, 136, 178, 180, 183; US retreat from, 101
US-Mexico War, 142, 174–75, 180, 181
US policymakers. *See specific policymakers and locations*

War for Independence (US), 2, 5, 16, 22, 30, 32, 37, 40, 41, 42, 48, 51, 58, 64, 131, 179, 180
War of 1812, 7, 41, 79, 80, 101, 102, 105, 106, 107, 108, 109, 111, 112, 124, 125, 127, 150
Washington, George, 2, 4, 11, 18, 28, 52, 55, 75; and proposed invasions of Bermuda, 31–33, 35; and westward expansion, 45, 51, 82, 83
Western Hemisphere, 26, 132–33, 134, 142, 154, 165, 178, 179, 182

# THE REVOLUTIONARY AGE

*Revolutionary Diplomacy: Spanish Connections and the Birth of the United States*
THOMAS E. CHÁVEZ

*Declarations of Independence: Indigenous Resilience, Colonial Rivalries, and the Cost of Revolution*
CHRISTOPHER R. PEARL

*Dishonored Americans: The Political Death of Loyalists in Revolutionary America*
TIMOTHY COMPEAU

*The American Liberty Pole: Popular Politics and the Struggle for Democracy in the Early Republic*
SHIRA LURIE

*European Friends of the American Revolution*
ANDREW J. O'SHAUGHNESSY, JOHN A. RAGOSTA, AND MARIE-JEANNE ROSSIGNOL, EDITORS

*The Tory's Wife: A Woman and Her Family in Revolutionary America*
CYNTHIA A. KIERNER

*Writing Early America: From Empire to Revolution*
TREVOR BURNARD

*Spain and the American Revolution: New Approaches and Perspectives*
GABRIEL PAQUETTE AND GONZALO M. QUINTERO SARAVIA, EDITORS

*The American Revolution and the Habsburg Monarchy*
JONATHAN SINGERTON

*Navigating Neutrality: Early American Governance in the Turbulent Atlantic*
SANDRA MOATS

*Ireland and America: Empire, Revolution, and Sovereignty*
PATRICK GRIFFIN AND FRANCIS D. COGLIANO, EDITORS

www.ingramcontent.com/pod-product-compliance
Lightning Source LLC
Chambersburg PA
CBHW030617230426
43661CB00053B/2030